MODERN THEOLOGY

MODERN THEOLOGY

ONE VOLUME EDITION

Selections from twentieth-century theologians
edited with an introduction and notes by

E. J. TINSLEY

1 KARL BARTH 1886–1968

2 RUDOLF BULTMANN 1884–

3 PAUL TILLICH 1886–1965

4 REINHOLD NIEBUHR 1892–1971

5 DIETRICH BONHOEFFER 1906–45

LONDON
EPWORTH PRESS

First published 1973 by Epworth Press
as a series of five books
entitled *Modern Theology*
1 Karl Barth 1886–1968
2 Rudolf Bultmann 1884–
3 Paul Tillich 1886–1965
4 Reinhold Niebuhr 1892–1971
5 Dietrich Bonhoeffer 1906–45

This One Volume Edition 1979

7162 0326 x

Enquiries should be addressed to
Methodist Publishing House
Wellington Road
Wimbledon
London SW19 8EU

PRINTED IN GREAT BRITAIN BY
THE GARDEN CITY PRESS LIMITED
LETCHWORTH, HERTFORDSHIRE
SG6 1JS

ACKNOWLEDGEMENTS

The author and publisher are grateful for permission to quote in this series from the following works:

Church Dogmatics, Vol. I, 2; IV, 2, T. and T. Clark
Deliverance to the Captives, by Karl Barth, SCM Press
Kerygma and Myth, Vol. I; II, edited by H. W. Bartsch, SPCK
Christology, by Dietrich Bonhoeffer, Collins Publishers
Ethics, by Dietrich Bonhoeffer, SCM Press
Letters and Papers from Prison, by Dietrich Bonhoeffer, SCM Press
Sanctorum Communio, by Dietrich Bonhoeffer, Collins Publishers
The Cost of Discipleship, by Dietrich Bonhoeffer, SCM Press
Form Criticism, by Bultmann and Kundsin, Harper and Row, New York
Theology of the New Testament, Vol. II, by Rudolf Bultmann, translated by F. Grobel, SCM Press
Word and Faith, by G. Ebeling, translated by J. W. Leitch, SCM Press
The Nature of Faith, by Gerhard Ebeling, Collins Publishers
Selections from Karl Barth's Church Dogmatics, by H. Gollwitzer, T. and T. Clark
The Systematic Theology of Paul Tillich, by A. J. McKelway, Lutterworth Press
Beyond Tragedy, by Reinhold Niebuhr, James Nisbet and Co. Ltd
Leaves from the Notebook of a Tamed Cynic, by Reinhold Niebuhr, Harper and Row, New York
The Nature and Destiny of Man, Vol. I; II, by Reinhold Niebuhr, James Nisbet and Co. Ltd
World Come of Age, edited by R. Gregor Smith, Collins Publishers
The Death of God, by Gabriel Vahanian, George Braziller, Inc., New York

CONTENTS

3 PAUL TILLICH 1886–1965

4 REINHOLD NIEBUHR 1892–1971

5 DIETRICH BONHOEFFER 1906–45

PREFACE TO THE SERIES

The theologians represented in this series of five volumes of selections are those who, one can confidently say, are already assured of an important place in the history of twentieth-century theology.

In the case of each theologian I have tried to give a fair representation of the author's work although, inevitably, there are important aspects of his thought which I have not always found it possible to illustrate. I have throughout preferred to give substantial selections rather than short extracts because the qualities of the writing of the theologians in this collection require this treatment for proper understanding and illustration. Even so selections are no substitute for the original, and it is my hope that readers will become sufficiently interested in what is given in this series to want to go to the full range of the authors' complete works.

As well as being representative of an influential group of theologians I hope that the selections provided will be found to provide something of an integrated discussion among the writers themselves. I have, therefore, in making the selections included some which give an idea how these theologians view each other. The reader is given some indication of the views, say, of Barth on Bultmann or Niebuhr on Barth, and there are cross-references in the introduction and notes so that he can have an idea of what subjects have been of continuing importance in modern theological discussion.

I have made this selection not only for those who have a professional interest in the study of theology (clergy and ministers, teachers, students) but also for the interested member of the general public who, whether believer or not, wishes to have a guide to a reading of some important phases of twentieth-century theology. A general introduction attempts to set the scene and for each author there is a biographical note and brief introductions to the selected passages. In each case also there are suggestions for further study and reading.

University of Leeds JOHN TINSLEY

INTRODUCTION TO THE SERIES

In this introductory chapter an attempt will be made to explain how the present theological situation in western Europe and the United States has come about. We shall trace very briefly the pedigree of contemporary ideas and attitudes. 'Theology' however is a word (like, e.g., 'mysticism', 'romanticism', 'philosophy') which is frequently and easily used without its meaning having first been made clear. It is not uncommon to find politicians and other public speakers using the word 'theology' to mean some recondite, antiquarian and hopelessly irrelevant intellectual pursuit involving, it is implied, a sad waste of mental energy. It is essential therefore to try first to clarify the meaning of the term 'theology'. A good way of doing this is to describe how theology is done. By describing the process of theology we shall more easily come to an understanding of what it essentially is.

Perhaps there have been as many attempts at a definition of theology as, for example, of art. The comparison with art is very relevant because theology is in one aspect, and a very important one, an instance of the perennial task of working with words to achieve lucidity and precision described by T. S. Eliot as 'the intolerable wrestle with words and meanings'. Even if we think we have found a more or less satisfactory language very often the cultural situation will have meantime so moved on that we find, in Eliot's words again, that we have only learned to get better words for the things we no longer want to say.

Nevertheless theologians have to keep on with this task not because they believe that it is possible, for instance, to describe 'God' or to find a language about God which is valid for all time, but because they believe that theology is a perennial human task. Man is a 'theologizing' animal: i.e., he must be constantly attempting to achieve in a significant pattern of words (or of words together with gestures and sound, as, for example, in liturgy) some way of rationalizing all those facets of his experience and history which point to a meaning beyond the visible and material. Because the most significant activity in religion, worship, involves among other things a particular use of language theology is, whether the fact be acknowledged by theologians or not, vitally linked with the arts and the problems raised by artistic creativity. Hence the amount of space taken up in this book with discussion of the nature of religious language, and the use of symbol, myth and metaphor in religion.

These subjects are of common interest to theologians and students of literature, and of the arts in general. The question of theology and language is however of special concern to the *Christian* theologian and the reason for this has never been better expressed than by St Augustine. In a famous passage in his *De Trinitate* he discusses the question why Christians should use trinitarian language when speaking about God. He is aware of the irritation and impatience of those who feel that theological language is attempting to make definitions precisely in a sphere where, in the nature of the case, such a thing is not possible. Augustine replies, however, that Christians have to be careful about language, especially language about God, *non ut diceretur sed ne taceretur*, which could be paraphrased 'not in order to define but because it is not possible just to say nothing'. Christians, of all people, cannot keep silence, adds Augustine, because God has broken silence in Christ and has spoken to mankind in him. We are bound therefore to make the best reply that we can.

More particularly theology invites comparison with what may properly be called the art of criticism, since it has the same relation to its subject matter (religion) as, for example, music criticism has to the symphony, art criticism to painting or sculpture, or literary criticism to poetry or prose. The best theology, like the best art, is that which so uses language that it sends the reader back with new and fruitful perspectives to the original (e.g., Christ, the Bible, etc.), or so speaks of the original that it affords a fresh and creative present experience of it.

Perhaps because of the great variety of approaches and methods possible for doing theology it is better, and here again the analogy from art is useful, not to think of what theology may be in the abstract but of actual types and styles of theology, and it is hoped that the selections given in this book will enable the reader to do this. The types and styles of theology are analogous to the types and styles of art. One could readily think in theology of the equivalents of, say, representational, impressionist, expressionist or abstract art. The 'quest of the historical Jesus' in the nineteenth century bears a resemblance to the 'pre-Raphaelite' school of painting in its attempt to portray Jesus in full and minute detail. Rudolf Bultmann and the 'existentialist' school of modern theology remind one of German 'expressionist' art where the subject of the painting is used as a means of expressing the commitment, feeling and attitudes of the artist. Further, like styles in art, theological styles continue to have significance even though they belong to an age now long past. The artist and the theologian are both in constant dialogue with their past traditions. To be a genuine contemporary, in both fields, means to have lived through, in imaginative experience, the outlook of previous practitioners. Theology belongs to the realm of human creativity and is therefore a dynamic and changing phenomenon. It is better, therefore, at the beginning of one's study of such a subject to look at the various methods of doing theology rather than to seek some distillation of it, some quintessential theology.

It would not be difficult to say something about what theology is from an analysis of the two words which make up the term theology—'theos' and 'logos'. Starting from these two components we might translate 'theology' as 'God-talk'. Theology as 'God-talk' takes its origin from two permanent features of human existence. There is first the fact that from time to time, in all sorts of ways, man finds himself wondering whether there is any meaning to his existence, whether the values and ideals which strike him in a cogent way in his many moral and aesthetic experiences are anything more than fine moments of feeling. There is further an impatience and a restlessness about human existence—we long for serenity, for wholeness and harmony, for unity and purpose, and continue to wonder whether in and behind material existence there is another order of reality.

These intimations of something beyond time and space have been variously expressed whether in the classical scheme of the values of 'truth, beauty and goodness', or in what Rudolf

Otto[1] has called the experience of the 'holy' or the 'numinous', or as far as aesthetic experience is concerned, in what Longinus[2] called the 'sublime'. Others have used the term 'mystery' for these features of human existence to express their sense of that which is mysterious, not in the way of a puzzle which is in principle solvable at some time or other, but as inducing, rather than the desire to solve, an overwhelming impression of awe, wonder, reverence, joy.

For the centre of this 'mystery' the Greek word would have been *theos,* sometimes translated 'god', but we may conveniently use it for any kind of transcendental reference given to human life. Man is a being who finds it difficult to undergo artistic, religious, scientific or moral experience and leave it just like that. He finds himself involved necessarily in the task of shaping this experience into significant patterns, trying to hold it in words or in some visual form. More particularly he is prompted to speech about it, to try and contain this experience in sentences. It is to this necessary use of language to analyse and explain *theos* that one can give the Greek word *logos.* Theology is, therefore, strictly speaking *theos-logos*— 'God-talk'. Theology results from the fact that on the one hand there is the 'mystery' and on the other the impulse to achieve understanding of it.

It is significant that many theologians have expressed a similar impatience with their task to that which we find in poets. We have already referred to Augustine and T. S. Eliot on the difficulties and frustrations of finding satisfactory words. This raises an important issue. Most frequently when we use the term 'theology' we think, inevitably and rightly, of verbal theology: that analysis of the 'mystery' of existence, that articulation of *theos* which can be done in words (*logos*). No doubt one would have to say that the best theology is that which approximates most closely to the character of its subject-matter. In the case of Christian theology this would mean the character of the Incarnation especially its 'signful', indirect, ambiguous, parabolic quality. Perhaps a more adequate kind of theology, a more satisfactory response to the *theos,* is that

[1] *The Idea of the Holy,* 1923.

[2] Cassius Longinus, Greek philosopher and critic of third century A.D., author of a treatise on literary criticism, *On the sublime.*

expressed in a concrete but non-verbal way in the arts, particularly the visual arts. If this is the case we ought to coin a new word for this reaction to *theos*. It would be a question not of *theos* and *logos* (=*verbal* theology) but of *theos* and *poiesis* ('making')—'theo-poetics'. The use of such a term as 'theo-poetics' would remind one of the saying of W. B. Yeats, specially appropriate to the Christian religion, that man cannot know the truth or express it in words. He can only *embody* (perhaps one could say 'incarnate') it. Even if we must continue to use the word 'theology' we need to think of it as a perennial attempt to *embody* human experience of *theos* rather than to translate it into some prose paraphrase.

This analysis of the meaning of the word 'theology' is a start, but it does not take us very far. We need to examine more closely how theologians have set about the task of 'God-talk', and the data which they have taken to be relevant. We must therefore turn now to a brief review of what theologians have been doing during the last two centuries. This will help us to understand the theological scene today, and to recognize more clearly some of the 'styles' being used by theologians at the present time.

1

A radical change came over the method of doing Christian theology in the eighteenth century. Up till then, broadly speaking, and certainly from the time when theology had been given its most comprehensive and systematic expression in the works of St Thomas Aquinas (*c*. 1225–74) the procedure had seemed straightforward and uncomplicated. The scheme of theological investigation had two main parts: (1) natural theology and (2) revealed theology.

To take the method of doing 'natural' theology first. It was thought possible to establish by the ordinary processes of human reasoning such great truths as the existence of God and the immortality of the soul. Furthermore the ordinary processes of argumentation could establish the truth of certain attributes of God, like his omnipotence and omnipresence. From the evidence provided by the natural world and human existence it was possible to establish the existence of God by 'proofs'. The existence of God could be demonstrated by the use of unaided human reason. This was a truth about God open to any enquirer and could therefore rightly be called 'natural' theology.

'Revealed' theology was an important supplement to this. It had two additional functions to those performed by natural theology. First of all it conveyed again the truths of natural theology but this time in a 'revealed' form (particularly in the Christian scriptures) which could be readily and easily understood by those who were not able to follow rational argument. Then, second, revealed theology presented truths which could not be demonstrated by human reason, such as, for instance, the trinitarian nature of God. The scriptures attested the divinity of Christ by showing that he fulfilled Old Testament prophecy and worked miracles. These were taken to be the two foundations of belief in the authority of Christ. They established his place in the Christian revelation.

There were thus two kinds of data at the disposal of the theologian, natural theology and revealed theology, or to put it shortly 'reason' and 'revelation'. From an investigation of the book of nature and the book of scripture the theologian could construct an integrated and systematic theology, like the *Summa Theologiae* of St Thomas Aquinas. This was the general pattern of Christian apologetics commonly accepted until comparatively recently, and has remained the official view of the matter in the Roman Catholic Church. This method of doing theology was enshrined in William Paley's *View of the Evidences of Christianity* (1794) which remained in use as a text-book until as late as the beginning of the present century. Various criticisms had been brought against this way of doing theology before the advent of modern developments in philosophy, the sciences, and in biblical criticism. Reformation theology in general was suspicious of the large claims made by natural theology for the use of man's 'unaided' reason. Not only did the Reformers insist on the fact that all reasoning is undergirded by grace but they questioned whether one could say that human reason, even when so supported, inevitably attained the truths of natural theology. This seemed to them to neglect the problem of 'fallen' human nature which is capable of perverting and corrupting even the process of reasoning. During the eighteenth century the unsatisfactory character of this traditional approach to theology became clearer still. Many Christian apologists in this period tried to develop a natural theology not by reading off from the book of nature but by searching, so to speak, the book of man's inner experience. This seemed to show that there was among human beings a general religious sense which lay behind all formally organized religions. So-called 'revealed' theology was therefore taken to be simply a sophisticated articulation of this universal natural theology. In this way the distinction between natural and revealed theology was blurred, to say the least. Christianity, for example, was seen not as a blend of natural and revealed theology but a particular version of the universal feeling for religion. To quote from the title of a book by a famous eighteenth-century Deist, Matthew Tindal, it was as 'old as creation', nothing more than 'a republication of the religion of nature'.

More dramatic in their effects on the traditional scheme of theology, however, were the developments in scientific investigation and historical criticism which gathered momentum during the eighteenth century and continued apace throughout the nineteenth century.

2

Research in the natural sciences during the nineteenth century, especially in the fields of geology and biology, produced a picture of the origin of the universe and its evolution radically different from that suggested by a literal acceptance of the early chapters of Genesis with a universe created in six days and an Adam and Eve as the first human beings. *The Bridgewater Treatises* (1833–40) showed, among other things, that it was quite impossible, from the evidence already made available by geological research, to subscribe to the view that Creation could be exactly dated, as Archbishop Ussher[1] had

[1] James Ussher (1581–1656), Archbishop of Armagh, worked out a complete biblical chronology in his *Annales Veteris et Novi Testamenti*, and the dates given in this book were inserted in editions of the Authorised Version of the Bible from 1701 onwards.

suggested, in 4004 B.C. For those who had been brought up on the idea that the Bible was itself the revelation of God, giving infallible truth as a series of propositions, this suggestion that the earth was millions rather than thousands of years old came as quite a shock. As late as 1851 John Ruskin could write: 'If only the geologists would let me alone, I could do very well, but those dreadful hammers! I hear the clink of them at the end of every cadence of the Bible verses.'

Following hard upon this shock came the news from the field of biological research. Charles Darwin's *The Origin of Species* was published in 1859 and his *The Descent of Man* in 1871. These made it clear not only that human life had evolved from sub-human species but that the whole process had been inconceivably longer than was generally supposed. Again for those brought up on the view that the Bible was a monolithic structure infallible on all subjects, including the science of human origins, this came as a great blow.

These shocks from outside the sphere of the Bible coincided with developments within biblical criticism which at the time seemed to undermine still further the status of the Bible as authoritative Scripture. As a result of literary and historical study it was no longer possible to maintain that the biblical literature was all of one kind, and all on the same level of authority or 'inspiration'. To take the Bible as an infallible oracle, to believe that in it the Word of God took print, was now seen to violate the nature of the biblical literature itself and to presuppose that the divine method of revelation is one which imposes rather than elicits, 'explains' rather than indicates, and forces rather than persuades.

Faced with these developments there were three possible reactions from Christian apologists. One could first simply refuse to recognize that any change had taken place and to carry on using the Bible as before, if anything hardening one's ideas about its authority and inerrancy. This is the approach which later on came to have the label 'fundamentalism' attached to it. Or, secondly, the attempt could be made to reconcile the new developments in knowledge with the traditional structure of theology. This was often taken to quite fantastic lengths like, for example, suggesting that the real significance of fossils in no way turned out to be a contradiction of the traditional dating of creation since they had been placed there by God to test faith! Similarly one remembers the notorious attempts to reconcile evolution with the scheme of creation in Genesis. Since the psalmist says that one day in the sight of the Lord is as a thousand years, 'days' in the Genesis account does not mean twenty-four hours but whatever extended period of time may be necessary to fit the case! Or, thirdly, one could accept the findings of research and in the light of them discard previous views of, for example, biblical inerrancy and look entirely afresh at the whole concept of revelation and the nature of the biblical literature. It was this latter reaction that has come to be known as nineteenth-century liberalism. Its main features were as follows.

First, a suspicion of the traditional schemes of dogmatic theology, and an attempt to reconstruct Christian belief in a way which took into account historical criticism. This could be illustrated by new procedures in such areas as christology or the doctrine of the Church. The traditional belief about the Christ as true God and true man, with two natures divine and human, as expressed in the traditional formula of the Council of Chalcedon 451 was put on one side, and an attempt made to construct a way of believing in Christ taking into account the results of historical criticism of the gospels, particularly the growing conviction that the fourth gospel, which had been a principal source for the formulation of traditional christology, was so much later than the synoptic gospels and so much less historical that it ought not to be used again in this way. The enigmatical Christ of the synoptic gospels, only indirectly indicating the meaning of himself, became the basis for a 'kenotic' christology. That is to say it was emphasized that whatever else the Incarnation was it meant an act of self-giving on the part of God which involved sacrificial self-limitation. Or again one could take the doctrine of the Church, especially in its relation to Christ. In the light of biblical and historical criticism it was felt by many nineteenth-century scholars that the Christ of history, the genuine Jesus of Nazareth, was one thing, and the Christ of Church doctrine quite another. It seemed to be self-evident that the historical Christ could not have intended the Church as an institution, but rather that he was an outstanding Hebrew prophet who was concerned with brotherly love, justice, and the inestimable worth of the human soul.

The second characteristic of nineteenth-century liberalism was the use made of the category of evolution, provided by developments in the biological sciences. Human history was seen in terms of evolutionary progress. Mankind was seen to be, indubitably, on the march of progress. By the use of reason and the intellectual tools at his disposal man would be able to fashion a better future for himself. 'Sin', if the word were used at all, ought to be put in inverted commas and translated to mean imperfection or ignorance. 'Salvation' consequently ought to be thought of in terms of education and enlightenment. Such biblical concepts as 'the kingdom of God' ought similarly to be reinterpreted in terms of some kind of evolutionary progressivism.

Out of all this came some new principles for theological method and the data to be used by theology. The Bible remained as a principal source for the Christian theologian but it had to be used critically in the light of the findings of literary and historical investigation. The Bible also needed to be detached from its traditional interpretation in the church. In particular allegorization and typology were discarded as both inappropriate and irrelevant to such a critical use of the Bible. The book of the universe, nature, was also a source to be used, especially since it provided such a category of interpretation as evolutionary development. Finally there was increasing use of human experience as a source for theology. Nineteenth-century theology was greatly influenced by the work of Friedrich Schleiermacher (1768–1834) who considered the essence of the religious sentiment to be the feeling of absolute dependence and interpreted Christ as the supreme example of such dependence and 'God-consciousness'.

As far as relations with philosophy were concerned it has to be remembered that in the nineteenth century the task of philosophy was taken to be, principally, to provide a 'metaphysics', that is an all-embracing interpretation of the universe and human existence. The philosopher was one who concerned himself with what Tillich (see Book 3, pp. 203ff.) called the 'ultimate questions of human existence'. The theologian's task was to keep on the look-out for philosophical schemes whose general outlook and vocabulary seemed to be particularly well-suited for the exposition of Christian beliefs. It was widely held during the nineteenth century, both on the Continent and in Britain, that such a congenial philosophical system had been found in the work of Friedrich Hegel (1770–1831). Hegel believed that existence could best be interpreted in terms of an evolutionary process, continually advancing from thesis to antithesis and fresh synthesis, whereby the Absolute Idea realized itself in ever more sharply focused ways. Adapting Christian trinitarian language he thought of the eternal Idea as God the Father. The eternal Idea as constantly passing from infinitude to finitude he thought of as God the Son. The Absolute Idea returning home, so to speak, enriched by this outgoing (Incarnation) he identified with the Christian God the Holy Spirit.

3

This was the background against which we can place all the theological movements represented in this series. Paul Tillich has described himself as a nineteenth-century figure, and certainly his concept of the relation between theology and philosophy as a 'correlation' (see Book 3, pp. 169ff.) makes him very much more akin to the philosophy of the last century than to the analytical anti-metaphysical philosophy which has dominated the academic scene in twentieth-century Britain. Karl Barth's theological thinking began as a strong reaction against the liberal theology of the nineteenth-century and particularly its alliance with philosophies which he believed prevented the unique and distinctive features of the Christian religion from being clearly expressed. Bultmann took up the issues raised by the development of biblical criticism in the nineteenth century, particularly the question of the relation between the Jesus of history and the Christ of faith. Bonhoeffer in his early period shared Barth's reaction to nineteenth-century theology but later came to believe that a quite new situation faces the twentieth-century Christian and that Barth was of decreasing usefulness to such a person. Niebuhr's theology of politics and society is a deliberate reaction to a liberal theology which he believed had seriously underplayed the doctrines of sin and original sin and had placed an ultimate trust in human intelligence and virtue. We now need to examine more fully the place in the history of twentieth-century theology likely to be occupied by these theologians.

All five of them were German or, in the case of Niebuhr, of German origin. As it happens they were also all of clerical or academic households. Further they all had experienced the age of Nazism and in most cases had suffered from it in one way or another.

The beginning of the theological movement associated with the name of *Karl Barth* can be dated from his shocked realization that the values of nineteenth-century liberalism as held by academics and intellectuals of his day left them incapable of recognizing tyranny when it appeared, much less of standing up against it. Academic education, even in theology, did not make men any more able to perceive the illiberalism and aggression implicit in the German policies which led to the outbreak of the 1914–18 war (see pp. 41ff.). The same inability of the liberal mind to believe in the recalcitrant and anti-rational possibilities of human conduct displayed itself again when the Nazis came to power in 1934. The theological charter which became the rallying point of church resistance to Hitler, the Barmen declaration, was mainly the work of Barth.

Certainly nothing could be more contrary to the theological method of nineteenth-century liberalism than that promulgated by Barth. For him the theological endeavour begins not with a series of questionings about human existence or the universe but by a realization that man is first confronted by an answer, a divine answer in the form of a revelation to which a unique witness is borne by the Bible. 'Religion' as the human enquiry after God, the human endeavour to attain God by the exercise of human reason is anathema to Barth (see *Karl Barth*, pp. 60ff.). It is impossible for man to take any initiative, strictly speaking, in his enquiries about God because by his very existence man is a potential recipient of a revelation which is one of the inescapable givennesses of life. God is essentially a prevenient God who has first spoken to man, and anything that man says, any enquiry that he may make, must necessarily take the form of a response to a God who has all the while been addressing him. This is a method of doing theology directly opposed to that of Paul Tillich who begins his theology precisely with human questions, the 'ultimate questions' posed by human existence.

This starting point led Barth to place a new kind of emphasis on the Bible and the place of scripture in the formation of dogmatic theology. This started a movement which later on came to be known as 'biblical theology'. The Bible was regarded as providing the categories for Christian theology. Barth's theology has been given different names. One of them, his own term, is 'kerygmatic' theology, namely a theology which has first and foremost to be proclaimed. It is not sensible to argue about revelation Barth believed; one can only proclaim it.

There is also in Barth a new emphasis on the indissoluble links between theology and the church. Academic theology in the nineteenth century, especially in Germany, was separated from the life of the Church and the work of the pastor. The Church as the believing community came to have a new meaning for Barth as the body which finds itself bearing the Word of God and being judged by it.

Barth's way of doing Christology, of tackling the problems raised by the person of Christ, seems at first sight to be very much in the traditional manner. He began from the traditional formulation of the Council of Chalcedon of Christ as true God and true man. But he soon showed himself to be suspicious of the historical method of the nineteenth-century 'quest of the historical Jesus'. Barth suspected that this really made faith dependent on the results of historical investigation and practically equivalent to acceptance of an agreed amount of reliable factual information about Christ. It is instructive at this point to compare Barth's attitude to the historical Jews with that of Bultmann, Tillich and Bonhoeffer. Barth treated more creatively and fruitfully than the nineteenth century the question of *kenosis* (self-emptying) in the Incarnation. This was not for Barth a matter of some loss of divinity, a downgrading of God. The *kenosis* in Christ is in fact the highest affirmation of the lordship of God over all. God is lord not only in transcendent glory but even in the form of the servant. God is free to be other personalities without ceasing to be himself. Whereas for so many 'kenotic' theologians in the nineteenth (and indeed twentieth centuries) the Incarnation had meant God revealing himself in a very qualified and impoverished way, for Barth the Incarnation is the expression (the Word) of a God who always had man, and the glorification of man, in mind. God in Christ revealed his majesty precisely in the humiliations, trials and sufferings of Christ which many theologians in the past had thought must conceal it.

The resulting shape of Barth's theological scheme gives central place to the Incarnation, Scripture, and the Church. All Christian theology turns out in the end, according to Barth, to be an aspect of Christology whether it be the doctrine of creation, or of the church, or of the sacraments.[1]

Barth may have been neo-Calvinist in his approach to the doctrine of man, emphasizing human impotence before God, but in the end his theology of man turns out to be more optimistic than, say, that of Tillich or Niebuhr. There is a warm glow about Barth's language when he writes about man as he is in Christ, re-created man. On the other hand his theology is distanced from cultural and social interests. Barth saw what he called a *diastasis,* a tension between theology and the arts where Tillich perceived the possibilities of 'correlation'.

For *Bultmann* too the 1914–18 war was a turning point. It was during this period that he was working as a New Testament scholar on the form-critical method (see Book 2, pp. 105ff.) and this proved to be determinative for his later work. He was sceptical about being able to get behind the 'kerygmatic' Christ of the gospels and sure that we do not have data for providing informed discussion about such subjects as the motivation of Christ or the self-awareness about his own mission. As well as the influence of Bultmann's scholarly investigations we need to reckon with his deep interest in the problem of communication, and his concern with the pastoral problems created by the fact that the tradition about Jesus comes down to us in a 'mythological' form. The extent of this problem was brought home to him by what he heard from army chaplains in the Second World War about their experiences in trying to preach and teach. This raised in an acute form the whole

[1] ***Church Dogmatics*, I, 2, pp. 123 ff.**

question of how the Christian gospel is to be communicated in the modern world. This involved a study of the status of 'mythology' in the Christian religion. Is it an essential form of human speech, or it is accidental, temporary, continually replaceable by more satisfactory translations or paraphrases into other kinds of language? Bultmann came to believe the latter and hence insisted upon the need for 'demythologizing' (see Book 2, pp. 132ff.).

Bultmann took over the language of 'existentialist' philosophy as that which is specially well equipped to express the kind of religious belief we find in the New Testament. 'Existentialist' thinking is that in which we are ourselves personally involved, the kind of thinking in which we are personally implicated. It calls for personal decision and genuine commitment. Existentialism is antipathetic to any philosophy which is merely theoretical or academic (in the bad sense). The debate started by Bultmann's transposition of New Testament belief into existentialist terms has centred on whether this emphasis on the subjective, on *my* decision and commitment here and now, is adequate to do justice to the many facets of Christianity. Is not the New Testament also concerned with certain objective facts, like the redemption wrought by Christ, which remain true irrespective of any personal decision and commitment. Sometimes after reading a lot of Bultmann one has the feeling that when the existentialist theologian says 'God' he really means 'me'. Or at least it sounds like that!

Bultmann shares the hesitations of Barth about exposing the Incarnation to the ambiguities and probabilities of historical investigation. This would make faith vulnerable to the hazards of historical criticism and Bultmann, like Barth, seems intent on finding some area for faith which is immune from that eventuality.

So the data for theology which is to determine one's starting point is not the world, nor is it the Bible in the way Barth takes it, although the New Testament plays a cardinal role in Bultmann's theology. Rather it is human existence, because this is where the whole question of faith is posed. The mythological idiom of the New Testament really relates to man in his existential predicaments, to the need for decision, and for turning from 'inauthentic' to 'authentic' existence.

When we turn to *Paul Tillich* we find a theologian who is very much closer than Barth or Bultmann to the liberal tradition and to principles of liberal investigation. Tillich's whole approach to theology is based on the assumption that man has a natural ability to apprehend truth and that there is in man 'a depth of reason'. He starts from anthropology, examining the implications of the questions which are set by human existence.

Tillich agreed with Barth that theology is 'kerygmatic' but he insisted that it is also 'apologetic'. He kept a place for 'natural theology'. If theology is treated as only 'kerygmatic' Tillich believed, and I think rightly, that it then becomes irrelevant outside the domestic circle of believers, and is only useful for 'revivalism', as he put it.

Tillich departed radically from Bultmann on the question of myth and symbol. 'Demythologizing' for Tillich was an impossible enterprise because the myth is by its very nature irreplaceable and untranslatable, and cannot be transposed into a paraphrase without serious distortion or reduction. 'Myth' is a significant pattern of symbols organized into a narrative story which has the peculiar power, whenever it is receptively read or heard of bringing with it a clearer perception and deeper understanding of some feature of human experience which can not be evoked or expressed in any other way. Tillich believed that myth was therefore fundamentally irreplaceable. Bultmann on the other hand does not see myth existing in its own permanent right, but rather as a temporary way of putting things in a certain culture, which may now be seen perhaps as striking and picturesque, but not a necessary form of human speech.

Tillich was outstanding among the group represented in this series, and indeed in the twentieth century generally, for the attention he gave to analysing the relation between theology and culture. On this issue he was far removed from Barth and closer to a thinker like Niebuhr.

Reinhold Niebuhr's work can also be seen as a reaction against the preceding liberal theology. He is specially critical of the tendencies in nineteenth-century theology to equate the 'kingdom of God' with social betterment or progress. His theological endeavour could be described as an essay in 'prophetic realism'. He sought, that is to say, to relate biblical insights into the meaning of history and God's judgement on and in it to the political and social situation of his day. His aim was 'realism' in the sense that he had a deep suspicion of what one American writer has called 'the men of the infinite', that is the idealists, the romantics, the men of abstract generalization'. Niebuhr preferred the company of 'the men of the finite', those with a careful eye for data, evidence, facts. A good example of this 'prophetic realism' is to be found in the essay 'The ultimate trust' in *Beyond Tragedy*.

Like Tillich, but unlike Barth, Niebuhr starts from the human situation. Here again one finds his work a marked contrast to nineteenth-century liberalism in the way he expounds afresh the doctrines of the 'fall of man' and 'original sin', and the place he gives to eschatology. The basic form of sin for Niebuhr is not finitude or imperfection but the anxiety about them which human freedom makes possible and which expresses itself in pride and envy.

Niebuhr takes up from liberal theology the results of biblical criticism, especially as it affects biblical history. 'Fundamentalist' approaches to the Bible blurred the distinction between different literary forms, and, most disastrously, between symbolic language and language of historical fact.

The theology of *Bonhoeffer*, fragmentary though it be, is of the greatest importance in showing a man struggling to free himself from various traditions in his early training, notably the influence of Karl Barth, and re-cast the whole structure of theology to face a new situation. Bonhoeffer came to believe that the theology of Barth and Bultmann had seriously neglected the social and political problems of the world. In this respect he found the theology of Niebuhr, which he came to know well as a result of his visits to America, very much more congenial.

Bonhoeffer was very much concerned with the significance of Christ, and especially the place of the historical Christ in Christian belief. His theology is, in one respect, an attempt to reconstruct a Christocentric theology and ethics just as thoroughgoing in its Christocentricity as Barth's. He does not, however, isolate the place and role of the Bible in the manner of Barth nor does he put the whole stress on inwardness in the existentialist fashion of Bultmann and Tillich.

4

The theologians represented in this series are already established figures on the twentieth-century theological scene, and their writings have by now attained the status of 'classics'. What developments have there been among a younger genera- of theologians? Recently a number of new movements have come into vogue which could be given the labels: 'The new theology', 'Secular Christianity' and 'The death of God theology'. There is space here only for a brief word about each of these developments.

One of the most astonishing phenomena in recent years has been the popular success of Dr John A. T. Robinson's *Honest to God*, first published in 1963, which has now sold well over one million copies, as well as being translated into a great number of foreign languages. The extraordinary circulation of this book is strange because it was not written for a popular audience, it contains long extracts from Tillich, Bultmann and Bonhoeffer which make severe demands on the general reader, and it could not be described as a piece of creative or lucid theological writing. The author would be the first to say that he was not attempting a new theology but to promote a discussion of the three thinkers just mentioned who had hitherto, especially in this country, been known only by academics and professional theologians. It was perhaps the tone of voice of this book rather than its contents which gave it such popular appeal particularly since the author was a bishop, with all that the image of such a person still implies in this country. The picture which the book suggested of a bishop not pontificating theological certainties in dogmatizing fashion, but exploring in a very tentative way and voicing his own doubts and uncertainties, struck a new note for many people. *Honest to God* appeared to be the manifesto of a movement of liberation, and to express the feeling that belief was a continuous dialogue with doubt within each person, and not an unchangeable certainty over against the unbelief of others.

Many critics have pointed out the obscurities and confusions in Dr Robinson's book. One of these is significant and worth pausing over. This is the question of the place and function of metaphor in religious language which he brings up in the first chapter on the God 'up there or out there'. He expresses his irritation with this kind of language but without making it at all clear what he takes a phrase like 'God is up there' to mean. If he is arguing that God is not 'up there' in the sense that God is not an entity that one could theoretically examine in, say, the course of space exploration, this is an assertion not to be found in traditional Christian theology. There is, however, a sense in which it is most true to say that God is 'up there' or 'out there' and that is that 'God' is not simply another word for human life or experience at its most profound or intense. It is not clear, on this basic issue, which of the two uses the bishop has in mind.

This is a very significant area of confusion and it pinpoints what is a real situation of crisis in contemporary theology. This is 'the crisis of metaphor', and it bears on the discussions about 'myth' and symbolism to be found in a number of the extracts given in this series. Man as a finite being is bound to be a metaphor-making animal so long as he experiences intimations of realities outside or beyond what can be measured scientifically. This means, at least, so long as he remains capable of aesthetic, moral, and mystical experience. The fact, for instance, that to indicate these experiences he uses the spatial language of a 'three-decker' universe ('up there', 'down there') is not the 'scandal 'that Bultmann and Dr Robinson take it to be. This is a serious misplacing of what is the real 'stumbling-block' for twentieth-century man as far as Christian language is concerned. In fact the 'three-decker' universe is not a bad image to use in any talk about values and religious beliefs, at least for finite man in a space-time universe which is likely to be the condition of most of mankind in the foreseeable future. For spaceless man no doubt another image would be necessary, but until it is demonstrated that spacelessness is to be the permanent human state to try and dispense with spatial or temporal metaphor or even to be coy about its use is not a sign of maturity or progress. It indicates an inhuman and senseless attempt to try and jump out of our finite skin. The momentum of the human mind, as the poet Wallace Stevens put it, is towards abstraction. Part of the appeal of a 'demythologized' version of Christianity, suggested by Bultmann and others, and commended by Dr Robinson, is that it takes one away from the trying particularities of the concrete. But 'concretizzation', to use Bonhoeffer's term, is a necessary undertaking for the Christian religion as long as it is firmly rooted in an historical and particular Incarnation. It is this feature of the Christian religion which indicates where the real 'stumbling-block' for modern man has to be placed. This is precisely where St Paul put it, in the enigmatical ambiguity of a Christ who is identified with the human scene as to be, seemingly, indistinguishable from it, except to the eyes of faith.

It would be generally true to say that all the theologians represented in this series took a view about the task of philosophy which has now become very unfashionable in Britain. They believed the job of the philosopher was to build up a world-view, a 'metaphysics'. Both Barth and Tillich shared this view. Barth suspected that the very 'world-view' inherent in philosophy would blur the distinctiveness of Christianity. Bultmann believed that 'existentialism' provided a coherent 'metaphysics' of human existence. Niebuhr and the earlier Bonhoeffer approached philosophy in the same way.

It is the special interest of Paul van Buren's *The Secular Meaning of the Gospel* (1963) that it discusses the relation between Christian theology and the type of linguistic or analytical philosophy which has developed in Britain and the United States. For philosophers like Ludwig Wittgenstein, G. E. Moore and A. J. Ayer the task of the philosopher is not to construct a 'world view' but to analyse and classify language. The philosopher studies how language works and the meanings which we attach to statements. He seeks to establish ways of verifying the truth of the various assertions we make.

In the first wave of linguistic analysis popularized by A. J. Ayer's *Language, Truth and Logic* (1936) it was asserted that the only kind of language which had meaning was that which was scientifically verifiable. All other types of language, poetry, for example, or moral exhortation or religion, were said to be meaningless because they were not susceptible to this kind of verification. Philosophical linguistic analysis has modified this position in recent years, and the concern now is how to classify the uses of language and to discuss the types of meaning appropriate to each in relation to the contexts in which they are used.

Paul van Buren seeks to relate the exposition of Christian theology to this kind of linguistic philosophical analysis. Also he has in mind the wish expressed by Bonhoeffer that one ought to be seeking for a 'non-religious interpretation' of biblical and theological concepts. van Buren's book has been nicknamed 'The case of the disappearing gospel'. Certainly in the process of re-stating Christianity in 'non-religious' language he so dissolves traditional Christian theology that it is difficult to see what if anything a believer of former times would recognize in it as familiar.

In *The Secular Meaning of the Gospel* van Buren contended that there is a residual Christianity, even when one has abandoned the idea that any meaning can be attached to 'God' or the 'transcendent'. This remainder he turns into a kind of moral heroism. Christ becomes for all men a model, *the* paradigm, of 'openness' and freedom. The significance of Christ is that he has shown himself, and continues to show himself to be a potent example of these qualities.

The most recent phase of theology has been called the 'death of God' movement. This is the title of a book by Gabriel Vahanian, and it has been used to describe the work not only of Vahanian but of Thomas Altizer (*The Gospel of Christian Atheism*) and William Hamilton, *The Essence of Christianity*.

If one complained about confusion in *Honest to God* this complaint would have to be brought even more sharply against some of these theologians, especially Altizer, whose work is irritatingly rhapsodic just at the points where clarity of expression is most required. It is not at all easy to be sure of what exactly is being said. In one way Altizer seems to be saying that Nietzsche's cry, 'God is dead', still needs repeating, particularly since as far as modern man in a technological society is concerned belief in God as a transcendent reality upon whom mankind depends has no meaning, and is hopelessly irrelevant. Man must now look to his own resources as he prepares to take charge of his own evolution.

Another side of Altizer seems to be saying, again in a very confused way, that Christians have been reluctant to come to realistic terms with the Incarnation, particularly with its corollary that Christ really died the death. This is a useful point because it is true that Christians have traditionally not only denied that Christ was born in the way that we are, but there remained for a long time in Christian theology, especially in the Greek church, the belief that Christ's human flesh was not mortal flesh as ours is.

Altizer wishes to press the reality of the *kenosis* or self-giving in Incarnation so that one can say with Charles Péguy, 'God too has faced death'. But Altizer seems to take *kenosis* to mean a literal self-annihilation. He speaks of the death of God as 'an historical event'. If these words mean anything Altizer is saying that in the Incarnation God, as it were, committed suicide. The death of God in Christ has freed us to become our own Christs, the result of the Incarnation being that God has diffused himself in the human race. This sounds like a new version of pantheism.

What is specially interesting in the 'death of God' theologians is the place which they are still willing to accord to Christ. In spite of form-criticism and the wave of scepticism which it produced both Altizer and Hamilton seem to believe that there is sufficiently reliable information available about Jesus to warrant our thinking again about the ideal of the 'imitation of Christ'. This is interpreted along very different lines from Bonhoeffer's presentation of the *imitatio Christi.* It reminds one of what Kierkegaard called 'admiration of Christ', a heroic endeavour to reproduce his 'openness' and 'freedom' by sheer effort of will.

5

It is hazardous to suggest what is likely to be the prospect for theology in the rest of this century. However, it seems to me that four areas will provide material for special clarification: (1) There is first what I have called the 'crisis of metaphor' in modern theology. Theology and religious language stand or fall by metaphor and all that it implies about human life and human perception. The impulse to metaphor, to speak of one thing in terms of another, prompts the question whether the relation between appearance and reality may not be of the kind which religious belief suggests. The surrender of metaphor means the end of religion and, significantly, the death of what we have come to regard as distinctively human feelings. The French 'anti-novelist' Alain Robbe-Grillet is perfectly right to detect an important link between metaphor and religion. Robbe-Grillet wishes to get rid of metaphor because it implies some hidden relationship between man and the universe, and this takes us half-way to religion. Indeed, there is a 'crisis of metaphor' in modern literature as well as in modern theology. Bultmann can speak disparagingly of 'mere metaphors' and advocates 'demythologization' because myth, metaphor and symbol can be taken in a crude literal way, or can become obsolete. These are certainly hazards in the human situation, which often necessitate a drastic process of unlearning. But a worse fate, a greater hurt to the soul is to attempt to bring about a state of affairs where such hazards are no longer possible. It is damaging either to identify metaphor and actuality or to romanticize pantheistically (in a way that alarms Robbe-Grillet), but it is worse to believe that as individuals and as a generation we have gone beyond the need for metaphor. At stake, therefore, in the present 'crisis of metaphor' in literature and religion is nothing less than the humanization or dehumanization of man.

(2) There needs to be very much more exploration of what Tillich called 'correlation' between religion and the arts. Christians have lived too long with the assumption that while art may have aesthetic or pedagogical value, it is no serious avenue to truth. Art has been regarded as useful for those who cannot read, and need pictures, but not for the literate who having mastered discursive reasoning and the manipulation of abstractions have no need of the image. Art has therefore been taken by many theologians to be inferior to philosophy, and on the whole Christian theologians have preferred to cultivate relations with philosophers rather than artists. This is, however, to beg the question whether art is a way of knowing which is

as truth-bearing, in its way, as philosophical or scientific method. Christians have surrendered with amazing ease to the notion that the image is a lesser form of truth than the concept, as if image and concept were simply alternative ways of saying the same thing, except that the image helps those who have more imagination than logic. It is arguable that the Christian religion would have gained as much (perhaps more) from association with art as it has from philosophy, not only for general apologetic reasons, but for intellectual arguments with what Schleiermacher called its 'cultural despisers'.

(3) Thirdly, there is the continuing work of interpreting afresh the significance of Christ and in the immediate future this will have to include a thorough exploration of what it means to talk about the uniqueness of Christ and his finality.

In spite of the central place which it occupies in the structure of their beliefs, it has proved persistently difficult for Christians to take the Incarnation with full realism and to follow through its implications in a rigorously realistic way. It took Christians a very long time indeed to accept the belief that the Incarnation meant taking a human biology exactly like ours. What a struggle there was in the early Church to get accepted the belief that Christ really died the death in the way that we do! The history of the iconography of the crucifixion in art shows that it took nearly five centuries before a body of Christ appeared on the cross, and then it is very much a live Christ who, eyes open, stands on the cross as a royal warrior looking through the scene. It took the Christian Church nearly ten centuries before a really dead body of Christ appeared on the cross, and even then it was not a death in suffering and agony. It is another century and a half before a bleeding, suffering emaciated Christ with a crown of thorns appears in the representation of the crucifixion. This is a long time, but it has taken Christians even longer to come anywhere near accepting that the Incarnation involved taking a genuine human psychology of the kind that might mean that Christ had to find his way to religious belief in exactly the same way as everybody else, through faith, through acting on signs which, because they are ambiguous and our freedom is real, can always be 'stumbling-bocks' ('scandals' in the New Testament) that offend. Just as dangerous as a theology based on the 'God of the gaps' has been a 'Christology of the gaps', that is, a tendency to insert a capacity for full divine self-awareness on the part of the historical Jesus in some 'gap' in his psyche, or, so it has sometimes been suggested, in his subconscious!

The question of the finality of Christ suggests the fourth area in which it is likely that theology will be specially engaged in the immediate future: comparative religion, and especially comparative theology.

(4) In the contemporary world it sometimes appears that the 'ecumenical' movement of unbelief grows faster than that of belief, so that all religions are finding themselves on the same side of the fence as far as faith that human life has a transcendental significance is concerned. In this situation there needs to be more conversation between the theologies of the religions, particularly those whose history gives them a special kinship: Judaism, Christianity and Islam. If the Christian has to start thinking again about the meaning of Incarnation and the unique place which he assigns to Christ there is no more bracing company in which he could explore this question than that of the Jew and Muslim.

The present-day student of the Christian doctrines of the Trinity and the Incarnation might well begin with reflection on the familiar strictures on these doctrines that come from the Jew and the Muslim: that they violate the concept of the unity of God, and, by involving God in human history in a finite way, blaspheme against the majesty of God. The Christian will want to have as rich a doctrine that God is one as the Jew or the Muslim, and that God is known in historical event, and perhaps this is now more likely to be attained by going to school theologically with these two religions. Further the three religions of Judaism, Christianity and Islam have much to give each other in working out afresh for our own day the meaning of what it is to be human. Bishop Kenneth Cragg has shown how profound a realization of the nature of man comes from relating the Jewish/Christian concept of man made in the 'image of God' to the Muslim concept of man as God's 'caliph'. [1]

Much needs to be unlearned and relearned in this field. Judaism, Islam and Buddhism have suffered from misleading

[1] Kenneth Cragg, *The Privilege of Man*, London, 1968.

propagandist slogans in the past like 'Jewish legalism', 'Islam is the most materialistic and least religious of the religions', 'Buddhism is insensitive to suffering or social justice'. These are Christian caricatures of the truth, and there is now a fresh chance, especially in those western countries which are now multi-religious, to rectify this distortion by mutual understanding in co-operative study.

1. Karl Barth

1886–1968

BIOGRAPHICAL INTRODUCTION

Karl Barth was born on 10 May 1886 at Basle in Switzerland where his father, Fritz Barth, was professor of New Testament and early Church history. When Karl was three the family moved to Berne where the father had been appointed to the chair of Church history. After school in Berne, Barth studied in the universities of Berne, Berlin, Tübingen and Marburg. At the University of Berlin he was taught by the famous Adolf von Harnack and at Marburg by Wilhelm Herrmann ('my unforgettable teacher'). At this time he became an enthusiastic student of Schleiermacher (see p. 22).

From 1909 to 1911 Barth was a junior pastor in Geneva, and then was appointed pastor of the village of Safonwil in Aargau. The ten years which he spent here were in fact the formative period of his life, and his discussions with fellow pastors in the area determined the shape of the theology which was to come.

Barth was profoundly shocked by a statement published in 1914 by university teachers in Germany endorsing German war policy. To his astonishment he saw in the list of signatories to this document some of his old theological teachers. The shock was the inability of these teachers to see that any gap existed between the values they professed to believe in and German nationalist policies during the 1914–18 war. To quote him: 'For me personally a day at the beginning of August in that year (1914) was the *dies ater* (the black day), when ninety-three German intellectuals published an endorsement of the military policy of Kaiser Wilhelm II and his councillors, on which to my horror I found the names of almost all the theological teachers whom hitherto I had confidently respected. If they could be so mistaken in ethos, I noted that it was quite impossible for me to adhere any longer to their ethics or dogmatics, to their exposition of the Bible or presentation of history. So far as I was concerned there was no more future for the theology of the 19th century.'[1]

This marked the beginning of Barth's distrust of nineteenth-

[1] Quoted in H. Gollwitzer, *Selections from Karl Barth's Church Dogmatics*, pp. 14–15.

century liberal theology (see pp. 21 ff.), particularly because of its inability to accept the possibility that the irrational and evil might be permanent features of human behaviour. During this period, he laid the foundations of his theology of the 'Word of God'. This takes as its starting-point acceptance of a unique divine revelation in Christ, witnessed to by the Bible. Not that the Bible is in itself the revelation of God (see p. 20) but that it points to the place of the revelation, Jesus of Nazareth. The first fruits of this theological thinking were to be seen in Barth's famous commentary on the epistle to the Romans which he published in 1919. This book had enormous influence on the continent and, following the publication of an English translation by Sir E. C. Hoskyns in 1933, in Britain also.

Following the publication of *Romans*, Barth was appointed to the chair of theology at Göttingen in 1921. Then followed appointments to chairs in Münster (1925) and in Bonn (1930).

The new theology of Barth provided the impetus behind the formation of the 'Confessing Church' in Germany which opposed the growth of Nazism and the Nazi-sponsored 'German Church' movement. It was Barth's theology also which informed the famous declaration of Barmen in 1934. In the following year he refused to swear allegiance to Hitler and was dismissed from his chair in Bonn. Barth then returned to his native Switzerland where he was appointed professor of systematic theology in Basle. There he taught until his retirement in 1962.

In 1932 he had begun work on what was to be his masterpiece. Originally entitled *Christian Dogmatics*, he changed the title to *Church Dogmatics*, indicating his now strong conviction of the indissoluble link between belief and community. This work in its magnificent sweep has caused it to be compared with the *Summa Theologiae* of St Thomas Aquinas. Pope Pius XII in fact described Karl Barth as the greatest theologian since St Thomas. Be that as it may, one would have to note that St Thomas and Barth differed radically in the way they thought theology should be done and in the place which they assigned to natural theology (see Introduction, pp. 17 ff.). More and more, Barth came to see Christology, belief about Christ, as the king-pin of the whole structure of Christian theology, whether it be the doctrines of creation, man, grace or atonement. So much so that he came to say that Christian theology is fundamentally Christology.

The early Barth so stressed the transcendence of God ('God as the wholly other') that it was difficult for his readers to see how he related God and man at all. The later Barth shows a considerable mellowing of this point of view. He admits to being only 'partially in the right' on this, and to having 'boxed man on the ears' too sharply. [1] His approach to the matter at this stage bears some likeness to later Greek theology which believed that there must be some antecedent kinship between God and man to make the Incarnation possible.

Barth exercised considerable theological influence on the growth of the ecumenical movement. His address at the first assembly of the World Council of Churches at Amsterdam in 1948 was a landmark in the history of the movement.

Karl Barth died on Monday, 9 December 1968 at the age of eighty-two.

[1] *The Humanity of God* (Fontana), 1961, p. 39.

SELECTIONS

1 'Saved by Grace

[Barth always saw a close connection between theology and preaching, theology being the explanation and clarification of the *Kerygma* which the preacher is commissioned to proclaim. While he was professor of theology at Basle University he used to visit prisoners in the gaol there, and preach to them. In this sermon, which gives his theology in a nutshell, he expresses in characteristic exultant language, the overwhelming sense of freedom and happiness that comes from realizing the wonderful givenness and courtesy of God's way with human beings, whether it is in salvation or grace.]

My dear brothers and sisters, I now read a passage from the Letter of the Apostle Paul to the Ephesians (2.5): *By grace have you been saved.* This, I think, is brief enough for it to be remembered by all, for it to impress itself upon you and, if it be God's will, to be understood.

We are gathered here this Sunday morning to hear this word: *By grace you have been saved!* Whatever else we do, praying and singing, is but an answer to this word spoken to us by God himself. The prophets and apostles wrote a strange book, called the Bible, for the very purpose of testifying to this fact before mankind. The Bible alone contains this sentence. We do not read it in Kant or in Schopenhauer,[1] or in any book of natural or secular history, and certainly not in any novel, but in the Bible alone. In order to hear this word we need what is called the Church—the company of Christians, of human beings called and willing to listen together to the Bible and through it to the word of God. This is the word of God: *By grace you have been saved!*

Someone once said to me: 'I need not go to church. I need not read the Bible. I know already what the Church teaches

[1] Immanuel Kant (1724–1804) and Arthur Schopenhauer (1788–1860), German philosophers. (Ed.)

and what the Bible says: "Do what is right and fear no one!"' Let me say this at this point: If this were the message at stake, I would most certainly not have come here. My time is too precious and so is yours. To say that, neither prophets nor apostles, neither Bible, Jesus Christ nor God are needed. Anybody is at liberty to say this to himself. By the same token this saying is void of any new, of any very special and exciting message. It does not help anyone. I have never seen a smile on the face of a person reassuring himself with this kind of talk. As a rule, those who use it are a sad-looking lot, revealing all too easily that this word does not help them, does not comfort them, does not bring them joy.

Let us hear therefore what the Bible says and what we as Christians are called to hear together: *By grace you have been saved!* No man can say this to himself. Neither can he say it to someone else. This can only be said by God to each one of us. It takes Jesus Christ to make this saying true. It takes the apostles to communicate it. And our gathering here as Christians is needed to spread it among us. This is why it is truly news, and very special news, the most exciting news of all, the most helpful thing also, indeed the only helpful thing.

'By grace *you* have been saved!' How strange to have this message addressed to us! Who are we, anyway? Let me tell you quite frankly: we are all together great sinners. Please understand me: I include myself. I stand ready to confess being the greatest sinner among you all; yet you may then not exclude yourself from the group! Sinners are people who in the judgement of God, and perhaps of their own consciences, missed and lost their way, who are not just a little, but totally guilty, hopelessly indebted and lost not only in time, but in eternity. We are such sinners. And we are prisoners. Believe me, there is a captivity much worse than the captivity in this house. There are walls much thicker and doors much heavier than those closed upon you. All of us, the people without and you within, are prisoners of our own obstinacy, of our many greeds, of our various anxieties, of our mistrust and in the last analysis of our unbelief. We are all sufferers. Most of all we suffer from ourselves. We each make life difficult for ourselves and in so doing for our fellowmen. We suffer from life's lack of meaning. We suffer in the shadow of death and of eternal judgement towards which we are moving. We spend our life in the midst of a whole world of sin and captivity and suffering.

But now listen. Into the depth of our predicament the word is spoken from on high: *By grace you have been saved!* To be saved does not just mean to be a little encouraged, a little comforted, a little relieved. It means to be pulled out like a log from a burning fire. You have been saved! We are not told: you may be saved sometimes, or a little bit. No you *have been* saved, totally and for all times. You? Yes, we! Not just any other people, more pious and better than we are, no, we, each one of us.

This is so because Jesus Christ is our brother and, through his life and death, has become our Saviour who has wrought our salvation. He is the word of God for us. And this word is: *By grace you have been saved!*

You probably all know the legend of the rider who crossed the frozen Lake of Constance by night without knowing it. When he reached the opposite shore and was told whence he came, he broke down, horrified. This is the human situation when the sky opens and the earth is bright, when we may hear: *By grace you have been saved!* In such a moment we are like that terrified rider. When we hear this word we involuntarily look back, do we not, asking ourselves: Where have I been? Over an abyss, in mortal danger! What did I do? The most foolish thing I ever attempted! What happened? I was doomed and miraculously escaped and now I am safe! You ask: 'Do we really live in such danger?' Yes, we live on the brink of death. But we have been saved. Look at our Saviour and at our salvation! Look at Jesus Christ on the cross, accused, sentenced and punished instead of us! Do you know for whose sake he is hanging there? For *our* sake—because of *our* sin—sharing *our* captivity—burdened with *our* suffering! He nails *our* life to the cross. This is how God had to deal with *us*. From this darkness he has saved *us*. He who is not shattered after hearing this news may not yet have grasped the word of God: *By grace you have been saved!*

But more important than the fear of sudden death is the

knowledge of life imparted to us: 'By grave you have been *saved!*' Therefore, we have reached the shore, the Lake of Constance is behind us, we may breathe freely, even though we still are in the grip of panic, and rightly so. This panic is but an aftermath. By virtue of the good news the sky truly opens and the earth is bright. What a glorious relief to be told that there I was, in that darkness, over that abyss, on the brink of death, but there I am no longer. Through this folly I lived, but I cannot and I will not do it again, never again. This happened, but it must not and it will not happen again. My sin, my captivity, my suffering are yesterday's reality, not today's. They are things of my past, not of the present nor of the future. I have been *saved!* Is this really so, is this the truth? Look once again to Jesus Christ in his death upon the cross. Look and try to understand that what he did and suffered he did and suffered for you, for me, for us all. He carried our sin, our captivity and our suffering, and did not carry it in vain. *He carried it away.* He acted as the captain of us all. He broke through the ranks of our enemies. He has already won the battle, our battle. All we have to do is to follow him, to be victorious with him. Through him, in him we are saved. Our sin has no longer any power over us. Our prison door is open. Our suffering has come to an end. This is a great word indeed. The word of God *is* indeed a great word. And we would deny him, we would deny the Lord Jesus Christ, were we to deny the greatness of this word: He sets us free. When he, the Son of God, sets us free, we are *truly* free.

Because we are saved by no other than Jesus Christ, we are saved *by grace.* This means that we did not deserve to be saved. What we deserved would be quite different. We cannot secure salvation for ourselves. Did you read in the newspapers the other day that man will soon be able to produce an artificial moon? But we cannot produce our salvation. No one can be proud of being saved. Each one can only fold his hands in great lowliness of heart and be thankful like a child. Consequently we shall never possess salvation as our property. We may only receive it as a gift over and over again, with hands outstretched. '*By grace* you have been saved!' This means constantly to look away from ourselves to God and to the man on the cross where this truth is revealed. This truth is ever anew to be believed and to be grasped by faith. To believe means to look to Jesus Christ and to God and to trust that there is the truth for us, for our lives, for the life of all men.

Is it not a pity that we rebel against this very truth in the depth of our hearts? Indeed, we dislike hearing that we are saved by grace, and by grace alone. We do not appreciate that God does not owe us anything, that we are bound to live from his goodness alone, that we are left with nothing but the great humility, the thankfulness of a child presented with many gifts. For we do not like at all to look away from ourselves. We would much prefer to withdraw into our own inner circle, not unlike the snail into its shell, and to be with ourselves. To put it bluntly: we do not like to believe. And yet grace and therefore faith as I just described it is the beginning of the true life of freedom, of a carefree heart, of joy deep within, of love of God and neighbour, of great and assured hope! And yet grace and faith would make things so very simple in our lives!

Dear brothers and sisters, where do we stand now? One thing is certain: the bright day *has dawned,* the sun of God *does shine* into our dark lives, even though we may close our eyes to its radiance. His voice *does call* us from heaven, even though we may obstruct our ears. The bread of life is *offered* to us, even though we are inclined to clench our fists instead of opening our hands to take the bread and eat it. The door of our prison *is open,* even though, strangely enough, we prefer to remain within. God has put the house in order, even though we like to mess it up all over again. '*By grace you have been saved!*'—this is true, even though we may not believe it, may not accept it as valid for ourselves and unfortunately in so doing may forego its benefits. *Why* should we want to forego the benefits? *Why* should we not want to believe? *Why* do we not go out through the open door? *Why* do we not open our clenched fists? *Why* do we obstruct our ears? *Why* are we blindfolded? Honestly, *why?*

One remark in reply must suffice. All this is so because perhaps we failed to pray fervently enough for a change within ourselves, on our part. That God is God, not only almighty, but merciful and good, that he wills and does what is best for us, that Jesus Christ died for us to set us free, that by grace, in him, we have been saved—all this need *not* be a concern of our prayers. All these things are true apart from our own deeds and prayers. But to believe, to accept, to let it be true for us, to begin to live with this truth, to believe it not only with our minds and with our lips, but also with our hearts and with all our life, so that our fellowmen may sense it, and finally to let our total existence be immersed in the great divine truth, *by grace you have been saved,* this is to be the concern of our prayers. No human being has ever prayed for this in vain. If anyone asks for this, the answer is already being given and faith begins. And because no one has ever asked for this in vain, no one may omit praying like a little child for the assurance that God's truth, this terrible, this glorious truth, is shining even today, a small, yet increasingly bright light. *By grace you have been saved.* Ask that you may believe this and it will be given you; seek this, and you will find it; knock on this door, and it will be opened to you.

This, my dear friends, is what I have been privileged and empowered to tell you of the good news as the word of God today. Amen.

(FROM: *Deliverance to the Captives*, pp. 36–41.)

2 'What is Dogmatic Theology'

[In this section we give some passages where Barth explains the task of theology as he sees it. He tries to answer the question 'Why theology?' and the objection that it is a needless complication of simple issues, the work of intellectuals who enjoy this kind of word spinning. For Barth the theologian needs to be a participant in the liturgy and prayer of a religious community, the Church. He touches also on the question of what he calls the 'invasion' of theology by philosophy.

This sequence of passages provides an illustration of a main theme in Barth—that Christian theology starts from *within* the Christian tradition, beginning, as he puts it, not from God nor man but from the God-man and the Bible, as witness to his divine revelation. It is interesting to compare this with the different starting-points of Tillich and the later Bonhoeffer.]

The special task of dogmatics implies that it is the place where, as nowhere else, theology comes into its own. But this situation has a two-edged character of which we ought to be aware. We have said that the work of dogmatics arises at the middle point between that of exegetical and that of practical theology. This means, on the one hand, that theology can exercise itself at this point in a certain security and independence, which is not self-evident elsewhere, but peculiar to it by reason of this middle position. Behind it theology has Holy Scripture as witness to revelation, and its attestation in the earlier confessions and knowledge of the Church. Before it, it has the Church and its activity of proclamation. Thus placed, theology can reveal, unfold and shape itself in dogmatics as a characteristic branch of knowledge. It can do so all the more, the more strictly it stands in this twofold relation and avails itself of the fact that here it is held, nourished and protected in this twofold way. When it asks concerning the content of the Church's proclamation in this sphere and framework, it is confronted by a whole world of problems, each of which is so rich and fruitful because we cannot seriously treat a single one of them without immediately having to treat the one central problem in a new and special way; for there is no real periphery, but each peripheral point immediately becomes another centre. And the details, too, form themselves automatically into a whole, the unity of which we do not merely surmise but also perceive, and then again merely surmise and fail to perceive. And, again, the more definitely we are placed within this sphere and framework, the more conversant we become with the details as such and with their cosmic totality as such: the more reason there is to be astounded, on the one hand, at the complete freedom with which we can work in every question of method, order or sequence of thought, apparently according to the peculiar disposition and talents of each individual worker, and, on the other hand, at the utter impossibility of arbitrariness either in approach or in the basic design, which the very nature of the thing determines. To engage in theology seriously means—and this in proportion to the seriousness with which the task is undertaken—to awaken as a theologian to scientific self-consciousness . . .

. . . But there is another aspect to the fact that in dogmatics, as nowhere else, theology comes into its own. For it undoubtedly involves a real burden and temptation, which we must also consider. It is not, of course, an accident that all the complaints and objections which arise both in the world and in the Church itself against theology are always aimed directly or indirectly at dogmatics. What does this mean? Is it not the case that the security and independence with which theology can be pursued in this middle position carry with them a relative impregnability for those who pursue it, that they are not immediately exposed, like the biblical theologian, to the direct assault of Holy Scripture, or, like the practical theologian, to the direct assault of the congregation and the world, that they are, indeed, contained and limited on both sides (and, it is to be hoped, most emphatically contained and limited), but that as the transition is there made from *explicatio* to *applicatio*, they are implicated in the necessary process of the reflection which both assimilates and then in the movement to *applicatio* utilizes? It is, of course, on this razor's edge that dogmatics appears in all its splendour as the central theological discipline, and we can never rate that splendour too highly. Here or nowhere, there awakes the self-awareness of the critical theologian. But how can this situation fail to be critical, two-edged and even actually dangerous? We are confronted immediately by the question whether that suspicion is not justified with which even in the Church itself the question is asked: What kind of abstraction and aloofness from life is this, in which dogmatics and therefore theology seems to move? Where are we really led by the innumerable formal reflections, distinctions and limitations, and all the indissolubly connected objections and negations, in which theology issues at this point? Is not the Bible much simpler than dogmatics? Is it not therefore possible and necessary that preaching and teaching should be much simpler? Must this middle course really be traversed? Are not unnecessary refinements and difficulties artificially introduced only at a later stage to be just as artificially resolved? Is there not at work in the practised analysis and synthesis a strong vein of humanistic aesthetics, which has no connexion with the seriousness of the Church's theological task? The temptation offered by such questions is twofold. It is certainly not a good thing arrogantly to exclude the probability that the open or tacit reproaches which such questions imply do always contain a *particula veri*. To the extent that in this middle position a man is really concerned with himself instead of with his subject matter, to the extent that he works himself out in this position, it is undoubtedly a misfortune, for speculations alien to the life of Scripture and the Church hold the attention, and these can only be aggravated by the natural brilliance of dogmatic activity, which in this case will immediately become unnatural. As dogmaticians, we continually have to put the question whether, in the whole of our work, we are not more concerned with ourselves than with the subject matter. This question will have to be asked the more urgently in proportion as we may feel our work to be successful. But, again, it is wrong if the questions suggested by this mistrust are allowed to alienate us from the task in hand, that task which is laid upon us in the middle position between the Bible and the Church, of critical and systematic reflection with a view to the discovery of pure doctrine. Dogmatics has not to be ashamed of its task as a discipline, its scholastic task. The reproaches may spring from inadequate insight into the seriousness and scope of this task. They may be philistine in character. Therefore we should not allow ourselves to be misled by them. We should treat them with friendly unconcern. Often enough there lies concealed behind them the error which has penetrated into the Church and which scents out in dogmatics its natural adversary. Often enough apparent simplicity is not merely complexity and sophistication, but also downright falsehood, which fears to be unmasked by dogmatics. And where this is the case dogmatics has even less occasion to allow itself to be confused by heckling from this source, and so diverted from its post.

But at this point a further question arises, for as dogmatics effects the transition from the Bible to preaching, and constitutes it by its own human reflection, it provides the occasion, as we have already seen in §21 on which the question of the relation between theology and philosophy becomes a burning issue. Is it not inevitable that at this point, where it seems that theology is no longer thinking and speaking exegetically and not yet practically, philosophy will present itself with instruction how critical and systematic thought is to be carried on in this process of transition? Is it not inevitable that in its suggestions—the suggestions which the theologian makes to himself in his capacity as a philosopher—the significant fact will again emerge that it is in dogmatics that the theologian can most easily lay an unauthorized emphasis on self? This is the classical point for the invasion of alien powers, the injection of metaphysical systems which are secretly in conflict with the Bible and the Church. And where this has taken place, it has only separated the Bible and the Church, and after lending to dogmatics a certain false independence, it has caused its disintegration and that of theology generally, at first inwardly and very soon outwardly as well. If the complaints about the aloofness and abstraction of dogmatics from life are justified, if in this matter man is more concerned about himself than his subject, then the reason or the effect will almost always be found in some such interpenetration. We must note again that there is a real source of danger at this point. When theology, as it were, snatches away the biblical word in order to press it into the framework of a scheme of thought which it has already prepared and regards as absolute, and to pass it on in this form to the preaching of the Church, then no matter what the scheme may be, the evil has already been committed, that is, the corruption of doctrine, which it is the task of theology, and of dogmatics at this middle point of theology, to prevent. The keeper himself has opened the gate to the enemy. The contingency needs only to be described to tell us that this is just what must not be allowed to happen. But, again, the opposite temptation must also be resisted. In dogmatics, personal schemes of thought must be shaped in accordance with the word of the Bible, which is now to become the word of the Church, and not conversely. There can never be any question of opposing them to the word of the Bible, as, so to speak, stable elements; nor can there ever be any question in dogmatics of maintaining such a scheme, however necessary and useful it may be, as a norm over against the preaching of the Church. But, again, it is not right to allow a fear of this interpretation, and therefore of the possible corruption of doctrine, to arrest human thinking, as it is no doubt controlled by the criterion of a philosophy, and with it the work of criticism and systematization which it has to perform. It cannot be good counsel to let an ascetic abstinence prevail at this point, because in practice this can only mean putting aside the work that has to be done here. It is quite wrong, of course, that at this point man should give rein to the arbitrariness of his thought and the philosopher prevails over the theologian. But it is even more wrong that at this point where he is challenged in his whole existence and therefore as a theological philosopher too, man should withdraw and refuse from fear of sin or of being suspected of sin, and should then pass from thinking to not thinking or to an idle and frivolous type of thinking. So long as dogmatics has heeded the warning, it can and must go forward in this respect too with a good conscience.

We now attempt briefly to outline its general task. Even the work of dogmatics can begin only with the hearing of the Word of God, and indeed the hearing of it in the proclamation of the Church. It, too, proceeds from the expectation and the claim which this proclamation arouses, that the human word which is heard may be not only man's word, but God's own

Word. Apart from this presupposition, it has no contribution to make, and the questions which it has to put, the criticism which it has to exercise and the counsels which it has to offer will be without root, object and meaning. The sphere in which it thinks and speaks does not lie outside but inside the Church. It does not think and speak, therefore, by ignoring but by acknowledging the promise given to the Church. For that reason it must not approach the preaching of the Church in a mood of distrust, as though the pure doctrine, about which it asks and concerns itself, cannot become a reality. The attitude of dogmatics towards Church proclamation must be critical, but it may not be sceptically negative. In spite of all the objections and scruples which it has to bring forward, in spite of all the changes, however significant, which it has to propose, it must proceed in the confidence that God's Word has never left itself without a witness in the Church, and will never do so. It will listen, expecting to hear pure doctrine and therefore not merely man's word but God's Word. It will listen to the Church's preaching, as listening in faith demands. In this way it will try to hear what the Church has to say about God to the world today in the whole scope of its activities. But just because of this presupposition it will listen critically. It will bear in mind the other presupposition that those who speak of God are men, that what happens is a matter of the ministry and liturgy of the Church which cannot as such be perfect and unassailable like the Word of God itself, but which by the Word of God, or, from the human point of view, by prayer and the work of the Church, always has to become what it is. For the Church to which this promise is given, and the preaching of which it therefore approaches with this first presupposition in mind, is undoubtedly a Church of sinners.

If dogmatics is particularly concerned with the work which from the Church point of view must be done in order that its divine worship may be divine worship not merely in form and appearance but in reality, then it cannot be sufficiently emphasized that this work cannot be properly done except in so far as the dogmatic theologian both assigns to prayer a much more important place in the solution of the problem confronting him, and also himself participates in the prayer of the Church for the correctness of its liturgy and the purity of its doctrine. About this, little need be said. The truth is that the quality of dogmatic work depends decisively on its not consisting, for example, merely in a series of conceptual manipulations, but on its being penetrated down to its last and apparently least important details by an unceasing supplication for the Holy Spirit, who is both for the purposes of the Church and for His own sake the *unum necessarium* which no technique nor toil can compel, but for which we can only pray . . .

. . . If we ask concerning the subject matter of dogmatics, the reply must be that it consists essentially in the totality of what it hears from the Church—the contemporary Church—as its human speech about God. In practice, however, it will consist in certain key-words and fundamental outlines which in this heterogeneous mass constitute that which is common to the whole and recurs in all its multiple forms. However searchingly, the critical inquiry into pure doctrine must be conducted, the fact of such common and recurrent features justifies us from the start in the corresponding faith (without which we cannot approach this task) that what the Church says about God is not just crude material without a pattern, but that by the unmistakable existence of such key-words and fundamental outlines it discloses itself as a system of doctrine, about the unity and therefore the purity of which it is not from the outset a hopeless undertaking to inquire . . .

. . . The material which the Church offers contemporary dogmatics will always be new, as will continually appear on a closer inspection, to the extent that both in content and expression the key-word and basic outlines are caught up in an unceasing movement which dogmatics, if its work is not to be too late, if it does not wish to present historical reports rather than the critical co-operation which it owes to the Church of the present, must meet in its most recent, contemporaneous stage. But, again, there is obviously no lack of continuity in this movement and so it is implied that the key-words and thoughts with which dogmatics has to deal today cannot in practice be any different from those with which it had to deal yesterday or four hundred or a thousand years ago. This continuity of basic words and outlines may sometimes be very formal and neutral, but in practice it does at least mean that dogmatics will find itself in conversation not only with the Church of its own generation, but also with that of all previous 'presents' which have now become 'past'. Indeed, it cannot take up its critical task in regard to its own present, if it refuses to bear in mind that it can be properly understood only when viewed as part of a single movement, of which it forms the most recent stage.

The task of dogmatics begins with the question with which it approaches this material. Dogmatics springs from the salutary unrest which must not and cannot leave the Church. It is the unrest of knowing that its work is not done simply by speaking somehow about God, or by speaking with some kind of consistency under the remarkable but undeniable compulsion of the basic words and outlines which supply its framework. As the Church occupies itself with dogmatics, it acknowledges that it is aware of the transformation in which its preaching constantly finds itself, in spite of the formal and neutral identity. It acknowledges that this transformation constitutes a problem. It acknowledges its fear that this transformation might be for the worse, but it acknowledges also its hope that it might be for the better. And finally it acknowledges that it cannot leave this matter to fate, or to the course of an immanent and inevitable development which it can comfortably watch as a spectator, but that it has itself a responsibility in this matter. This sense of responsibility arises, as we have seen, from its realization of the promise given to it that it can and must speak the Word of God. And from the same realization there also arises the impossibility of confining itself to establishing the material contents of dogmatics, the broad facts of a speech about God which 'somehow' takes place and 'somehow' finds unity. From it again, therefore, there arises the seriousness of the question with which dogmatics approach this material.

The task of dogmatics consists generally in a critical examination of its material, which means in fact of these key-words and basic outlines of the Church's speech about God. To examine does not mean to reject. It means to take up, in order to test, or weigh, or measure. Its purpose is to see whether the matter to be tested is what it promises to be and really should be. Dogmatics tests the Church's speech about God, in order to find out whether as man's word it is fitted to serve the Word of God. It considers it in the light of the promise that its essential character, order and task are to serve the Word of God and so to be pure doctrine. It does not allow the changing situation in which it stands, and the confusing multiplicity of its meaning and expression, to mislead it into supposing that the Church's speech about God is not worth examining. But, again, it will not wrongly suppose, that, because in its reality and its apparent unity this speech would prefer not to be exposed to criticism, it therefore does not need it. About the fulfilment of this criticism we shall have to speak in the last two sections of this chapter. Obviously, an examination of this kind cannot be carried out arbitrarily. As we have seen, the danger is not ruled out that a bad examination of the Church's preaching and therefore bad dogmatics may do more harm than good to preaching. Therefore there is every reason that dogmatics should prove itself to be competent for this task, examining itself first in regard to the method to which it must subject itself if it is to be a good examination and good dogmatics. And if in this preliminary self-examination it is a question of measuring and weighing, it is clear what the questions which dogmatics must first of all put to itself should be: (1) the question concerning the criterion or standard with which it is to conduct its examination; and (2) the question concerning the right use of this criterion and standard. We can call the first the question of the dogmatic norm, the second that of dogmatic thinking. The dogmatic norm is the objective possibility, dogmatic thinking the subjective possibility of the Church's proclamation, of which the reality is the Word of God itself.

(FROM: *Church Dogmatics*, I, 2, pp. 771, 772–6, 778–9, 779–80, 781.)

2 'Religion as Unbelief'

[This section gives an idea of what would have been Barth's contribution to what is now called 'religionless Christianity (see Book 5, pp. 331ff.). It illustrates Barth's antipathy to the idea that the Christian theologian ought to begin by analysing religion in general and then go on to treat Christianity as an example, albeit a preeminent one, of the genus 'religion'. The extracts given here also illustrate Barth's approach to the question of the relation of Christianity to other religions.]

A theological evaluation of religion and religions must be characterized primarily by the great cautiousness and charity of its assessment and judgements. It will observe and understand and take man in all seriousness as the subject of religion. But it will not be man apart from God, in a human *per se*. It will be man for whom (whether he knows it or not) Jesus Christ was born, died and rose again. It will be man who (whether he has already heard it or not) is intended in the Word of God. It will be man who (whether he is aware of it or not) has in Christ his Lord. It will always understand religion as a vital utterance and activity of this man. It will not ascribe to this life-utterance and activity of his a unique 'nature', the so-called 'nature of religion', which it can then use as a gauge to weigh and balance one human thing against another, distinguishing the 'higher' religion from the 'lower', the 'living' from the 'decomposed', the 'ponderable' from the 'imponderable'. It will not omit to do this from carelessness or indifference towards the manifoldness with which we have to do in this human sphere, nor because a prior definition of the 'nature' of the phenomena in this sphere is either impossible or in itself irrelevant, but because what we have to know of the nature of religion from the standpoint of God's revelation does not allow us to make any but the most incidental use of an immanent definition of the nature of religion. It is not, then, that this 'revealed' nature of religion is not fitted in either form or content to differentiate between the good and the bad, the true and the false in the religious world. Revelation singles out the Church as the *locus* of true religion. But this does not mean that the Christian religion as such is the fulfilled nature of human religion. It does not mean that the Christian religion is the true religion, fundamentally superior to all other religions. We can never stress too much the connexion between the truth of the Christian religion and the grace of revelation. We have to give particular emphasis to the fact that through grace the Church lives by grace, and to that extent it is the *locus* of true religion. And if this is so, the Church will as little boast of its 'nature', i.e., the perfection in which it fulfils the 'nature' of religion, as it can attribute that nature to other religions. We cannot differentiate and separate the Church from other religions on the basis of a general concept of the nature or religion . . .

. . . A truly theological treatment of religion and religions, as it is demanded and possible in the Church as the *locus* of the Christian religion, will need to be distinguished from all other forms of treatment by the exercise of a very marked tolerance towards its object. Now this tolerance must not be confused with the moderation of those who actually have their own religion or religiosity, and are secretly zealous for it, but who can exercise self-control, because they have told themselves or have been told that theirs is not the only faith, that fanaticism is a bad thing, that love must always have the first and the last word. It must not be confused with the clever aloofness of the rationalistic Know-All—the typical Hegelian belongs to the same category—who thinks that he can deal comfortably and in the end successfully with all religions in the light of a concept of a perfect religion which is gradually evolving in history. But it also must not be confused with the relativism and impartiality of an historical scepticism, which does not ask about truth and untruth in the field of religious phenomena, because it thinks that truth can be known only in the form of its own doubt about all truth. That the so-called 'tolerance' of this kind is unattainable is revealed by the fact that the object, religion and religions, and therefore man, are not taken seriously but are at bottom patronized. Tolerance in the sense of moderation, or superior knowledge, or scepticism is actually the worst form of intolerance. But the religion and religions must be treated with a tolerance which is informed by the forbearance of Christ, which derives therefore from the knowledge that by grace God has reconciled to Himself godless man and his religion. It will see man carried, like an obstinate child in the arms of its mother, by what God has determined and done for his salvation in spite of his own opposition. In detail, it will neither praise nor reproach him. It will understand his situation—understand it even in the dark and terrifying perplexity of it—not because it can see any meaning in the situation as such, but because it acquires a meaning from outside, from Jesus Christ. But confronted by this object it will not display the weak or superior or weary smile of a quite inappropriate indulgence. It will see that man is caught in a way of acting that cannot be recognized as right and holy, unless it is first and at the same time recognized as thoroughly wrong and unholy. Self-evidently, this kind of tolerance, and therefore a theological consideration of religion, is possible only for those who are ready to abase themselves and their religion together with man, with every individual man, knowing that they first, and their religion, have need of tolerance, a strong forbearing tolerance.

We begin, by stating that religion is unbelief. It is a concern, indeed, we must say that it is the one great concern, of godless man . . .

. . . In the light of what we have already said, this proposition is not in any sense a negative value-judgement. It is not a judgment of religious science or philosophy based upon some prior negative judgement concerned with the nature of religion. It does not affect only other men with their religion. Above all it affects ourselves also as adherents of the Christian religion. It formulates the judgement of divine revelation upon all religion. It can be explained and expounded but it cannot be derived from any higher principle than revelation, nor can it be proved by any phenomenology or history of religion. Since it aims only to repeat the judgement of God, it does not involve any human renunciation of human values, any contesting of the true and the good and the beautiful which a closer inspection will reveal in almost all religions, and which we naturally expect to find in abundant measure in our own religion, if we hold to it with any conviction. What happens is simply that man is taken by God and judged and condemned by God. That means, of course, that we are struck to the very roots, to the heart. Our whole existence is called in question. But where that is the case there can be no place for sad and pitiful laments at the non-recognition of relative human greatness . . .

. . . To realize that religion is really unbelief, we have to consider it from the standpoint of the revelation attested in Holy Scripture. There are two elements in that revelation which make it unmistakably clear.

1. Revelation is God's self-offering and self-manifestation. Revelation encounters man on the presupposition and in confirmation of the fact that man's attempts to know God from his own standpoint are wholly and entirely futile; not because of any necessity in principle, but because of a practical necessity of fact. In revelation God tells man that He is God, and that as such He is his Lord. In telling him this, revelation tells him something utterly new, something which apart from revelation he does not know and cannot tell either himself or others. It is true that he could do this, for revelation simply states the truth. If it is true that God is God and that as such He is the Lord of man, then it is also true that man is so placed towards Him, that he could know Him. But this is the very truth which is not available to man, before it is told him in revelation. If he really can know God, this capacity rests upon the fact that he really does know Him, because God has offered and manifested Himself to him. The capacity, then, does not rest upon the fact, which is true enough, that man could know Him. Between 'he could' and 'he can' there lies the absolutely decisive 'he cannot', which can be removed and turned into its opposite only by revelation. The truth that God is God and our Lord, and the further truth that we could know Him as God and Lord, can only come to us through the truth itself. This 'coming to us' of the truth is revelation. It

does not reach us in a neutral condition, but in an action which stands to it, as the coming of truth, in a very definite, indeed a determinate relationship. That is to say, it reaches us as religious men; i.e., it reaches us in the attempt to know God from our standpoint. It does not reach us, therefore, in the activity which corresponds to it. The activity which corresponds to revelation would have to be faith; the recognition of the self-offering and self-manifestation of God. We need to see that in view of God all our activity is in vain even in the best life; i.e., that of ourselves we are not in a position to apprehend the truth, to let God be God and our Lord. We need to renounce all attempts even to try to apprehend this truth. We need to be ready and resolved simply to let the truth be told us and therefore to be apprehended by it. But that is the very thing for which we are not resolved and ready. The man to whom the truth has really come will concede that he was not at all ready and resolved to let it speak to him. The genuine believer will not say that he came to faith from faith, but—from unbelief, even though the attitude and activity with which he met revelation, and still meets it, is religion. For in faith, man's religion as such is shown by relevation to be resistance to it. From the standpoint of revelation religion is clearly seen to be a human attempt to anticipate what God in His revelation wills to do and does do. It is the attempted replacement of the divine work by a human manufacture. The divine reality offered and manifested to us in revelation is replaced by a concept of God arbitrarily and wilfully evolved by man.

'Arbitrarily and wilfully' means here by his own means, by his own human insight and constructiveness and energy. Many different images of God can be formed once we have engaged in this undertaking, but their significance is always the same . . .

. . . The image of God is always that reality of perception or thought in which man assumes and asserts something unique and ultimate and decisive either beyond or within his own existence, by which he believes himself to be posited or at least determined and conditioned. From the standpoint of revelation, man's religion is simply an assumption and assertion of this kind, and as such it is an activity which contradicts revelation—contradicts it, because it is only through truth that truth can come to man. If man tries to grasp at truth of himself, he tries to grasp at it *a priori*. But in that case he does not do what he has to do when the truth comes to him. He does not believe. If he did, he would listen; but in religion he talks. If he did, he would accept a gift; but in religion he takes something for himself. If he did, he would let God Himself intercede, for God: but in religion he ventures to grasp at God. Because it is a grasping, religion is the contradiction of revelation, the concentrated expression of human unbelief, i.e., an attitude and activity which is directly opposed to faith. It is a feeble but defiant, an arrogant but hopeless, attempt to create something which man could do, but now cannot do, or can do only because and if God Himself creates it for him: the knowledge of the truth, the knowledge of God. We cannot, therefore, interpret the attempt as a harmonious co-operating of man with the revelation of God, as though religion were a kind of outstretched hand which is filled by God in His revelation. Again, we cannot say of the evident religious capacity of man that it is, so to speak, the general form of human knowledge, which acquires its true and proper content in the shape of revelation. On the contrary, we have here an exclusive contradiction. In religion man bolts and bars himself against revelation by providing a substitute, by taking away in advance the very thing which has to be given by God.

He has, of course, the power to do this. But what he achieves and acquires in virtue of this power is never the knowledge of God as Lord and God. It is never the truth. It is a complete fiction, which has not only little but no relation to God. It is an anti-God who has first to be known as such and discarded when the truth comes to him. But it can be known as such, as a fiction, only as the truth does come to him.

Revelation does not link up with a human religion which is already present and practised. It contradicts it, just as religion previously contradicted revelation. It displaces it, just as religion previously displaced revelation; just as faith cannot link up with a mistaken faith, but must contradict and displace it as unbelief, as an act of contradiction . . .

2. As the self-offering and self-manifestation of God, revelation

is the act by which in grace He reconciles man to Himself by grace. As a radical teaching about God, it is also the radical assistance of God which comes to us as those who are unrighteous and unholy, and as such damned and lost. In this respect, too, the affirmation which revelation makes and presupposes of man is that he is unable to help himself either in whole or even in part. But again, he ought not to have been so helpless. It is not inherent in the nature and concept of man that he should be unrighteous and unholy and therefore damned and lost. He was created to be the image of God, i.e., to obedience towards God and not to sin, to salvation and not to destruction. But he is not summoned to this as to a state in which he might still somehow find himself, but as one in which he no longer finds himself, from which he has fallen by his own fault. But this, too, is a truth which he cannot maintain: it is not present to him unless it comes to him in revelation, i.e., in Jesus Christ, to be declared to him in a new way—the oldest truth of all in a way which is quite new. He cannot in any sense declare to himself that he is righteous and holy, and therefore saved, for in his own mouth as his own judgement of himself it would be a lie. It is truth as the revealed knowledge of God. It is truth in Jesus Christ. Jesus Christ does not fill out and improve all the different attempts of man to think of God and to represent Him according to his own standard. But as the self-offering and self-manifestation of God He replaces and completely outbids those attempts, putting them in the shadows to which they belong. Similarly, in so far as God reconciles the world to Himself in Him, He replaces all the different attempts of man to reconcile God to the world, all our human efforts at justification and sanctification, at conversion and salvation. The revelation of God in Jesus Christ maintains that our justification and sanctification, our conversion and salvation, have been brought about and achieved once and for all in Jesus Christ. And our faith in Jesus Christ consists in our recognizing and admitting and affirming and accepting the fact that everything has actually been done for us once and for all in Jesus Christ. He is the assistance that comes to us. He alone is the Word of God that is spoken to us. There is an exchange of status between Him and us: His righteousness and holiness are ours, our sin is

His; He is lost for us, and we for His sake are saved. By this exchange (καταλλαγή, 2 Cor. 5:19) revelation stands or falls. It would not be the active redemptive self-offering and self-manifestation of God, if it were not centrally and decisively the *satisfactio* and *intercessio Jesu Christi.*

And now we can see a second way in which revelation contradicts religion, and conversely religion necessarily opposes revelation. For what is the purpose of the universal attempt of religions to anticipate God, to foist a human product into the place of His Word, to make our own images of the One who is known only where He gives himself to be known, images which are first spiritual, and then religious, and then actually visible? What does religious man want when he thinks and believes and maintains that there is a unique and ultimate and decisive being, that there is a divine being (θεῖον), a godhead, that there are gods and a single supreme God, and when he thinks that he himself is posited, determined, conditioned and overruled by this being? Is the postulate of God or gods, and the need to objectify the Ultimate spiritually or physically, conditioned by man's experience of the actual superiority and lordship of certain natural and supernatural, historical and eternal necessities, potencies and ordinances? Is this experience (or the postulate and need which correspond to it) followed by the feeling of man's impotence and failure in face of this higher world, by the urge to put himself on peaceful and friendly terms with it, to interest it on his behalf, to assure himself of its support, or, better still, to enable himself to exercise an influence on it, to participate in its power and dignity and to co-operate in its work? Does man's attempt to justify and sanctify himself follow the attempt to think of God and represent Him? Or is the relationship the direct opposite? Is the primary thing man's obscure urge to justify and sanctify himself, i.e., to confirm and strengthen himself in the awareness and exercise of his skill and strength to master life, to come to terms with the world, to make the world serviceable to him? Is religion with its dogmatics and worship and precepts the most primitive, or better perhaps, the most intimate and intensive part of the technique, by which we try to come to terms with life? Is it that the experience of that higher world, or the need to objectify it in the thought of God and the representation of God, must be regarded only as an exponent of this attempt, that is, as the ideal construction inevitable within the framework of this technique? Are the gods only reflected images and guarantees of the needs and capacities of man, who in reality is lonely and driven back upon himself and his own willing and ordering and creating? Are sacrifice and prayer and asceticism and morality more basic than God and the gods? Who is to say? In face of the two possibilities we are in a circle which we can consider from any point of view with exactly the same result. What is certain is that in respect of the practical content of religion it is still a matter of an attitude and activity which does not correspond to God's revelation, but contradicts it. At this point, too, weakness and defiance, helplessness and arrogance, folly and imagination are so close to one another that we can scarcely distinguish the one from the other. Where we want what is wanted in religion, i.e., justification and sanctification as our own work, we do not find ourselves—and it does not matter whether the thought and representation of God has a primary or only a secondary importance—on the direct way to God, who can then bring us to our goal at some higher stage on the way. On the contrary, we lock the door against God, we alienate ourselves from Him, we come into direct opposition to Him. God in His revelation will not allow man to try to come to terms with life, to justify and sanctify himself. God in His revelation, God in Jesus Christ, is the One who takes on Himself the sin of the world, who wills that all our care should be cast upon Him, because He careth for us . . .

. . . It is the characteristically pious element in the pious effort to reconcile Him to us which must be an abomination to God, whether idolatry is regarded as its presupposition or its result, or perhaps as both. Not by any continuing along this way, but only by radically breaking away from it, can we come, not to our own goal but to God's goal, which is the direct opposite of our goal . . .

. . . We cannot make this point without insisting expressly that it is only by the revelation of God in Jesus Christ that we can characterize religion as idolatry and self-righteousness, and in this way show it to be unbelief. Religion can, of course, be called in question from within, and we have to be aware of this and to distinguish it from the abolishing of religion by revelation. It is an observation which we can more or less clearly verify from the history and phenomenology of every religion that the religious man does not at all face up to his theoretico-practical aims, like a man who is sure of his business, straightforwardly. In his striving, then, he involves himself in a peculiar inward dialectic. He strangely contradicts himself. He scores through his thinking and willing, and uplifts and outbids it by a thinking and willing which he believes to be higher and better. In this way he necessarily calls himself in question, unsettling himself and plunging himself into uncertainty. But he also jeopardizes more or less radically the whole of his religious activity—although without abandoning the religious attitude and appetite—but also without directing it to its real goal in this new and critical turn in the matter. The observation will not surprise us if we know the judgement which revelation has pronounced upon all religion. It is a confirmation of the fact that the verdict is true: Religion is always self-contradictory and impossible *per se*. But we have to note that the critical turn at which the self-contradiction and impossibility are brought out is itself a moment in the life of religion. It has only an immanent significance. It does not give any ultimate or definitive answer to the question which it tries to answer. Therefore—and this is the point—it must not be confused with revelation. It does not show religion to be unbelief. For it falls under the same judgement. Even at the supposedly higher level where it tries to overcome idolatry and self-righteousness in its own strength and its own way, religion is still idolatry and self-righteousness. To be more specific, religion is called in question by a twofold movement which at root is only one: by mysticism on the one hand and atheism on the other. Our task is to show that even in these two supposedly higher and apparently inimical forms, whether in good or evil, in failure or success, religion is still thoroughly self-centred.

The two primitive and as it were normal forms of religion are, as we have seen, the conception of the deity and the fulfilment of the law. It is always in these two forms that religious need first seeks its satisfaction. But it seeks satisfaction because it already has it—and that is why religious need differs from the need of man for faith in God's revelation. It is, of course, the need of man for a truth above and a certainty within, both of which he thinks he can know and even create for himself. Since the need is there, have not the starry heaven above and the moral law within long since brought this truth and certainty into the range and realm of his perception? He is not in any way lacking in advice or help. He knows that truth and certainty exist and are attainable, and he is confident of his own ability to achieve them. His need is not an absolute need, a strictly needy need, in face of which he does not know where to turn. His need is not in the least like the neediness of the believer, who with empty heart and hands finds himself thrown back entirely upon the revelation of God. To satisfy this need, he steps out in a bold bid for truth, creating the Deity according to his own image—and in a confident act of self-assurance, undertaking to justify and sanctify himself in conformity with what he holds to be the law. And in so doing he betrays the fact that even as he seeks satisfaction, potentially at least, in respect of his religious capacity he is already satisfied. He is like a rich man, who in the need to grow richer (which cannot, of course, be an absolute need) puts parts of his fortune into an undertaking that promises a profit.

From this it follows that there is always an ultimate non-necessity about the origin and exercise of all religion. The life of religion, in which religious need seeks satisfaction and provisionally finds it, is fundamentally only an externalization, an expression, a representation and therefore a repetition of something which previously existed without form or activity, but still quite powerfully, as the real essence of religion and to that extent as the peculiar religious possession of man.

(FROM: *Church Dogmatics*, I, 2, pp. 297–8, 299–300, 301–3, 307–9, 310, 314–15.)

4 'Scripture as the Word of God'

[In these passages Barth sets out his belief about the nature of the Bible and the normative rôle which it must play in Christian theology. The Bible is not itself revelation ('direct impartation', as Barth puts it) but the unique irreplaceable witness to revelation. It comes to be seen as such through faith, in the context of life in the Church.]

In the statement: we believe that the Bible is the Word of God, we must first emphasize and consider the word 'believe'. Believing does, of course, involve recognizing and knowing. Believing is not an obscure and indeterminate feeling. It is a clear hearing, apperceiving, thinking and then speaking and doing. Believing is also a free human act, i.e., one which is not destroyed or disturbed by any magic; but, of course, a free act which as such is conditioned and determined by an encounter, a challenge, an act of lordship which confronts man, which man cannot bring about himself, which exists either as an event or not at all. Therefore believing is not something arbitrary. It does not control its object. It is a recognizing, knowing, hearing, apperceiving, thinking, speaking and doing which is overmastered by its object. Belief that the Bible is the Word of God presupposes, therefore, that this over-mastering has already taken place, that the Bible has already proved itself to be the Word of God, so that we can and must recognize it to be such. But when and where there is this proof, it must be a matter of the Word of God itself. We must say at once, that of itself the mere presence of the Bible and our own presence with our capacities for knowing an object does not mean and never will mean the reality or even the possibility of the proof that the Bible is the Word of God. On the contrary, we have to recognize that this situation as such, i.e., apart from faith, only means the impossibility of this proof. We have to recognize that faith as an irruption into this reality and possibility means the removing of a barrier in which we can only see and again and again see a miracle. And it is a miracle which we cannot explain apart from faith, or rather apart from the Word of God in which faith believes. Therefore the reality and possibility of it cannot be maintained or defended at all apart from faith and the Word. Nor can there be any assurances of it apart from faith and the Word. It is not only that we cannot attribute to ourselves any capacity or instrument for recognizing the Word of God either in the Bible or elsewhere. It is also that if we are serious about the true humanity of the Bible, we obviously cannot attribute to the Bible as such the capacity—and in this it is distinguished, as we have seen, from the exalted and glorified humanity of Jesus Christ—in such a way to reveal God to us that by its very presence, by the fact that we can read it, it gives us a hearty faith in the Word of God spoken in it. It is there and always there as a sign, as a human and temporal word—and therefore also as a word which is conditioned and limited. It witnesses to God's revelation, but that does not mean that God's revelation is now before us in any kind of divine revealedness. The Bible is not a book of oracles; it is not an instrument of direct impartation. It is genuine witness. And how can it be witness of divine revelation, if the actual purpose, act and decision of God in His only-begotten Son, as seen and heard by the prophets and apostles in that Son, is dissolved in the Bible into a sum total of truths abstracted from that decision—and those truths are then propounded to us as truths of faith, salvation and revelation? If it tries to be more than witness, to be direct impartation, will it not keep from us the best, the one real thing, which God intends to tell and give us and which we ourselves need? But if it does not try to do this, if it is really witness, we must understand clearly what it means and involves that in itself it is only witness. It means the existence of those barriers which can be broken down only by miracle. The men whom we hear as witnesses speak as fallible, erring men like ourselves. What they say, and what we read as their word, can of itself lay claim to be the Word of God, but never sustain that claim. We can read and try to assess their word as a purely human word. It can be subjected to all kinds of immanent criticism, not only in respect of its philosophical, historical and ethical content, but even of its religious and theological. We can establish lacunae, inconsistencies and over-emphases. We may be alienated by a figure like that of Moses. We may quarrel with James or with Paul. We may have to admit that we can make little or nothing of large tracts of the Bible, as is often the case with the records of other men. We can take offence at the Bible. And in the light of the claim or the assertion that the Bible is the Word of God—granting that the miracle of faith and the Word does not intervene—we are bound to take offence at it. But this is a miracle which we cannot presuppose. We can remember it. We can wait for it. But we cannot set it up like one chessman with others, which we can 'move' at the right moment. Therefore we are bound to take offence at the Bible in the light of that claim. If we do not, we have not yet realized the importance of that claim. Only the miracle of faith and the Word can genuinely and seriously prevent us from taking offence at the Bible. But the *theopneustia*[1] of the Bible, the attitude of obedience in which it is written, the compelling fact that in it true men speak to us in the name of the true God: this—and here is the miracle of it—is not simply before us because the Bible is before us and we read the Bible. The *theopneustia* is the act of revelation in which the prophets and apostles in their humanity became what they were, and in which alone in their humanity they can become to us what they are . . .

. . . But now in order to see the full acuteness of the problem, we must also emphasize and consider the concept 'Word of God' in the statement: We believe that the Bible is the Word of God. What we have said so far cannot mean that the miracle just mentioned consists in our having to believe in a sort of enthusiastic rapture which penetrates the barriers of offence by which the Bible is surrounded. Of course, the whole mystery of this statement rests on the fact that faith is not for everybody, and that even if we have it, it is a small and weak and inadequate because not a true faith. Therefore the miracle which has to take place if the Bible is to rise up and speak to us as the Word of God has always to consist in an awakening and strengthening of our faith. But the real difficulty of the

[1] *Theopneustia:* the fact of the Bible being *inspired by God.* (Ed.)

statement does not rest in the side which concerns us men, but in that which concerns God Himself. It does not rest, therefore, in the severity of the offences caused by the humanity of the Bible. Although the question of faith of which we have just been speaking is central, it is only the secondary form of the question which has to be decided at this centre. Faith can in fact only be obedience and cling to the Word as a free human decision. And it can do so only because the Word has come to it and made and introduced it as faith. Therefore faith cannot simply grasp at the Bible, as though by the energy of its grasping, perhaps that highest energy which may even rise to enthusiasm, the Word of God would come to it in spite of all the offences (which are therefore overcome by the enthusiasm). Rather, the energy of this grasping itself rests on the prior coming of the Word of God. Faith does not live by its own energy and therefore not even by its arousing and strengthening by the Word of God. It lives by the energy of the movement in which the Word of God in Holy Scripture has come to us in spite of all the offences which we might take at it, and has first created our faith. Whether this has happened or not is the objective mystery which confronts and precedes the question of faith, the mystery of the statement that 'the Bible is the Word of God.' In the statement that 'the Bible is the Word of God,' we cannot suddenly mean a lesser, less potent, less ineffable and majestic Word of God, than that which has occupied us in the doctrine of the Trinity and in the doctrine of Christ and of the Holy Spirit. There is only one Word of God and that is the eternal Word of the Father which for our reconciliation became flesh like us and has now returned to the Father, to be present to His Church by the Holy Spirit. In Holy Scripture, too, in the human word of His witnesses, it is a matter of this Word and its presence. That means that in this equation it is a matter of the miracle of the divine Majesty in its condescension and mercy. If we take this equation on our lips, it can only be as an appeal to the promise in virtue of which this miracle was real in Jesus Christ and will again be real in the word of His witnesses. In this equation we have to do with the free grace and the gracious freedom of God. That the Bible is the Word of God cannot mean that with other attributes the Bible has the attribute of being the Word of

God. To say that would be to violate the Word of God which is God Himself—to violate the freedom and the sovereignty of God. God is not an attribute of something else, even if this something else is the Bible. God is the subject, God is Lord. He is Lord even over the Bible and in the Bible. The statement that the Bible is the Word of God cannot therefore say that the Word of God is tied to the Bible. On the contrary, what it must say is that the Bible is tied to the Word of God. But that means that in this statement we contemplate a free decision of God—not in uncertainty but in certainty, not without basis but on the basis of the promise which the Bible itself proclaims and which we receive in and with the Church. But its content is always a free decision of God, which we cannot anticipate by grasping at the Bible—even if we do it with the greatest faith of which we are capable, but the freedom of which we will have to recognize when we grasp at the Bible in the right way. The Bible is not the Word of God on earth in the same way as Jesus Christ, very God and very man, is that Word in heaven. The being of Jesus Christ as the Word of God even in His humanity requires neither promise nor faith. The act in which He became the Word of God in His humanity requires neither repetition nor confirmation. But in His eternal presence as the Word of God He is concealed from us who now live on earth and in time. He is revealed only in the sign of His humanity, and especially in the witness of His prophets and apostles. But by nature these signs are not heavenly-human, but earthly- and temporal-human. Therefore the act of their institution as signs requires repetition and confirmation. Their being as the Word of God requires promise and faith—just because they are signs of the eternal presence of Christ. For if they are to act as signs, if the eternal presence of Christ is to be revealed to us in time, there is a constant need of that continuing work of the Holy Spirit in the Church and to its members which is always taking place in new acts. If the Church lives by the Bible because it is the Word of God, that means that it lives by the fact that Christ is revealed in the Bible by the work of the Holy Spirit. That means that it has no power or control over this work. It can grasp at the Bible. It can honour it. It can accept its promise. It can be ready and open to read and understand and expound it. All these things it can and should do. The human side of the life of the Church with the Bible rightly consists in all these things. But apart from these things, the human side of its life with the Bible can consist only in the fact that it prays that the Bible may be the Word of God here and now, that there may take place that work of the Holy Spirit, and therefore a free applying of the free grace of God. Over and above that: the fulfilment of this prayer, that the Bible is the Word of God here and now in virtue of the eternal, hidden, heavenly presence of Christ—that is the divine side of the life of the Church. Its reality cannot be doubted: the fulness of the reality of the life of the Church with the Bible lies in this its divine aspect. Also the certainty of the perception of it cannot be doubted: it is mediated to us in the promise, it can be grasped in faith. But the very fact that this happens, that the promise speaks to us and that we are obedient in faith, is always before us as the question which has to be answered again and again by the work of the Holy Spirit. This is the event we look to, if—here on earth in the Church non-triumphant, but militant—we confess that the Bible is God's Word. For in doing so we acknowledge God and His grace, and the freedom of His grace.

(FROM: *Church Dogmatics*, I, 2, pp. 506–8, 512–14.)

5 'Sin as Sloth'

[In Christian theology sin has often been characterized principally as pride (*superbia* in the mediaeval list of the seven deadly sins), a promethean defiance not unlike the *hybris* of Greek tragedy. As Barth says, this presentation of sin has attractions. It is dramatically impressive and appeals to the Prometheus in all of us. There is, however, another side to sin much less fascinating. This is the sluggishness of sin as sloth, a being gripped by self-reference to the point of inaction. As always for Barth these facts come out in attitudes to Christ.]

We now turn to the material question: What is sin as seen from the standpoint of the new man introduced in Jesus Christ? What is the action of the old man overcome in the death of Jesus Christ? What is the character of this man as he is subsequently revealed in Christ's resurrection, in the light of the divine direction which falls on him from this source? Our present answer is that the sin of man is the sloth of man. The christological aspect which now occupies us calls for this or a similar term. We might also describe it as sluggishness, indolence, slowness or inertia. What is meant is the evil inaction which is absolutely forbidden and reprehensible but which characterizes human sin from the standpoint presupposed in the deliberations of our first sub-section.

There is a heroic, Promethean[1] form of sin. This is brought to light—as the pride of man which not only derives from but is itself his fall—when we consider man in his confrontation with the Lord who humbled Himself and became a servant for him, with the Son of God made flesh. Sin was unmasked as this counter-movement to the divine condescension practised and revealed in Jesus Christ when we reached the correspond-

[1] Prometheus in Greek mythology was punished by Zeus for giving the arts to mankind and has become a symbol of human freedom and the defiance of arbitrary divine laws. (Ed.)

ing point in the first part of the doctrine of reconciliation. In its unity and totality human sin always has this heroic form, just as, in its unity and totality, the free grace of God addressed to man always has the form of the justification which positively encounters this pride. But as reconciling grace is not merely justifying, but also wholly and utterly sanctifying and awakening and establishing grace, so sin has not merely the heroic form of pride but also, in complete antithesis yet profound correspondence, the quite unheroic and trivial form of sloth. In other words, it has the form, not only of evil action, but also of evil inaction; not only of the rash arrogance which is forbidden and reprehensible, but also of the tardiness and failure which are equally forbidden and reprehensible. It is also the counter-movement to the elevation which has come to man from God Himself in Jesus Christ.

In Protestantism, and perhaps in Western Christianity generally, there is a temptation to overlook this aspect of the matter and to underestimate its importance. The figure who claims our attention is Prometheus who tries to steal the lightning from Zeus and turn it to his own use: the man who wants to be as God, not a servant but the Lord, his own judge and helper; man in his hybris as a defiant insurrectionary. We do well to consider this figure, and constantly to realize how powerfully he is contradicted by the grace of God which justifies the sinner and exalts the abased and only the abased; how decisively he is routed by Jesus Christ, the Son of God, the Lord who became for us a servant. But the man of sin is not simply this insurrectionary, and his sin has more than the heroic form in which (however terrible it may seem to be) we can hardly avoid finding traces of a sombre beauty—the beauty of the Luciferian man. We are missing the real man, not only in the mass but individually, not only in the common herd but in the finest and most outstanding of all times and places, and especially in ourselves, if we try to see and understand his sin consistently and one-sidedly as hybris, as this brilliant perversion of human pride. At a hidden depth it certainly is this brilliant perversion in all of us. But sober observation compels us to state that, as it may be seen and grasped in the overwhelming majority, it has little or nothing of this Luciferian or Promethean brilliance, this sombre beauty; and that even among those who may be regarded as exceptions there is a hidden depth at which, although they are still sinners, they are not at all insurrectionaries, but something very different and much more primitive, in which sin is merely banal and ugly and loathsome. It gives evidence of a very deficient or, from the Christian standpoint, very unenlightened self-knowledge if we try to deny that, beyond all that we may see and bewail in ourselves as pride, we have also to confess this very different and much more primitive thing in which there is nothing at all even of that doubtful beauty. And is it really 'beyond' what we call price? Sin may have different dimensions and aspects, but it is a single entity. Ought we not to say, therefore, that this different form is there at the very heart of our pride and forms its final basis? And yet the connexion between the two forms cannot easily be reduced to a common denominator. We might equally well say that this other, more primitive form has its final basis in human pride. The important thing is that we have every reason closely to scrutinize this second form. If we consider sin only in its first and more impressive form it might easily acquire an unreal and fantastic quality in which we do not recognize the real man whose heart, according to Luther's rendering of Jer. 17, 9,[1] is not merely desperate but also despairing. And the result would be to obscure the concrete point at issue in the sanctification or exaltation of sinful man. The sin of man is not merely heroic in its perversion. It is also—to use again the terms already introduced in the first sub-section—ordinary, trivial and mediocre. The sinner is not merely Prometheus or Lucifer. He is also—and for the sake of clarity, and to match the grossness of the matter, we will use rather popular expressions—a lazy-bones, a sluggard, a good-for-nothing, a slowcoach and a loafer. He does not exist only in an exalted world of evil; he exists also in a very mean and petty world of evil (and there is a remarkable unity and reciprocity between the two in spite of their apparent antithesis). In the one case, he stands bitterly in need of humiliation; in the other he stands no less bitterly in need of exaltation. And in both cases the need is in relation to the totality of his life an action. We will gather together

[1] 'The heart is deceitful above all things, and desperately corrupt; who can understand it?' (RSV.)

what we have to say on this second aspect under the term or concept 'sloth.'

The forbidden or reprehensible tardiness and failure of man obviously fall under the general definition of sin as disobedience. In face of the divine direction calling him to perform a definite action, man refuses to follow the indication which he is given. Even in this refusal to act, however, and therefore in this inaction, he is involved in a certain action. The idler or loafer does something. For the most part, indeed, what he does is quite considerable and intensive. The only thing is that it does not correspond to the divine direction but is alien and opposed to it. He does not do what God wills, and so he does what God does not will. He is disobedient and he does that which is evil. In all that follows we must keep before us the fact that because sin in its form as sloth seems to have the nature of a vacuum, a mere failure to act, this does not mean that it is a milder or weaker or less potent type of sin than it is in its active form as pride. Even as sloth, sin is plainly disobedience.

Again, this form obviously falls under the even more penetrating definition of sin as unbelief. For the disobedience in which man refuses the divine direction and does positively that which God does not will has its basis in the fact that he does not grasp the promise given him with this direction, but refuses to trust in the One who demonstrates and maintains His faithfulness in this overwhelming way, not claiming his obedience with the severity and coldness of an alien tyrant but as the source of his life, in the majesty and freedom of the love with which He has loved him from all eternity. He hardens himself against the divine benevolence addressed to him in the divine demand. The sloth of man, too, is a form of unbelief.

But we must define the term rather more closely as we use it of human sloth. In its form as man's tardiness and failure, sloth expresses much more clearly than pride the positive and aggressive ingratitude which repays good with evil. It consists in the fact, not only that man does not trust God, but beyond this that he does not love Him, i.e., that he will not know and have Him, that he will not have dealings with Him, as the One who first loved him, from all eternity. In relation to God there is no middle term betwen love and hate. The man who does not love God resists and avoids the fact that God is the One He is, and that He is this for him. He turns his back on God, rolling himself into a ball like a hedgehog with prickly spikes. As every point, as we shall see, this is the strange inactive action of the slothful man. It may be that this action often assumes the disguise of a tolerant indifference in relation to God. But in fact it is the action of the hate which wants to be free of God, which would prefer that there were no God, or that God were not the One He is—at least for him, the slothful man. This hatred of God is the culminating point of human pride too. The overweening pride of man, which consists in the fact that he wants to be and act as God, may at a pinch be understood—and this is perhaps the reason for its sinister beauty—as a perverse love of God, whose frivolous encroachment and usurpation, whose illegitimate attempt to control its object, do of course culminate in a desire that the object should disappear as such, that there should be no God or that God should not be God, that man should be able to sit unhindered on his throne. But sin as man's subservient and obsequious sloth is from the very outset his desire not to be illuminated by the existence and nature of God, not to have to accept Him, to be without God in the world. The slothful man, who is of course identical with the proud, begins where the other leaves off, i.e., by saying in his heart: 'There is no God.' This is the characteristic feature of sin, of disobedience, of unbelief, in this second form. It is from this root that all the constitutive elements of human sloth grow.

Sin in the form of sloth crystallizes in the rejection of the man Jesus. In relation to Him the rejection of God from which it derives finds virulent and concrete and forceful expression. For it is in Him that the divine direction and summons and claim come to man. It is in Him that the divine decision is made which he will not accept, which he tries to resist and escape. It is to be noted that in the main there is no radical opposition to the idea of God as a higher or supreme being to whom man regards himself as committed, nor to the thought of a beyond, of something which transcends his existence, nor to the demand that he should enter into a more or less conscious or unconscious, binding or non-binding connexion with it. He will never seriously or basically reject altogether religion or piety in one form or another, nor will he finally or totally cease to exercise or practise them in an open or disguised form. On the contrary, an escape to religion, to adoring faith in a congenial higher being, is the purest and ripest and most appropriate possibility at which he grasps in his sloth, and cannot finally cease from grasping as a slothful man. His rejection of God acquires weight and seriousness only when it is made with a final and concentrated piety. But that in this piety it is really a matter of rejecting God, of rendering Him innocuous, emerges clearly in the fact that man definitely will not accept in relation to himself the reality and presence and action of God in the existence of the man Jesus, and the claim of God which they involve. He definitely will not accept them as the reality and presence and action of God which refer absolutely and exclusively and totally and directly to him, and make on him an absolute, exclusive, total and direct demand. As one who worships a higher being, as a religious or pious man, he is able to resist this. It does not matter what name or form he gives to the higher being which he worships; he finds that he is tolerated by it, that far from being questioned and disturbed and seized he is strengthened and confirmed and maintained in equilibrium by it. And he for his part can always show equal toleration to this being—and in this form to 'God.' It does not cause him any offence, and so he has no need to be offended at it. But he is not tolerated, let alone confirmed, by the reality and presence and action of God in the existence of the man Jesus. He is basically illuminated and radically questioned and disturbed and therefore offended by the deity of God in the concrete phenomenon of the existence of this man. His own tolerance is thus strained to the limit when he has to do with God in this man. His rejection of God finds expression in his relation to this man. Tested in this way, he will unhesitatingly avoid God even as the religious or pious man. But this means that he will unhesitatingly resist God. In his relation to God he will show himself to be slothful man, turned in upon himself and finding his satisfaction and comfort in his own ego.

Why is it that this is expressed in the rejection of the man Jesus? The reason is that in this man, as opposed to all the higher beings and transcendencies which he knows to be congenial and to which he may therefore commit himself, he has to do with the true and living God who loved this man, and was His God, from all eternity, and who will love this man, and be His God, to all eternity; the God whose outstretched hand of promise and preservation of deliverance and command, has always been, and always will be, the existence of this man. The reason is that what God always gave to all men, what He was and is and will be for them, is simply a demonstration of the free grace which became an historical event in the appearance and work, the dying and rising again, of this man. The God of this man, and therefore concretely this man, offends us. Our sloth rejects Him. In relation to Him it is our great inaction, our hesitation, our withdrawal into ourselves. Man rejects Him because he wants to elect and will himself, and he does not want to be disturbed in this choice. For he is disturbed, and he finds that he is disturbed by Him; by the will of God which always has and will have the name of Jesus, which has in this name its unalterable goal and ineffaceable contour. When he comes face to face with the will of God in Him he comes to the frontier which he can cross only if he will give up himself and his congenial deities and find God and himself in this Other. At this point he can only protest, for he is not tolerated and therefore he cannot tolerate. He regards it as vitally necessary to be free of this man, i.e., of the God of this man. This is a pious act which he must execute in his reverence for the higher being which does tolerate him. 'There is no God' means concretely that there is no God of this kind; that a God of this kind cannot and may not be.

Why not? Why is it that human disobedience, unbelief and ingratitude in sloth have this culmination? Why is the sin of man revealed in this opposition? Our first and general answer is that it is because in himself and as such man will not live in the distinctive freedom of the man Jesus and is therefore forced to regard this Fellow and Brother as a stranger and interloper, and his existence as an intolerable demand.

He wants to be left alone by the God who has made this man a neighbour with His distinctive freedom, and therefore by this neighbour with His summons to freedom. He regards the renewal of human nature declared in His existence as quite unnecessary. He sees and feels, perhaps, the limitation and imperfection of his present nature, but they do not touch him so deeply that he is not finally satisfied with this nature and the way in which he fulfils it. A serious need, a hunger or thirst for its renewal, is quite foreign to him. He therefore sees no relevance in the man Jesus with His freedom to be a new man. Again, he thinks he has a sober idea of what is attainable, of what is possible and impossible, within the limits of his humanity. This leads him to question the real significance of this renewal, of man's exaltation. The limited sphere with which he is content seems to him to be his necessary sphere, so that its transcendence in the freedom of the man Jesus is an imaginary work in which he himself can have no part.

Behind the indifference and doubt there is a definite mistrust. In the freedom of the man Jesus it seems that we have a renewal and exaltation from servitude to lordship. But this is an exacting and dangerous business if it necessarily means that we acquire and have in Jesus a Lord, and if His lordship involves that we are demanded to leave our burdensome but comfortable and secure life as slaves and assume responsibility as lords.

Again, if the freedom of the man Jesus as the new and exalted and lordly man has its basis and meaning in the fact that he is the man who lives in fellowship with God, the indifference and doubt and mistrust in which we confront Him have their basis and meaning, or lack of meaning; in the fact that we regard it as unpractical, difficult and undesirable to live in fellowship with God. A life which moves and circles around itself, which is self-orientated but also self-directed, seems to hold out far greater promise than one which is lived in this fellowship.

It is for this reason that our brother Jesus is a stranger, and His existence among us is an intolerable demand, and the God who is His God is unacceptable. This is, in very general terms, the deployment, or rather the rigid front which human sin presents to Him, and in which it is actual and visible in face of Him, in the form of human sloth.

(FROM: *Church Dogmatics*, IV, 2, pp. 403–8.)

6 'Barth on Bonhoeffer'

[This letter, gives an interesting, though fragmentary example of Barth's critical appreciation of Bonhoeffer. Barth does not argue fully any of the points made by Bonhoeffer, notably the latter's strictures on 'theological positivism' (see Book 5, pp. 335ff.) contenting himself with a statement of his bewilderment to know what the phrase meant.]

The letters, whatever one may make of their individual sentences (and I have let them work on me once again in their whole context since the beginning of your correspondence[1]), are a particular thorn; to let them excite us can only do us all good—for, unlike 'demythologizing', this is unrest of a spiritual kind.

What an open and rich and at the same time deep and disturbed man stands before us—somehow shaming and comforting us at the same time. That is how I also personally remember him. An aristocratic Christian, one might say, who seemed to run on ahead in the most varied dimensions. That is why I always read his earlier writings, especially those which apparently or in reality said things which were not at once clear to me, with the thought that—when they were seen round some corner or other—he might be right. So too with these letters, parts of which of course astonish me too. One cannot read them without having the impression that there might be something in them. You are therefore certainly right to call your pastors' attention to them and to make some suggestions about their meaning.

But as always with Bonhoeffer one is faced by a peculiar difficulty. He was—how shall I put it?—an impulsive, visionary thinker who was suddenly seized by an idea to which he gave lively form, and then after a time he called a halt (one never

[1] This extract is from a letter of Karl Barth to Landessuperintendent P. W. Herrenbrück, 21 December 1952. (Ed.)

knew whether it was final or temporary) with some provisional last point or other. Was this not the case with *The Cost of Discipleship*? Did he not also for a time have liturgical impulses—And how was it with the 'Mandates' of his *Ethics*, with which I tussled when I wrote [*Dogmatics*] III/4? Do we not always expect him to be clearer and more concise in some other context, either by withdrawing what he said, or by going even further? Now he has left us alone with the enigmatic utterances of his letters—at more than one point clearly showing that he sensed, without really knowing, how the story should continue—for example, what exactly he meant by the 'positivism of revelation'[1] he found in me, and especially how the programme of an unreligious speech was to be realized.

As to the first, I have certainly been disturbed by the question of when and where I have asked anyone to 'take' or 'leave' the virgin birth, and by the question of what my neo-Calvinist well-wishers in Holland would think of me portrayed as a 'positivist of revelation'. But I am somewhat embarrassed by the thought that so sensible and well-meaning a man as Bonhoeffer somehow remembered my books (which he certainly did not have with him in his prison cell) in terms of this enigmatic expression. The hope remains that in heaven at least he has not reported about me to all the angels (including the church fathers, etc.) with just this expression. But perhaps I have indeed on occasion behaved and expressed myself 'positivistically', and if this is so then Bonhoeffer's recollections have brought it to light. Without being able to ask him personally, we shall have to make do with remaining behind, somewhat confused.

Similarly with the postulate of un-religious speech. I think that you have dealt rather too severely with him when (on your page 9) you tend to explain this in terms of existentialism, pre-understanding, etc. On the other hand you are right to indicate that he did not show any sign of putting the kerygma into 'other words', that is, doing what in practice Bultmann ends up with. Can he really have meant anything other than a warning against all unthought-out repetition of biblical and traditional images, phrases, and combinations of ideas, meaningless to the 'world' because the 'religious' speaker or writer

[1] See Book 5, pp. 335ff.

does not think at all, or does not think properly, about what he is saying? But in the opinion that the stuff will somehow be God's Word he just lets fly—in much the same style as you will find happening about now—oh, I don't mean it in a bad sense, and how many of us really have the time and capacity to think things out in an orderly way?—under thousands of Christmas trees?

Certainly, Bonhoeffer has left us nothing tangible in this respect, and I almost think that it was not tangible to him either. What then remains for us but to take the best from him—in the way I have indicated or in some other way—without searching for a deeper meaning which he himself did not offer us, and perhaps had not even thought through himself? And what he says about sharing in the suffering of God, and so on, seems to me to be clearly a variation of the idea of *imitatio* which he rightly stressed. Why should one not allow oneself to be addressed like this by a man of whom it was asked and to whom it was also given that he not only thought it and said it, but also lived it? It has long been clear to me that I will have to devote a lot of room to this matter in the *Church Dogmatics*. Was it Bonhoeffer's view that the whole of theology must be put on this basis? It is possible that in his cell he did at times think this. But again he has left us no clues about details and about how he regarded the questions which touch upon his thesis. Well, you understand that I do not want to dismiss him when I ascribe to him, 'more or less', as one so nicely puts it, what I call 'the melancholy theology of the North German plain'. I am thankful enough that I myself lived there for fifteen years, and that I have absorbed a good deal of this Lutheran melancholy. That is how I understand Bultmann, too. But it is not yet clear, and neither Bultmann nor Bonhoeffer has been successful in making it clear, that we have to look for the last word in his direction.

None of this is meant as criticism of your concern with Bonhoeffer. All you have said has to be pondered. A lessening of the offence he has provided for us would be the last thing I should wish . . .

(FROM: *World Come of Age*, edited by R. Gregor Smith, p. 89.)

7 'Barth on Bultmann and demythologizing'

[This section illustrates the general direction of Barth's criticism of Bultmann and his demythologizing enterprise. Barth calls it into question because it violates literary principles for appreciating the meaning of a text and seems to suggest that a translation can replace the original. Notice also Barth's stricture on the view that myth is valueless for modern man, and his suggestion that Bultmann is not willing to accept the fact that the Incarnation meant God exposing himself to genuine history (and all the probabilities of human historical investigation), becoming, in fact, 'datable'.]

I thought it best to concentrate to begin with on the positive aspect of Bultmann's work, his presentation of the New Testament message. I have not yet mentioned the word by which his work has become so widely known and discussed, not only among German theologians, but all over the world. I refer, of course, to the demythologizing of the New Testament. This is, of course, no nickname given to it by a third party. It was invented by Bultmann himself; and not only is it a barbarism,[1] but it is unnecessarily provoking. And it was Bultmann who bandied the term about so much, e.g., in his primary essay, 'The New Testament and Mythology',[2] which is of crucial importance for the whole subject. If the wicked (Christian) world fails to understand him, much of the blame is due to his invention of this word, so uninspiring and negative. But we must not be put off by the word itself, for that would not do him justice. It is not itself the real clue, or at any rate not the only clue to his position. I, for one, would regard the demythologizing of the New Testament of secondary importance compared with the positive results of his exegesis, and the positive principles by which he reaches them. It is, in fact, the

[1] Demythologizing' certainly sounds more barbaric in the German 'entmythologisierung'! (Ed.)

[2] *Kerygma and Myth*, Vol. I, pp. 1–44.

positive side which disturbs me even more if anything, than the negative side, or demythologizing proper. But since Bultmann himself has introduced the term and evidently sets such store by it, I shall have to give it due attention and follow him along this path too.

Once again I shall begin with his positive account of the New Testament message, at first in purely general terms, and simply point out Bultmann's omission of certain elements which are characteristic of it in its original form. He has no use for those elements at all, and he tells us so quite plainly. He suggests—and in his original essay with almost frantic insistence—that the primary task of exegesis and translation as he sees it is to circumvent these elements and eliminate them. Let me hasten, however, to correct this impression. He expressly contrasts himself with the older liberals on this point. His aim is not, except in a few border-line cases, to suppress or circumvent these elements. Rather, they must be translated out of the language, imagery and terminology of the New Testament into our own, into those of contemporary man. For, says Bultmann, it is just these elements which require translation. We can hardly complain that he actually omits them except in a few marginal instances. They are certainly there, though in a new guise. What has been allowed to disappear, what is missing, he claims, is the forms in which the New Testament expresses those elements, not their essential meaning. This, then, is the crucial question about Bultmann's work, taken as a whole. Is the essential meaning of these elements and the function they fulfil still recognizable in spite of the different form in which they are expressed? And if so, to what extent? Or, to put it in Bultmann's own terms, does the removal of the New Testament form of expression enable us to recognize more clearly the intention of the elements in question? More than this, is it the case that their intention can only be recognized when they have been transformed and the New Testament forms of expression replaced by another? Can I, therefore, claim that the questions I raised under section III were posed correctly, at least in a formal sense, from Bultmann's point of view? In that section I was in fact concerned with the problem of recognizing in Bultmann's presentation the New Testament message itself. Since this presentation was at least partly—and Bultmann sometimes gives the impression that it is absolutely—determined by his transformation of them, it is reasonable to suppose that it is just the transformation of them which makes it difficult, if not impossible for me at least to recognize the original message. That is what I was trying to explain there.

What kind of elements does Bultmann find room for in his restatement? He divides them into two groups, though how he does so I find difficult to understand. First, we have those elements in the language of the New Testament which directly or indirectly reflect the distinctive world view of late Judaism and Hellenistic gnosticism. There is the three-stored universe, the intervention of supernatural powers, and their influence in human existence. There is Satan and the demons, sin and death on the one hand, and God, angels and miracles on the other. There is imminent end of all things in a cosmic catastrophe, the resurrection of the dead, and divine sentence of salvation or damnation directly pronounced upon them. Secondly, there is everything that corresponds to that world view in the New Testament portrayal of salvation. This includes the idea that the end is ushered in with the mission of the pre-existent Son of God, his birth of a virgin, his bodily resurrection from the dead as the first stage in the dethronement of Satan, sin, death, and the demons; his exaltation as king and Lord and his reign in heaven; his visible return to consummate his saving work—an event which Paul himself expected to experience; the Church, baptism and the Lord's Supper as means of uniting believers to their Lord, the indwelling spirit as the pledge of their final status as sons of God.

Does this mean that a viable translation of the New Testament depends on the proper treatment of these respective elements? That in some cases they should be eliminated, and in others transformed? Here I must pause for a moment to ask Bultmann why he has raised these elements to central importance in his exegesis. As we can see from what he has written elsewhere, and particularly in what his disciples have written, there is a tendency to describe these elements a little crudely, a little ironically, even to caricature them. Does he do it in the interest of the spirit, content and scope of what the New Testament says? If so, he should pay more attention to the context in which these elements occur, and the value attached to them in their context. That would give him elbow room to consider them, more patience and inclination for doing so. He would look at them with less irritation (pardon me for saying so), less detachment, less temptation to lump them all together as a series of curiosities. He would be less inclined to exalt them into a problem for their own sake, still less to make them the main problem of his exegesis.

Why this procedure? Where does he find his common denominator? Is it the core of the New Testament message as he conceives it? Or is it some kind of historical analysis which makes him feel free, or rather compelled to turn such a detached interest to the structural idiosyncrasies of the New Testament statements? For it is clearly historical analysis which provides him with the clue to the common features in these various elements. What is not clear to me is what kind of transformation this is if Bultmann, as he seems to have done, had taken just one of the possible results of historical analysis and elevated it into the problem of all problems for New Testament exegesis, and made it into the sole criterion for its solution. Hence, even if we were merely concerned with Bultmann's *modus operandi*, I feel I can hardly go along with him thus far with a good conscience.

Assuming that he is right first in lumping all these elements together and then treating them separately, what does he actually do to them? Let me repeat that he does not deny, eliminate or expunge them from the kerygma, except those elements which are untranslatable, such as the three-storied universe, Satan and the demons, the angels, the virgin birth, the empty tomb and the ascension. He interprets them. Let us examine the way he presents them. Some of the important elements are certainly there. There is sin, Death; God, his revelation in Christ and in Christ alone; the Holy Spirit, the divine sonship of the believers, the Church and even the sacraments and the eschatological hope, the last being the dominant principle. All these are there, each in its proper place and each duly translated and 'interpreted'. He does it with an earnestness which puts many a more orthodox expositor to shame. No wonder many liberals think Bultmann is too orthodox to be one of themselves. He has on more than one occasion disowned the name of liberal; he is not eliminating these indigestible elements but interpreting them! This may not be quite fair to some of the early liberals like Biedermann. And did not Schleiermacher, who was also suspected of being too orthodox, aim chiefly to interpret and to confine himself to that? But who reads Schleiermacher nowadays, let alone Biedermann?

It is good to remind ourselves that there is nothing new under the sun—only the names have changed, that's all. But enough of that!

But why do these particular elements in the New Testament need interpretation? That is the first and foremost question here. And supposing they do, how far should we go? Bultmann's answer is that they need it—and here is his cardinal principle of criticism—because they are couched in the thought and language of the world of those days. They are mythological expressions of the truths they seek to convey. Myth and mythological language, according to Bultmann, are to be found wherever the divine is described in terms of this world, the other side in terms of this side, the non-objective as objective. In this form myth speaks of the power or powers which man allegedly experiences as the ground and limit of his world and of his own activity and sufferings. In this form myth is an expression of man's self-understanding. Thus the New Testament message, Bultmann thinks, in the historical forms in which it is enshrined in the texts, is a mythological expression of a distinctive human self-understanding. That is why the New Testament demands interpretation and its records require translation. This implies, on the negative side, that they must be demythologized, i.e., removed from their present form and placed in another. Such a procedure is possible since the mythological form was at best only a temporary necessity. There is nothing specifically Christian about it, and it can easily be detached from the message itself, which is the specifically Christian self-understanding. This operation is necessary since the mythological form obscures the real meaning of the New Testament message. Why? Because the mythological view of the world and of man is as obsolete as the age which produced it. Another view of the world and man, the modern one, is irresistibly forcing itself upon us, and we cannot avoid presupposing it in our thinking. It would be senseless and impossible for the Christian preacher to expect modern man to swallow the ancient world view, or to accept those features in the New Testament's presentation of the redemptive event which conform to that world view and which he can only regard as obsolete. Such a *sacrificium intellectus* would be as impossible as it would be downright dishonest. It would reduce faith to a human achievement, which, as Wilhelm Herrmann[1] pointed out, would be immoral. It would in no way confront man with the real stumbling-block, or challenge him to a genuine decision between faith and belief. We must, therefore, stop expecting it of him. The task of exegesis, shared as it is by the dogmatic theologian and the preacher, is thus in the first place a negative one. It is to show from the texts themselves that the New Testament message is couched in imagery derived from late Judaism and Gnosticism. This imagery must then be removed on the ground that it is irrelevant for the understanding of the message, so as to make room for an exposition of the message itself. The demythologizing of the texts is the *sine qua non* for their understanding. This process. thinks Bultmann, is all the more justified since there are in the New Testament not only obvious contradictions between the various images, but also a process of interpretation which itself tends towards demythologizing. We can see that as we compare Paul, and especially John, with the Synoptic gospels. Bultmann claims that this is just what he has provided by his presentation in its positive aspect: he has met the need which the New Testament itself requires.

As I listen I am amazed; I should like to follow but I cannot. Is it possible to understand any text, be it ancient or modern, if we approach it with preconceived notions about the extent and the limit to which it can be understood? Is it not preferable to come to it with an open mind, and patiently follow what it has to say? Can we undersand it if we think we have some criterion to enable us to know in advance what parts of the text are intelligible, and thus differentiate the outward imagery from the actual substance? Are we to suppose that the text can only be made intelligible and gain a hearing if it is first translated? Surely, if we want to understand any given text, the provisional clue to its understanding must be sought from the text itself,

[1] Wilhelm Herrmann (1846–1922), German theologian, once described by Barth as 'my unforgettable teacher'. (Ed.)

and moreover from its spirit, content and aim. Surely we should be condemning our text to silence in advance if we approached it with such a criterion, alien alike to its spirit, content and aim. How can we decide even before we have read the text what it actually says, and what is only temporary imagery? And what happens if we use this alien criterion as an infallible instrument rather than as a provisional clue? Is not Bultmann's very concept of myth, the infallible criterion which dominates his hermeneutics, quite alien to the New Testament? Whether or not it is the contemporary fashion, as Bultmann claims it is, the question is how can it be used to decide what belongs to the substance of the New Testament and what is merely outward imagery?

Bultmann says the exegete must be honest and sincere. To whom does he owe this obligation primarily? To what is he responsible, the presuppositions of his own thought and of the contemporary world, and to a principle of understanding determined by that thought, or to the actual text he is trying to understand, and to the criterion to be derived from its spirit, content and aim? I do not mean to suggest that this canon should be applied rigidly; it is only a flexible rule for further research.

From another point of view it may be asked whether it is right to stigmatize everything mythological as though it were *ipso facto* absolutely useless for modern man. Why should not the divine be described in terms of human life, the otherworldly in terms of this world, the non-objective as objective? And is not this too formal a definition of myth to cover all the different kinds we know in history, the Indian, Babylonian, Egyptian and Teutonic mythologies? Or the myths of the modern world, the myth of the twentieth century, the Marxist myth, the myth of the Christian west, etc.? Has myth always been the representation of some general relationship and correspondence within the realm of nature or history, decked out as a superhuman tale of the gods? The controversy over the meaning of myth is not without its importance. For if Bultmann used a definition which covered the content rather than the form, he could still find plenty of mythological imagery and terminology incidentally accepted and used in the New Testament. As for the actual content of the New Testament message, however, he could hardly describe it as mythological in form, proceed to dismantle it from top to bottom and replace it by some other form, supposedly more intelligible and relevant to modern man. However much the New Testament writers borrowed their imagery and language from the surrounding world, it could hardly have occurred to them to produce their message as the proclamation of general cosmic truths disguised as a tale about the gods and their doings. After all, that was just the kind of thing they were attacking. Perhaps demythologizing the New Testament would have made more sense if Bultmann had not chosen this curiously formal definition of myth and made it the criterion with which to distinguish between the form and substance of the New Testament. I wonder what voice from heaven it was that led him to choose this crude definition of myth to describe the dubious elements of the New Testament. He would have done better to reserve his fire for the supernaturalism of the Bible, as it used to be called, if indeed he had to attack anything at all.

Since, however, he has chosen that definition all I can do is to put to him the real theological question on which everything devolves. Is the demythologized kerygma allowed to say anything about God's having condescended to become this-worldly, objective and—horror of horrors!—datable? Apparently it is not allowed to say that the New Testament God is the kind of God who is capable of such condescension. Nor can it admit that it originated in the concrete fact that the disciples saw with their own eyes, heard with their ears, touched with their hands, in space and time, not only the dereliction of the Word made flesh hanging on the cross, but also the glory of the same Word made flesh risen from the dead. Nor apparently can it say that the disciples' faith was born, not by a kind of parthenogenesis, but through a revelation, the revelation of one who had been crucified on Golgotha, a revelation occurring not in some invisible, supra-historical, celestial sphere, but in their own visible, historical, earthly sphere, a revelation as human, worldly, this-worldly and objective as the cross itself? Apparently the demythologized kerygma must remain silent about what causes faith. It has a cause, it is not just a paradox, but it is not 'susceptible of proof'. Apparently the kerygma must suppress or even deny the fact that the cross and resurrection of Jesus Christ, the total Christ event, is the event of our redemption, that it possessed an intrinsic significance of its own, and that only because it has that primary significance has it a derived significance here and now. Yet this event is the ground of our faith and of the kerygma, and faith and kerygma are only secondary to it and derivative from it. Apparently the kerygma must suppress or even deny the fact that the Christ event has founded a community which throughout its history has had a Lord distinct from itself, a Lord whom it follows in discipleship. All this would, it seems, have to go by the board if we demythologized the New Testament *à la* Bultmann. What is the purpose of the alleged mythological elements if not to demonstrate that we are not left alone in this human, worldly, this-worldly, objective existence of ours, that our faith does not depend on some unknown distant deity, some supra-cosmic transcendent, non-objective reality? On the contrary, are they not meant to show that he who was crucified and rose again at a particular time and place is our divine Lord and human brother whom we are privileged to know as one who is both near and far, as one who lives and reigns over us even before we come to believe in him and even in our unbelief, as the one in whom God first loved us. How else can all this be expressed except in the way Bultmann calls mythological? It is just this truth—or am I mistaken?—that Bultmann has left out in his demythologizing. What service is it to modern man, ourselves included, to suppress the cardinal truth of the kerygma like this? I am most embarrassed: much as I am loath to charge Bultmann with heresy, I cannot deny that his demythologized New Testament looks suspiciously like docetism.[1] Perhaps this has something to do with his inability to make anything of the Old Testament. It is too historical, too down to earth for him! Schleiermacher had just the same difficulty with it. And perhaps it also has something to do with his difficulties over the synoptic Jesus, with his ministry of word and deed and his course from Jordan to Gethsemane. I cannot as yet see how this all fits together, but I must confess

[1] 'Docetism', from tne Greek doēko 'to seem', is used of a tendency in Christian theology to underplay the genuine humanity of Jesus, especially his possession of a real human biology and psychology. (Ed.)

that if interpreting the New Testament means demythologizing it, and if demythologizing means what Bultmann with his definition of myth means by it, it seems to have singularly little to do with the gospel of the New Testament.

(FROM: *Kerygma and Myth* II, edited by H. W. Bartsch, pp. 102–11.)

FOR STUDY AND DISCUSSION

1 Does Barth's way of doing theology have any 'apologetic' value?
2 Why does Barth come to characterize 'religion' as unbelief? Is there more to be said for religion than Barth allows? Can Christianity be differentiated from religion in this way?
3 Is the Christian Bible totally different in kind from the scriptures of other religions?
4 Does the historical Jesus matter for religious belief, according to Barth?

FOR FURTHER READING

PRINCIPAL WORKS OF KARL BARTH
(in English translation)

1936 *Credo* (translated by J. Strathearn McNab), 1964.
1947 *Dogmatics* in outline (translated by G. T. Thomson), 1949.
1932–59 *Church Dogmatics.*
1953 *The Humanity of God* (translated by J. N. Thomas and T. Wieser), 1961.
1956 *Shorter Commentary on Romans* (translated by D. H. van Daalen), 1959.
1959 *Deliverance to the Captives* (translated by M. Wieser).
1963 *Evangelical Theology* (translated by Grover Foley), 1962.
1964 *God Here and Now* (translated by Paul van Buren).

SOME BOOKS ABOUT KARL BARTH

T. F. Torrance, *Karl Barth, an introduction to his early theology,* London, 1962. (A study by a former pupil of Karl Barth, who sympathizes with his general standpoint, of the development of his thinking up to the publication of *Church Dogmatics.*)
Herbert Hartwell, *The Theology of Karl Barth: an introduction,* London, 1964. (A useful exposition of the whole scheme of Barth's theology, again by a sympathizer.)
H. A. Meynell, *Grace Versus Nature,* London, 1965. (A valuable and lucid survey of the *Church Dogmatics* by a young Roman Catholic philosopher and theologian who provides an excellent critical assessment of Barth.

FOR GENERAL BACKGROUND READING

John Macquarrie, *Twentieth-century Religious Thought*, 1963.
——, *God-talk*, 1967.
——, *God and Secularity*, 1968.
Frederick Ferré, *Language, Logic and God*, 1962.
——, *Basic Modern Philosophy of Religion*, 1968.
David E. Jenkins, *Guide to the Debate about God*, 1966.
Colin Williams, *Faith in a Secular Age*, 1966.
E. L. Mascall, *The Secularisation of Christianity*, 1965.
H. Gollwitzer, *The Existence of God as Confessed by Faith*, 1964.
A. M. Ramsey, *God, Christ and the World*, 1969.
T. W. Ogletree, *The Death of God Controversy*, 1966.

2. Rudolf Bultmann

1884–

BIOGRAPHICAL INTRODUCTION

There is an astonishing contrast between the uneventful life of Bultmann and the dramatic and controversial role which he has played in biblical studies and Christian theology in the first half of the twentieth century. He was born in 1884 in Wiefel-stede which was then part of the Grand Duchy of Oldenburg in north-west Germany. He came from clerical stock, both sides of the family having produced pastors. He had a country up-bringing and speaks of his schooldays as a time of happiness. Outside his religious interests he read a good deal of German and Greek literature, and he was keen on music concerts and the theatre.

He decided to study theology at the University and was a student at Tübingen, Berlin and Marburg. He began his academic career at Marburg when he was appointed to a lectureship.

He has known the scars of his generation. He had one brother killed in the First World War, and another in a Nazi concentration camp in the Second World War.

In 1916 he was appointed assistant professor at Breslau, where Bonhoeffer was born, and in 1920 became full professor at Giessen. The following year he returned as professor to his old university of Marburg in which he remained until his retirement in 1951.

He took up a pronounced anti-Nazi attitude but was not involved in underground activity in the way Bonhoeffer was.

Since his retirement he has lectured in the United States and elsewhere.

SELECTIONS

1 Form-criticism

[The work of the later Bultmann, especially his programme of 'demythologizing', can only be understood in the light of his earlier researches as a New Testament critic. He was one of the 'founding-fathers' of New Testament 'form-criticism' and these extracts give some illustration of its methods.

Bultmann discusses first the comparative literary study of the gospels. This showed that Mark was the first of the New Testament gospels to achieve written form, and that it had been used (with adaptations) as one of their sources by the authors of *St Matthew* and *St Luke*. Following this discovery, Mark's gospel was used to try and reconstruct the historical mission of Jesus and, in particular, the development of his 'messianic self-consciousness'. The results of this effort were however inconclusive.

Bultmann then turns to a description of form-criticism, pointing out first the amplifications and modifications which any tradition undergoes as it is handed on by word of mouth. Form-criticism tries to isolate and analyse characteristic units of the tradition about Christ, like, for example, 'miracle-stories' and 'sayings-stories' (apothegms), and to place them in the history of the formation of the gospels.]

(*a*) *The Literary study of the Gospels*

The second feature of contemporary Gospel research is the new literary-historical method of approach which has come to be known as Form-criticism. As we have noted, research had already arrived at the result that the Gospel of Mark was the oldest of the three Synoptics, and that by its side was to be found the collection of Sayings as another old source. It was assumed in the generation of such experts as H. J. Holtzmann, A. Julicher, and J. Weiss that one could make out from Mark and Q (the Sayings-document) the course of the life of Jesus and the content of his preaching with relative certainty. The inner development of the life of Jesus was inferred from the development of his Messianic consciousness: that is, from his steadily advancing claim to Messiahship, of which he was not entirely certain at the beginning and accordingly kept secret, and which he publicly acknowledged only at the end of his life; which consciousness as it gradually ripened in himself he permitted gradually to ripen likewise in his disciples. The outward development of his life, on the other hand, was characterized by an initial success and then by a gradual desertion on the part of the people, whose hopes he had disappointed, and most of all by the opposition of the scribes and Pharisees. The chief content of the preaching of Jesus was his message of the Kingdom of God, which was neither a purely spiritual state nor a society of the pious realizing itself historically in the midst of this world, but was the heavenly Kingdom expected to come miraculously and catastrophically in the immediate future. These scholars scarcely recognized the problem, viz., how the moral demands of Jesus were related to this 'eschatological' message—the former receiving expression in many of his sayings (e.g., Matt. v. 20–45; vi. 1–34) and in the controversies with the scribes, and containing practically no traces of the eschatological expectation.

On the other hand, W. Wrede had already demonstrated in his book *The Messianic Secret in the Gospels* (*Das Messiasgeheimnis in den Evangelien*, 1901), undoubtedly the most important work in the field of gospel research in the generation now past, that although Mark is indeed the oldest gospel, its narrative cannot be accepted as an exact account of the history of Jesus; that Mark is really dominated by the theology of the Church and by a dogmatic conception of Christ; and that he arranged and revised the old traditional material out of which his gospel is composed in accordance with his own ideas, so that one cannot make out from his narrative either the development of the Messianic consciousness and claim of Jesus or the course of his activity, nor the reasons for his failure and death. Wellhausen[1] in his *Commentaries on the Gospels* (1905 and following) reinforced and demonstrated essentially the same conclusion: in each of the gospels one must distinguish between the old tradition and the redactional

[1] Julius Wellhausen (1844–1918), distinguished German biblical scholar. (Ed.)

contribution of the evangelists; the former consists essentially in single brief units; the latter not only altered many of the details but first gave its continuity to the whole, thus creating the artificial effect of a historical development. Especially important is Wellhausen's demonstration that the Sayings-document, like Mark, has been influenced by the theology of the primitive Church : it grew out of the primitive community and is steeped in its views and interests, and therefore gives us no infallible reflection of the preaching of Jesus.

The result of these works was at once a widespread but perfectly futile discussion of the Messianic consciousness of Jesus. To what extent had Jesus looked upon himself as Messiah in the Jewish sense, to what extent did he transform the Jewish Messianic conception? Did he look upon himself as Messiah from the very beginning—say from the time of his baptism—or did his Messianic consciousness grow gradually, first developing, perhaps, towards the end of his ministry? Was the Messianic consciousness for him a matter of pride and of consolation in the midst of opposition, or was it a burden hard to bear? Was it essential or was it a relatively indifferent form of his sense of vocation? These were the typical questions, and all of these tantalizing possibilities were investigated by individual scholars and variously affirmed and denied; one can scarcely gain a stronger impression of the uncertainty of our knowledge concerning the person of Jesus than by putting together what the various investigators of the Messianic consciousness of Jesus have thought. It is noteworthy that little attention has been given to the outward course of the life of Jesus and the grounds of his condemnation. The assurance with which formerly it was assumed that the ministry of Jesus was limited to one year has indeed weakened since it has come to be recognized that the outline of Mark is not historical. But what were the actual external factors determining his fate, and what it was that led him to the cross—these questions are scarcely asked, as if it were self-evident that the enmity of the scribes and Pharisees compassed his death. The problem, how the eschatological and the ethical teaching of Jesus are related one to the other, has come at last to be recognized. It is in truth far from easy to say how an eschatological prophet who sees the end of the world approaching, who senses the arrival of the Kingdom of God, and accordingly pronounces blessed those of his contemporaries who are prepared for it (Matt. 13 : 16–17; 5 : 3–9; 11 : 5–6 etc.)—to say how such a person could argue over questions of the Law and turn off epigrammatic proverbs like a Jewish rabbi (since to practically all the moral directions of Jesus there are parallel and related words of Jewish rabbis), in words which contain simply no hint of eschatological tension (e.g., Matt. 6 : 19–21, 25–34; 7 : 1, 2, 7; 10 : 29; Luke 14 : 7–11; Mark 2 : 27; 4 : 21). Wellhausen looked upon the ethical teaching as the genuine historical nucleus, and believed that the eschatological sayings were for the most part of the products of the primitive Christian community, which after Jesus' death was strongly influenced by the Messianic expectations. Others, like J. Weiss and A. Schweitzer, held, contrariwise, the eschatological preaching to be the characteristic message of the historical Jesus, and either ignored the moral directions or explained them as 'interim ethic', that is, as requirements which lacked general validity but which held good for this last brief space of time which was to precede the end.

(*b*) *The Method of Form-criticism*

Form-criticism begins with the observation that, especially in primitive literature, literary expression (oral or written) makes use of more or less fixed forms, which have their own laws of style. In the Old Testament we have long been accustomed to recognize this feature and to apply the form-historical method. The forms of psalm, prayer, prophetic address, fable, story, and historical narrative have been recognized and their stylistic laws have been described. Is it possible to identify similar literary forms in the Synoptic tradition? If this be the case, one must recognize and reckon with the fact that the tradition possesses a certain solidarity, since the form would naturally oppose itself to any serious alterations. On the other hand, it will be possible to determine in the individual sections whether the appropriate form was purely expressed or somewhat revised, and so one should be able to determine the age of the section. This would be the more true if it were possible to recognize not only the appropriate laws of style of a specified literary form but also the laws by which the further development of material takes place, i.e., a certain orderliness in change by which a body of tradition is always controlled in its growth. There are various means available to this end. The first is this, that we may accurately observe how the Marcan material is altered and revised by Matthew and Luke, and how Matthew and Luke have presumably edited the text of Q (the Sayings-document). If we are able to deduce a certain regularity in this procedure, then we may certainly assume that the same laws held good even earlier, and we may draw conclusions as to the state of the tradition prior to Mark and Q. It is clear that this is a very difficult process and one to be pursued with great caution. One may, however, test his skill by studying the manner in which the evangelical material was handed down in the later Church, especially in the apocryphal gospels, and likewise the general laws governing popular narrative and tradition, such as stories and anecdotes. In order, however, to identify the peculiar stylistic laws governing the forms of the Synoptic tradition, we must remind ourselves that certain forms were found close at hand in the environment of the early Christian community, and offered themselves for purposes of tradition. Similar sayings and brief narratives were handed down in Jewish literature, and their forms show remarkable similarity to those of the evangelical material.

(*c*) *The Laws Governing Popular Narrative and Tradition*

The laws governing the formulation of popular narrative and tradition may be studied in detail in the material which the Synoptists hand down. The first thing we observe is that the narrators do not give us long unified accounts but rather small single pictures, individual scenes narrated with the utmost simplicity. These always occupy but a brief space of time; apart from the Passion Narrative no event or proceeding is narrated which covered more than two days. As a rule only two speaking characters appear in these scenes, or at most three; involved proceedings are beyond the powers of the simple story teller. Where groups or crowds are present, they are treated as a unity. As such narratives pass from mouth to mouth, or when one writer takes them over from another, their fundamental character remains the same, but the details are subject to the control of fancy and are usually made more explicit and definite. So, for example, Mark 9 : 17 relates that the father brought his demoniac son to Jesus; in Luke's version is added the statement that he was an only son (9 : 38). The palsied hand which Jesus healed (Mark 3 : 1) is described by Luke as the right hand (6 : 6). The ear of the high priest's servant which was struck off in Gethsemane (Mark 14 : 47) was according to Luke 22 : 50 the right ear. One may observe in the account of this scene which appears in the Gospel of John another important law at work: though the Synoptists do not name either the servant or the disciple who struck him, John gives the names, Malchus and Peter.

In the apocryphal tradition the process may be followed still further since here legend creates the names of hitherto unnamed persons; for example, those of the three Wise Men from the East, the woman with an issue of blood, the crucified robbers, the officer on guard at Jesus' tomb, and so on. However, one may see such supplying of names already at work in the Synoptics. The disciples who are sent to prepare for the Last Supper are unnamed in Mark (14 : 13); in Luke their names are given, Peter and John (22 : 8). Instead of the disciples as in Mark 7 : 17, it is Peter who asks the question of Jesus in Matthew 15 : 15. The name of the ruler of the synagogue, whose daughter Jesus raised from death, is given as Jairus in Luke 8 : 41; in Mark there is a whole series of manuscripts in which the name is omitted, and it is not at all unlikely that in the others it was added to complete the text. For this reason one must be a little sceptical even of the names given in Mark (e.g., 10 : 28, 46; 11 : 21).

Still another example of the way in which fancy has elaborated the older material is the account of the robbers crucified with Jesus (Luke 23 : 39–43) : Mark knows nothing of this but says simply that the two men crucified with Jesus mocked him (15 : 32).

Another characteristic trait is that the narrator prefers to give in direct discourse what his source gave indirectly. For example, Mark 8 : 32 states that when Jesus announced his coming Passion, Peter upbraided him; Matthew 16 : 22 reports him as saying, 'Be it far from Thee, Lord!' Instead of the narrative of Mark 14 : 1, 'After two days was the feast of the Passover and of unleavened bread', Matthew 26 : 1 f. reads, 'And it came to pass when Jesus had finished all these sayings, he said unto his disciples "Ye know that after two days is the feast of the passover . . ."' While Mark 14 : 23 relates that when the cup was passed around at the Last Supper 'they all drank of it,' Matthew makes Jesus say 'Drink ye all of it' (26 : 27). In the account of the kiss of Judas, Mark says nothing of any words of Jesus; Matthew (26 : 50), however, and Luke (22 : 48), each introduce a saying, though each brings forward a different one—it is easy to see how imagination has elaborated this scene. The last inarticulate cry of Jesus (Mark 15 : 37) becomes in Luke the saying, 'Father, into Thy Hands I commend my spirit' (23 : 46).

Still another important fact deserves to be mentioned. Along with the tendency to characterize more definitely the dim figures in the tradition goes the inclination to impose a schematic idea of the course of Jesus' activity, viz., the opponents with whom Jesus engages in disputation are almost invariably scribes and Pharisees, who interrogate him with malicious intent. One may often observe or infer that the earliest tradition had to do with unspecified questioners, whom the later narrators transformed into ill-disposed scribes or Pharisees. In the original Sayings-document (Q) it was only stated that 'some of them' accused Jesus of collusion with the devil (Luke 11 : 15); according to Matthew (12 : 24) these were Pharisees, according to Mark (3 : 22) they were scribes. Similarly the demand for a sign was made originally by some of the crowd (Luke 11 : 16); in Matthew (12 : 38) and Mark (7 : II) the demand comes from the Pharisees (and scribes). It is quite characteristic that Mark has retained in its old form the story of the question concerning the greatest commandment, in accordance with which the inquirer is entirely honest, and in the end is praised by Jesus as not far from the Kingdom of God (12 : 28–34). In Matthew this word of praise has fallen away, and the questioner appears from the outset as crafty and hypocritical (22 : 34–40; cf. Luke 10 : 25). Of course, many a polemic word of Jesus addressed to the scribes and Pharisees may be entirely historical (Mark 12 : 38–40; and most of Matt. 23 : 1–31), but the schematic representation according to which the Pharisees and scribes are from the outset the sworn enemies of Jesus is certainly unhistorical.

(*d*) *Two types of traditional material*

(*i*) *Miracle stories*

It may further be demonstrated that the evangelical material is set forth in the forms of distinct literary types. It is self-evident that the laws of style governing a literary type are more or less elastic; at the same time each type has its own definite characteristics which may be observed in every example of the type, even though these characteristics are not all present in any one example.

This may be seen for example in the miracle stories. Professor O. Weinreich has gathered together a body of material suitable for comparison under the title *Ancient Miracles of Healing* (*Antike Heilungswunder,* 1909), as have also P. Fiebig, *Jewish Miracle Narratives of the New Testament Period* (*Judische Wundergeschichten des neutestamentlichen Zeitalters,* 1911), and others. The lay reader may obtain an impression of such ancient miracle stories from a translation of the writing of Lucian of Samosata (second century A.D.), *The Friend of Lies* (Greek 'Philopseudes'). A comparison of the two makes it clear that the miracle stories of the gospels possess a remarkable resemblance to the Hellenistic miracle narratives; the latter accordingly throw significant light upon the problem of their origin or at least of their formulation.

The following seem to be characteristic of the style observed in the narratives of miracles. As a rule the narrative is given in three parts. First, the condition of the patient is described. Just as, for example, in Mark 9: 18 we read, 'I have brought unto thee my son who hath a dumb spirit; and wheresoever he taketh him, he teareth him : and he foameth and gnasheth with his teeth and pineth away'—so Lucian tells the story (Philops. 16) of a certain 'Syrian from Palestine,' a 'wise man' who had understanding in these matters: he was known to have healed many, 'who fell down in fits, rolled their eyes, and foamed at the mouth'. Typical also is the emphasis upon the gravity of the illness (e.g., Mark 5 : 3–5) or its long duration (e.g., Mark 5 : 25 f.; 9 : 12; Luke 13 : II). Just as in the Greek stories, so Mark 5 : 26 describes the futile efforts of physicians to heal the illness, and also the scornful attitude of the people when the true healer first appeared (Mark 5 : 40). Just as here it is said that the crowd standing about the house of mourning laughed Jesus to scorn, so, for example, the inscriptions in the temple of the healing God Asclepios at Epidauros tell of a sick woman who laughed sceptically when she heard of the marvellous deeds of the God, or how the crowd ridiculed the folly of a man totally blind who hoped for divine healing.

In the second section of the story the healing itself is narrated. Often the peculiar manipulations of the healer are described, as in Mark 7 : 33; 8 : 23. In general, however, the New Testament miracle stories are extremely reserved in this respect, since they hesitate to attribute to the person of Jesus the magical traits which were often characteristic of the Hellenistic miracle worker. In Hellenistic stories we are told, for example, how an exorcist drove the spirit out of a demoniac by holding a ring to the patient's nose so that he might smell a marvellous root that has been set in it; or how another healed a person of snake-bite by placing upon the wounded foot a tiny piece of the gravestone of a virgin, to the accompaniment of an appropriate magic formula. In the gospels as a rule it is simply stated, as likewise in the Hellenistic narratives, that the wonder worker approaches the patient—perhaps coming to his bedside—lays his hand upon him or takes him by the hand and utters the healing word. It is also characteristic that these words are as a rule given in an unknown foreign tongue, like 'Talitha kumi' (Mark 5:41) and 'Ephphatha' (Mark 7:34). Where the view prevails that the patient is possessed by a demon we are told how the demon sensed the presence of his master, disputed with him, but was finally threatened and driven out, as in the genuine folk-tale contained in Mark 5 : 1–20. Finally, it may be noted as characteristic that not infrequently it is said that no one was present at the miracle proper; e.g., Mark 7:33; 8:23. We find some examples in the Old Testament; I Kings 17 : 19; II Kings 4 : 4, 33. The original implication of this is doubtless that no one may witness an act of deity, as in the story of Lot's wife (Genesis 19 : 26).

Two characteristics are found in the third section, as a rule. First of all it was naturally often pointed out that witnesses of the wonderful results of the miracles broke out in exclamations of wonder or approval. Not infrequently it is related of the person healed that he gave some clear demonstration of the fact : for example, the lame man taking up his bed and walking, as in Mark 2 : 11 f., and in a miracle story that Lucian relates. To the same effect is the statement that the restored daughter of Jairus was given something to eat (Mark 5 : 43); by this anyone could see that she was completely restored to life. Following the exorcism of the demons the demonstration often consists in some spiteful and destructive act of the departing demon, like the shattering of a pillar or the overturning of a bowl of water, or, as in Mark 5 : 13, the sudden frenzy of a herd of swine who dash over a cliff and fall into the sea.

(*ii*) *Apothegms*

Among the sayings of Jesus it is possible to distinguish various groups. There are those, for example, which have been handed down in association with a little scene, in which according to the tradition they were originally spoken. Dibelius calls such fragments of tradition 'paradigms', since he assumes that they served as illustrations in Christian preaching. I prefer to call them apothegms, since in their structure they are closely related to the narratives of Greek literature which have hitherto borne this name. It is characteristic that the narrated scene serves only as the framework for an important saying; the whole point lies in the saying, and the frame simply gives the situation in which the word was spoken, and its occasion. The occasion may be the question of a disciple or a scribe; and the question, in turn, may have been occasioned by some deed of Jesus such as a healing on the Sabbath, or by the conduct of the disciples who ate without first performing the ritual washing of hands. In such a classification belong the controversies of the Synoptic tradition, such as those in Mark 2 : 1–12, 23–

28; 3 : 1–6; 7 : 1–23 etc.; conversations with eager inquirers, as in Mark 10 : 17–22; 12 : 28–34; Matthew 11 : 2–19; Luke 17 : 20–21 etc.; and scenes of a biographical character, like Mark 6 : 1–6; 10 : 13–16; Luke 9 : 57–62; 11 : 27–28 etc. Such apothegms are to be found in Jewish literature as well as in Greek, but a closer consideration shows that there were characteristic differences between Jewish and Greek literature on this point. For the Jewish story, it is significant that the saying of the hero which is given in response to a question usually appears either as a counter-question or as a brief parable (or both at once). This is true of most of the apothegms of Jesus. A story of Rabban Gamaliel may serve as a Jewish example (Fiebig, *Erzählungsstil*, p. 103). A heathen philosopher once asked him why it was that God should be angered at idolatry, and he replied: 'Suppose a man calls his dog by the name of his father, and when he makes a vow uses the words, "By the life of this dog"; with whom will the father be angry, with the son or with the dog?' Another example is a dispute over the resurrection of the dead (Strack-Billerbeck, *Kommentar*, I, p. 895): 'The Emperor Hadrian said to Rabban Gamaliel, "You say that the dead will come back to life again; on the contrary they have turned to dust, and can dust come to life again?" Then Gamaliel's daughter spoke up and said to her father, "Never mind, let me answer him! In our city", she said, "there were two potters. One made his vessels out of water and the other out of clay. Which of these two deserves the greater praise?" The Emperor replied, "The one who made vessels out of water", and she said, "If God is able to create man out of moisture, how much more can he do so out of clay!"' This is the way the Synoptic controversies go. For example, Jesus replies (Mark 2 : 19) to the question, why his disciples do not fast, with the parabolic question, 'Do the sons of the bride-chamber (the bridegroom's companions) fast while the bridegroom is still with them?' To the invidious question whether or not he will heal on the Sabbath (Mark 3 : 4), he replies with the counter-question, 'Is it lawful to do good on the Sabbath day, or to do evil?' Similar counter-questions and parables are given in reply to the accusation of collusion with Satan in Mark 3 : 24–26 (cf. Mark 2 : 25 f.; 11 : 30; Luke 13 : 15, 14 : 5; Matthew 17 : 25). One may safely infer that these narratives have almost all been formulated in a Jewish environment and do not belong to the later Hellenistic period of development.

It is characteristic of the Greek apothegm that it is introduced with some such formula as, 'When he was asked by ...', or 'Once when he observed how....' We may give an example or two of this style. 'When asked by the Tyrant Dionysius why it was that philosophers visited the rich rather than the rich the philosophers, Aristippus replied: "The philosophers realize what they lack, but the rich do not".' 'Anaxagoras of Klazomenai, when he was asked why we are here, replied, "To behold the works of nature".' 'Once when Demonax saw two philosophers engaged in a thorougly discreditable argument, in which one of them asked foolish questions, and the other replied with irrelevancies, he said, "My friends, do you not realize that one of you is milking a ram and the other is holding up a sieve?"' 'As Diogenes once saw a child drinking out of its hands, he threw away the cup that he had in his wallet and said, "A child has exceeded me in doing without things".' The passage in Luke 17:20–21 is formulated in this manner: 'And when he was demanded of the Pharisees, when the Kingdom of God should come, he answered them and said, "The Kingdom of God cometh not with observation: neither shall they say, Lo here! or lo there! for, behold, the Kingdom of God is [at once] among you".' Similar to this is the narrative contained in one manuscript of Luke 6:5: 'On the same day when he saw a man working on the Sabbath he said to him. "Man, if you know what you are doing you are happy! but if you do not know, then you are accursed and a breaker of the law."' It may accordingly be concluded that these two accounts were first formulated in the Hellenistic church. However, it is not only possible but really probable that in Luke 17:20–21 only the framework, the scene, is a later creation and that the saying of Jesus is derived from the older tradition. One must therefore distinguish carefully between those apothegms in which the framework and the saying are so closely related that one cannot be told without the other (e.g., Mark 2:18–19; 3:1–5; Luke 12:13–14—'And one of the company said unto him, "Master speak to my brother, that he divide the inheritance with me", but he said unto him, "Man, who made me a judge or a divider over you?" '), and others, in which the framework and the saying are only loosely connected. Among the latter it is often only the saying of Jesus which is original and the frame has been supplied later; e.g., Mark 7:1–23; 10:2–12. Especially significant is Mark 2:15–17, Jesus' saying reads, 'They that are whole have no need of the physician but they that are sick; I come not to call the righteous but sinners'; the setting in vv. 15 f. has been artistically supplied later. This is indicated by the wholly unmotivated, and literally impossible, appearance of the Pharisaic scribes at a dinner attended by publicans, and further by the remarkable fact that it is the disciples who are questioned and Jesus who replies—and the same is true of other sayings in the series. The effort was made to introduce the traditional words of Jesus as completely as possible into scenes in his life, and in this case the setting of a meal seemed to be the most appropriate situation, since fellowship at table easily symbolized fellowship in general. One may further observe in other cases that unattached sayings of Jesus have been introduced into older apothegms or fastened on to them; examples of the former are found in Matthew 12:11 f.; Luke xiv. 5; of the latter in Mark 2:27 f.; 7:9–23; 10:23–27.

Striking also is a further observation that may be made: in Mark 2:18–19, 23–26; 7:1–8, it is related that the disciples did not fast, that they rubbed out kernels of grain on the Sabbath, and that they did not observe the ritual washing before meals. How are we to explain the fact that all these things are told of the disciples and not of Jesus himself, and that Jesus is called upon to defend their conduct rather than his own? It is impossible to assume that in all these instances his own conduct was correct; for the disciples can have learned their free attitude only from him! Nor may one suppose that the opponents hesitated to attack him directly; since in other cases, e.g., with reference to the healings on the Sabbath, they had no such hesitation.

Apparently the situation is to be understood only as follows: these traditions first arose in the Christian community and are to be explained by its situation. The 'disciples', i.e., the primitive Christian Church, have broken with the old customs in this matter, and they are defending themselves against criticism by means of the stories, through which they make their appeal to a saying of Jesus. It is certainly possible that the saying of Jesus enshrined in such a setting is old and authentic, as, for example, probably Mark 2:19. In the other cases it is less probable, since here argumentative use is made of sentences from the Old Testament, and since most of the words of Jesus which cite the Old Testament are suspected of originating in the theological debates of the primitive community. Just as the Messiah was defended by an appeal to Old Testament passages, so likewise an effort was made to found Christian practice upon a similar appeal.

Those apothegms which are of a biographical character are likewise for the most part creations of the community, since they give expression to what Christians had experienced of their Master or what he had experienced at the hands of his people. It is accordingly clear that the calling of the disciples in Mark 1:16–20 reflects no historical situation; the story completely lacks motivation and psychological probability. The scene sets forth symbolically and picturesquely the common experience of the disciples as they were raised by Jesus' wonderful power out of their previous spheres of life. It is in this way that we must also explain Mark 3:31–35 (Jesus' true relatives); 12:41–44 (the widow's mite); Luke 9:57–62 (various followers); 10:38–42 (Mary and Martha). Even the scene in Nazareth (Mark 6:1–6) may perhaps not reflect a particular historical event, but is rather a symbolical picture, setting forth the attitude of the people as a whole to the preaching of Jesus. As evidence for this may be cited the saying of Jesus found in one of the papyri:

'No prophet is welcome in his own home town;
And no physician can cure those who know him well.'

It may be that the scene in Mark has been created out of this saying.

(*e*) *Our Knowledge of the Historical Jesus*

What then is the final solution of the three involved problems described above: the Messianic consciousness of Jesus, the outward course of his life (and especially the grounds of his condemnation), and the relation between his eschatological and his ethical message?

Regarding the origin and development of his Messianic consciousness, we are, generally speaking, unable to say anything definite. Indeed, it must remain questionable whether Jesus regarded himself as Messiah at all, and did not rather first become Messiah in the faith of the community. The majority of scholars remain convinced of the first alternative. To me it appears rather that the second is the necessary consequence of the analysis of his words. At any rate, one may clearly see that Jesus did not come forward with the claims which from the Jewish point of view the Messianic title involved, but rather that his ministry was rightly characterized when it was said he was a prophet. Nevertheless, the movement which he inaugurated among the Jewish people may, and really must, be described as a Messianic movement, since it was carried on with the conviction that the Messianic prophecies were about to be fulfilled, that the Kingdom of God was about to appear, and that the signs of its arrival were to be seen in the mighty works of Jesus, chiefly in the banishment of the evil spirits. To those who stood outside it, this movement must have appeared like any of the other Messianic movements which in those decades convulsed the Jewish people and finally led to the war with Rome and the destruction of Jerusalem. The Roman procurators suppressed such movements with blood, and Jesus fell a victim to the intervention of the procurator Pilate. As he came up to Jerusalem with his followers his arrival was viewed by the procurator as politically dangerous. Whatever part the Jewish authorities took therein cannot now be made out, since the Passion Narrative is too thickly overgrown with legend. For the later Christians the real enemies were the Jews; since they were found to be their standing enemies and accusers, in the work of the Christian mission (note the representation in the Book of Acts), they were also made responsible for the death of Jesus. It is, of course, possible that the Jewish court in Jerusalem, in order to demonstrate its own political innocence, had some part in the tragedy; but at all events we are not entitled to assume that Jesus' ethical teaching so roused the Pharisees and scribes against him that he finally fell victim to their enmity. That the steady opposition of the Pharisees and scribes rests upon the artificial and schematic conception of later Christians has already been shown.

The most important question is that concerning the content of Jesus' preaching. The investigation has shown that both the eschatological and the ethical teaching of Jesus belong equally to the oldest stratum of the tradition, so that one can hardly call either one of them secondary. Nor can we view the ethical precepts of Jesus as 'interim-ethic'[1] for his demands have an absolute character, and are by no means influenced in their formulation by the thought that the end of the world is near at hand. Consequently, both sides of the message of Jesus, the eschatological and the ethical, must be conceived as belonging together. Did Jesus preach the new ethic simply as a condition of entrance into the Kingdom of God? In form this is certainly true again and again; and yet this would be no real union of the two elements, but only a superficial and external relation, which, precisely in view of the earnestness of his moral demands, would be hard to conceive. Or is the announcement of the coming Reign of God only the mythological or symbolical form, in which he set forth his general faith in God as the Judge and Rewarder? One can scarcely combine this with the moral earnestness of his prophetic mission.

We must probably conclude that in the eschatological as in the ethical teaching of Jesus the same fundamental view of God and of man is presupposed. The eschatological expectation arose out of the conviction that God is the final Reality, before whom everything earthly fades away, and before whom man in his unworthiness and worthlessness sinks to nothing. Only the future, which is God's, can bring salvation to man; and this future still faces man, in the present, and requires of him the decision for the world or for God. This is exactly the sense that Jesus' moral demands held. Jesus sets forth neither an individual nor a social ethics; that is, he measured the deeds of men neither according to an ideal conception of human personality nor of human society, but he taught men that the present instant is the moment of decision, in which it is

[1] An ethic not for all time but only for the interval between Jesus's own time and the 'End' which he believed to be imminent. The phrase was first used by Albert Schweitzer. (Ed.)

possible to yield up every claim of one's own and submit obediently to the will of God. It is this way of the good will, that Jesus preached, which leads man directly to the awareness of his own unworthiness and worthlessness in the sight of God, and of his own situation as faced with inevitable decision; it is only here that he learns the profoundest meaning of God's forgiveness, which one can receive only as a little child.

(FROM: *Form Criticism*, Harper Torchbooks, 1962, pp. 20–4, 28–30, 32–5, 36–46, 71–4.)

2 The Offence of the Incarnation

[Some of Bultmann's best writing has been on St John's gospel. A good example of this is the extract given here from his *Theology of the New Testament*. A first reading of St John's gospel might give the reader the impression that the enigmatic, ironic Christ of the synoptic tradition had disappeared, to be replaced by a Christ who openly reveals himself unambiguously from the start. Bultmann shows how even what might seem the most startling example of this, the miracles of St John, are in fact presented in a very 'misunderstandable', 'signful' way. There is a 'messianic secret' about the Christ of the fourth gospel, just as there is in the earlier tradition. Bultmann is also illuminating in the way he shows that the Christ of the fourth gospel is presented in language which is deliberately intended to carry a double-meaning, and suggest simultaneously both the historical Jesus of Nazareth and the present Christ of Christian belief.]

1. How does God's Son come into the world? As a human being. The theme of the whole Gospel of John is the statement: 'The word become flesh' (1 : 14). This statement is defended by I and II John against the false teachers. These are evidently Christian Gnostics[1] who deny the identity of the Son of God with the human Jesus either by asserting that their union was only temporary or by flatly rejecting the reality of the human

[1] Gnostics (literally 'those who know') tended to qualify or deny the real humanity of Christ (Ed.).

Jesus and docetically[1] regarding the human form of the Son of God as only a seeming body. John's answer to them is: every spirit that does not confess that Jesus Christ came in the flesh, that does not confess Jesus (the man as the Son of God) is not 'from God'; indeed, such false doctrine is nothing less than the work of Antichrist (I John 4:2 f.; II John 7). Just because John makes use of the Gnostic Redeemer-myth for his picture of the figure and activity of Jesus, a demarcation of his own position from that of Gnosticism is particularly incumbent upon him.

It is clear to begin with that for him the incarnation of the Son of God is not, as it is in Gnosticism, a cosmic event which sets into motion the eschatological occurrence (the unfolding of redemption) as a process of nature by which the union of the essentially opposite natures, light and darkness, is dissolved. The Gnostic Redeemer releases the pre-existent human selves, who by virtue of their light-nature are related to him, out of the matter (body and 'soul') that trammels them, and then leads them to the world of light above. John eliminated both the Gnostic concept of φύσις ('nature') and the Gnostic notion of the pre-existence of human selves and their unnatural imprisonment in the material world. He does not accept the Gnostic trichotomy of man, according to which man's true self is imprisoned in a body and a soul. Neither is the incarnation of the Son of God for John a device for transmitting 'Gnosis' to men in the form of teachings about cosmogony and anthropology or for bringing them secret formulas and sacraments, on the strength of which their selves can safely make the journey to heaven.

The Revealer appears not as man-in-general, i.e., not simply as a bearer of human nature, but as a definite human being in history: Jesus of Nazareth. His humanity is genuine humanity: 'the word became flesh.' Hence, John has no theory about the pre-existent one's miraculous manner of entry into the world nor about the manner of his union with the man Jesus. He knows neither the legend of the virgin birth[2] nor that of Jesus'

[1] See note in Book 1, p. 96

[2] In some Latin witnesses to the text of John 1:13 'qui . . . natus est' (who . . . was born) is found instead of 'who . . . were born'; this is certainly a 'correcting' of the original text. (Ed.)

birth in Bethlehem—or if he knows of them, he will have nothing to do with them. Jesus comes from Nazareth, and this fact, offensive to 'the Jews', is emphasized (1:45; 7:52) rather than deprecated. 'The Jews', knowing Jesus' place of origin and his parents (7:27 f.; 6:42), are not in error as to the facts, but err in denying the claim of this Jesus of Nazareth to be the Revealer of God. They err not in the matter upon which they judge but in making a judgement at all *κατὰ σάρκα* (according to the 'flesh'—according to external appearances).

Neither does the Revealer appear as a mystagogue communicating teachings, formulas, and rites as if he himself were only a means to an end who could sink into unimportance to any who had received his 'Gnosis.' Though Jesus says in departing from the earth, 'I have manifested thy name to the men whom thou gavest me out of the world' (17:6; cf. v. 26), still he has imparted no information about God at all, any more than he has brought instruction about the origin of the world or the fate of the self. He does not communicate anything, but calls men to himself. Or when he promises a gift, he is, himself, that gift: he himself is the bread of life that he bestows (6:35); he himself is the light (8:12); he himself is life (11:25; 14:6).

Jesus, the Son of God who has become man, is a genuine man—which again does not mean that in his personality the divine became visible so as to fill men with enthusiasm and touch their feelings or to fascinate and overwhelm them. If that were the case, the divine would then be conceived of simply as the human exalted and intensified. But according to John, the divine is the very counter-pole to the human, with the result that it is a paradox, an offence, that the Word became flesh. As a matter of fact, the divinity of the figure of Jesus in John is completely lacking in visibility, and the disciples' relation to him as 'friends' (15:14 f.) is by no means conceived of as a personal relation of human friendship. It is the farewell discourses especially that strive to teach this distinction by making clear that the disciples will not achieve the right relation to him until he has departed from them—indeed, that he is not in the full sense the Revealer until he has been lifted up and glorified (see especially 14:28; 16:7).

2. In what sense, then, can it be said of the incarnate Word,

'We have beheld his glory' (1:14)? Is his human figure, so to speak, a translucent picture through which his divinity gleams? On first thought it might seem so, for many passages of the evangelist represent Jesus as the 'divine man' (*θεῖος ἀνήρ*) in the Hellenistic sense—a man who has miraculous knowledge at his command, does miracles, and is immune to the plottings of his enemies.

It is as a 'divine man' that Jesus sees through the people he meets (Peter, 1:42; Nathanael, 1:47 f.) and knows the past of the Samaritan woman (4:17 f.). But to the evangelist these stories taken from tradition are symbolic pictures which indicate that the believer feels himself searched and known by God and that his own existence is exposed by the encounter with the Revealer. When 2:42 f., generalizing, says that Jesus sees through men, the author is not thinking of a supranatural ability but of the knowledge about man which arises from knowing God, and therefore knows what a stumbling-block God is to men. The same motif underlies the words, 'But I know that you have not the love of God within you' (5:42)—Jesus deduces this from the unbelief of the 'Jews'; he knows that face to face with the divine Revelation human resistance to God comes to light. Thus he knows that men mutter when they hear the Revealer's 'hard saying' (6:60 f.) and knows what oppresses believers and limits their comprehension, so long as they have not freed themselves from the notion that the Revelation ought to cause an alteration within this world (16:19).

Jesus' omniscience is confirmed by the disciples: 'Now we know that you know all things' (16:30)—but not because he has demonstrated it by miraculous knowledge, but because now at his farewell he has spoken 'plainly' (*παρρησία*) without any 'figure' (*παροιμία*, 'riddle,' 16:29). But in reality it is not some progress in Jesus' conduct that is characterized in the transition from 'riddles' to 'openness' but a change in the disciples' situation. For in the end Jesus has not said anything materially different from what he had always been saying, but what he had previously said now is seen in a new light; for in the light of Jesus' departure it now appears as something provisional for which only the future can bring a definite unveiling—that is to say, a genuine understanding (16:12–28, especially vv. 25 f.). The disciples' confession therefore anticipates this future and simply means that in Jesus' work as Revealer, which has now reached its end, all knowledge is contained. In keeping with this the confession continues not, 'and you need to question no one', but: 'And no one needs to question you.' The 'omniscience' of Jesus is therefore not understood to be his super-human ability, but his knowledge which is transmitted to the believer: whoever has recognized him as the Revealer by knowing that one thing knows everything, and Jesus' promise is fulfilled: 'On that day you will ask me no questions' (16:23).

The mention of Jesus' miraculous knowledge in the story of Lazarus is the result of unconsidered adoption of tradition (11:4, 11–14). Naturally, Jesus knows of his coming betrayal by Judas before the event (6:64, 70; 13:18). Perhaps this is due to an apologetic motif (if it is allowable even to look for such in this Gospel). But in addition to this possible motif, it is probably another idea that is dominant here: the idea that in the very nature of the Revelation—because it arouses man's resistance—there lies the possibility for the apostasy even of a disciple. Faith has no guarantee, and the Church must surmount the stumbling-block created by the fact that the devil finds his tool even in her own midst. Jesus' prediction of the disciples' flight and of persecution for the Church (16:32; 15:18–16:4a) is to be interpreted in a similar fashion: it is a foreknowledge which results from insight into the nature of the Revelation. That is also the way in which Jesus' knowledge of the fate that awaits him is to be understood. He is both the bringer of the Revelation and is himself the Revelation. Therefore he knows what is to befall him (2:19, 21); he knows 'the hour' (13:1; 18:4; 19:28). For him the perfect 'Gnostic' (i.e., knower), fate is no riddle.

Several times Jesus eludes harm or is snatched out of his enemies' hands until his hour is come (7:30, 44; 8:20, 59; 10:39). This motif has the purpose of demonstrating the fact that the Revealer's fate is not determined by human will but is in the hands of God.

3. Jesus performs miracles, a fact that is sometimes mentioned in general terms (2:23; 3:2; 4:45; 7:3, 31; 10:41, 11:47; 12:37; 20:30) and sometimes is depicted in accounts of specific miracles (2:1–12; 4:46–54; 5:1–9; 6:1–25; 9:1–7; 11:1–44).

The term used for these miracles is σημεῖα ('signs' and, secondarily, 'miracles'), and in John this word retains its true meaning of 'sign.' The 'signs' reveal Jesus' glory (2:11 cf. 9:3; 11:4), and the disbelief that refuses to be convinced by so many miracles is reproved (12:37). On the other hand, however, Jesus says in rebuke: 'Unless you see signs and wonders you will not believe' (4:48). And the risen Jesus addresses to Thomas the reproving word: 'Do you believe now because you have seen me? Blessed are those who see (me) not and yet believe' (20:29 tr.). It is an indication of disbelief when 'the Jews' ask: ('Then what sign do you do, that we may see, and believe you? What work do you perform)?' (6:30; cf. 2:18). They ask for a miracle analogous to the manna-miracle of Moses, and have no understanding of the work Jesus is performing. The fact that their question chronologically follows the sign of the bread-miracle makes it clear that the meaning of the sign does not lie in the miraculous occurrence. In fact, this had already been said in v. 26: 'You seek me, not because you saw signs, but because you ate some of the loaves and were filled' (6:26 tr.).

As 'signs' the miracles of Jesus are ambiguous. Like Jesus' words, they are misunderstandable. Of course, they are remarkable occurrences, but that only makes them indicators that the activity of the Revealer is a disturbance of what is familiar to the world. They point to the fact that the Revelation is no worldly occurrence, but an other-worldly one. They are pictures, symbols. The wine-miracle, an epiphany (2:1–12) symbolizes what occurs in all Jesus' work: the revelation of his 'glory'—not the glory of a miracle-worker, but that of him by whom the gift of 'grace and truth' is made. The cure of the official's son (4:46–54) and the healing of the lame man at the pool (5:1–9), both miraculous, are 'signs' only in the general sense that they point to the Revealer's work as of life-promoting kind. But the bread-miracle (6:1–15), the cure of the blind man (9:1–7), and the raising of Lazarus (11:1–44) have specific symbolic meaning: they represent the Revelation as food, light, and life respectively. It can hardly be decided whether the walking on the water is appended to the multiplication of the loaves only by the force of tradition or whether it is meant to convey that the Revealer and the Revelation are not subject to the laws of natural life.

We have already seen how 6:26 and 30 indicate that the 'signs,' though they are miraculous occurrences, do not furnish Jesus with legitimating credentials. The remark that the faith of the many, which rests upon the miracles, is no trustworthy faith (2:23–25) indicates the same thing. John's whole presentation shows, rather, that if the miracles are not understood as signs, they are an offence! The healing of the lame man and the cure of the blind man both elicit enmity and persecution, and the raising of Lazarus brings Jesus to the cross. The miracles may be for many the first shock that leads them to pay heed to Jesus and so begin to have faith—for this purpose, miracles are, so to speak, conceded; nevertheless, for the leaders of the people, the representatives of 'the world', the miracles are the offence that leads them to condemn him to death (11:47; cf. 12:18 f.).

4. Just because the miracles are 'signs' which require understanding, they also provide the possibility of misunderstanding. After the bread-miracle which raises the question whether he is 'the prophet who is to come into the world' (6:14), the crowd wants to make him king (6:15) because it expects material benefits of him (6:26). His brothers want to take him to Jerusalem to the Feast of Tabernacles so that he may make himself conspicuous there, saying: 'For no man works in secret if he seeks to be known openly. If you do these things, show yourself to the world' (7:4). They do not understand the way in which the Revelation works. They do not understand that from the world's standpoint the Revelation must always be a 'hidden thing' (cf. 'in secret' 7:4) and that it nevertheless occurs 'openly'—not, however, with demonstrative obtrusiveness but with the unobtrusiveness of everyday events. What is true of the miracles is true of all that Jesus does: it is not understood. Even the disciples understand the cleansing of the temple no more than 'the Jews' do. Not until after the resurrection does its meaning dawn upon them (2:17); likewise with the entry into Jerusalem (12:16). Peter does not grasp the meaning of the foot-washing (13:4 ff.).

As Jesus' actions are misunderstood, so are his words so long as they are conceived in the categories of worldly thought.

'The Jews' cannot but grossly misunderstand the saying about the destruction and rebuilding of the temple (2:20). As Nicodemus is able to understand re-birth only in the external natural sense (3:4), so the woman of Samaria misunderstands the saying about 'living water' first to mean running water and then to mean miraculous water (4:11, 15). The disciples cannot conceive what food Jesus means as his secret nourishment (4:33), nor can 'the Jews' guess what the bread from heaven is that Jesus bestows (6:34). Jesus' saying about his departure is misunderstood as an intention to go to the Dispersion (7:35 f.) or even to kill himself (8:22). The disciples misunderstand the sentence addressed to Judas: 'What you are going to do, do quickly' (13:27 f.). And Thomas cannot cope with the statement that the disciples know the way which Jesus will take (14:4). The disciples do not understand the 'little while' used by Jesus of his approaching departure and return (16:17 f.). They do not see why Jesus does not wish to manifest himself to the world (14:22). The incomprehension of the crowd is symbolically illustrated by the fact that some misunderstand the heavenly voice in answer to Jesus' prayer as thunder and others understand it as the angel voice which it is, but without perceiving that it is really speaking not to Jesus but to them (12:28–38).

In all these misunderstandings the offence of the assertion, 'the word became flesh' finds expression. This offence lies in the fact that the Revealer appears as a man whose claim to be the Son of God is one which he cannot, indeed, must not, prove to the world. For the Revelation is judgement upon the world and is necessarily felt as an attack upon it and an offence to it, so long as the world refuses to give up its norms. Until it does so, the world inevitably misunderstands the words and deeds of the Revealer, or they remain a riddle for it (10:6; 16:25, 29), even though Jesus has said everything openly all along (18:20). The world's inner capacity to understand comes most crassly to expression in the demand, 'If you are the Christ, tell us plainly'. Jesus, of course, had been telling them for a long time, so he can only answer, 'I told you, and you do not believe' (10:24 f.). Evidently he is to the world a foreigner whose language it does not understand. Why not? Not because he is not a real man, but because he, a mere man, demands credence for his claim to be the Revealer: 'Why do you not understand what I say? Because you cannot hear my word' (8:43 tr.). Why do 'the Jews' who know him and his home town, nevertheless not know who he is nor where he comes from? Because they do not know God (7:28)! So, on the one hand, Jesus can say that he does not bear witness for himself; if he did, his testimony would not be true (5:31 f.). On the other hand, he is constantly bearing witness for himself by claiming to be the Revealer, and can assert that his testimony is true when he does so (8:14). Each statement is true, according to which point of view is adopted: such a testimony as the world demands, a legitimation, he cannot and must not give. But there is a testimony which consists of his claim to be the Revealer, a claim which denies the world's competence to judge; in the world's opinion this cannot be considered true testimony (8:13). But this testimony he must bear.

The offence of the assertion 'the word became flesh', comes most clearly to light in the direct contradiction of Jesus' claim. It can only appear as an insane blasphemy that he, a man, makes himself equal to God, and the authorities seek to kill him (5:17 f.). His claim calls forth the accusation that he is demon-possessed and a 'Samaritan' (8:51 f.). So does his assertion that whoever keeps his word will not see death (8:51 f.). And when he claims that he is older than Abraham (8:57), they want to stone him (8:59). His assertion that he and the Father are one fills them with such indignation that once more they want to stone him (10:30 f.). In short, his 'hard word' is intolerable to hear. And his persistence in his claim results in the apostasy of all but a few of his very disciples (6:66). What a scandal (σκάνδαλον) his cross will one day be to men, he hints in the words: 'Does this (his "hard word") scandalize you? What, then, if you see the Son of Man ascending where he was at first?' (6:61 f., tr.)—a saying of remarkably double meaning, for the world will, of course, perceive only the outward form of his 'ascending': his crucifixion. John at the end brings this *skandalon* drastically into view when he has Pilate present the scourged and thorn-crowned Jesus to the crowd with the words, 'Behold the man!' (19:5) and, 'Behold your king!' (19:14). Here and in the incription over the cross (19:19) the paradoxical stumbling-block of

Jesus' claim is presented in a symbol of tremendous irony. 5. By his presentation of Jesus' work as the incarnate Son of God John has singularly developed and deepened Mark's theory of the Messiah-secret[1] (4, 4). Over the figure of Jesus there hangs a mystery, even though—or rather just because—he quite openly says who he is and what claim he makes. For to the world he is still in spite of all publicity the hidden Messiah, not because he conceals anything or commands anything to be kept secret, but because the world does not see with seeing eyes (12:40). His hiddenness is the very consequence of his self-revelation; his revealing of himself is the very thing that makes 'those who see' become 'blind' (9:39).

His work as a whole, which forms a unity framed by his coming and his departure, is both revelation and offence. His departure or 'exaltation' (i.e., upon the cross) not only belongs to the whole as its culmination but is that which makes the whole what it is: both revelation and offence. The possibility considered by Jesus in the meditation which is John's substitute for the Gethsemane scene of the synoptic tradition, 'What shall I say? "Father, save me from this hour"?' Jesus immediately rejects: 'No, for this purpose I have come to this hour' (12:27). In his passion the meaning of the sending of Jesus is fulfilled. And by his conceiving and accepting it as the fulfilment of the mission enjoined upon him by the Father (14:31), it becomes the hours of exaltation, the hour of glorification. Seen from the vantage-point of this fulfilment the whole work of the man Jesus is a revelation of the divine glory. Whereas in the Gospel of Mark we can recognize the historical process by which the unmessianic life of Jesus was retrospectively made messianic, in John the inner appropriateness of that process is made clear. This is expressed by the evangelist by means of the petition of Jesus which follows the deliberation mentioned above: 'Father, glorify thy name' (12:28) and by the heavenly voice which answers this prayer, 'I have glorified it, and I will giorify it again' (12:28). Hence, the glorification of God's name which begins with Jesus' exaltation by crucifixion and the glorification of God's name by the ministry of the earthly Jesus (17:4) are a unity. Neither exists without the other; each exists only through the other. But the glorification of the name

[1] See p. 106

of God is also the glorification of Jesus himself, and Jesus' other prayer, 'Father, the hour has come; glorify thy Son' (17:1), corresponds to this one ('Father, glorify thy name'). And the motive for this prayer—'that the Son may glorify thee'—makes the unity of God's glory and Jesus' glory evident. And when the motive is further developed in the words 'since thou hast given him power over all flesh' (17:2), the unity of his glory after the exaltation with that before it is once again made clear. Both unities are once more expressed in the words which pronounce the granting of this prayer:

> 'Now is the Son of man glorified,
> and in him God is glorified;
> if God is glorified in him,
> God will also glorify him in himself
> and glorify him at once' (13:31 f.).

In the 'now' of the 'hour' when the Son of God departs from the world the past and the future are bound together, as it were. And since not until the future will the past be made into what it really is (viz., the revelation of the 'glory'), the disciples can only be glad that Jesus is going away (14:28; 16:7).

Faith in Jesus, then, is faith in the exalted Jesus, but not as if he were a heavenly being who had stripped off the garment of earthly-human existence as the Gnostic Redeemer was conceived to do. Rather, the exalted Jesus is at the same time the earthly man Jesus; the 'glorified one' is still always he who 'became flesh'. In other words, Jesus' life on earth does not become an item of the historical past, but constantly remains present reality. The historical figure of Jesus, i.e., his human history, retains its significance of being the revelation of his 'glory' and thereby of God's. It is the eschatological occurrence. Of course, this is not visible to the world, for the exalted Jesus does not reveal himself to it (14:22)—indeed he cannot, for it cannot receive the Spirit of truth which gives knowledge to those who believe (14:17; 16:13 f.). But those who believe can now look back upon Jesus' earthly life and say, 'We have beheld his glory (1:14).

(FROM: *Theology of the New Testament*, London 1955, Volume II, pp. 40–9.)

3 DEMYTHOLOGIZING

[Bultmann's work as a form-critic made him sceptical about what one could say with certainty about the historical Jesus, beyond the fact that he existed, the 'Christ-event'. The latter he believed still had unique and vital significance but unfortunately it was clothed by the New Testament writers in 'mythological' terms. In the first extract given here, originally a talk broadcast by the BBC, Bultmann explains why he thinks the New Testament material must be 'demythologized' and re-presented in a way which is 'independent of every picture of the world'.

The second extract gives a sample of the kind of 'demythologizing the event of Christ', especially the crucifixion and resurrection, which commends itself to Bultmann. Readers will find it instructive to compare this with Tillich's treatment of the crucifixion and resurrection in Book 3, pp. 222ff.]

(a) *What is Demythologizing?*

What does 'demythologizing the Bible' mean? There are many passages in the Bible, especially those about God and God's action which for the thought of modern man bear the stamp of mythological expressions. To demythologize does not mean to eliminate those passages, but rather to make them understandable to modern thought. Demythologizing is not a process of subtraction, but a method of interpreting Scripture. It is a method which questions the mythological expressions of Scripture about the truth they contain, because the mythological form in which this truth is clothed makes the passages incomprehensible to modern thought. For this is, in fact, the state of affairs; people today find the statements of the Bible largely incomprehensible, and therefore reject them with scorn or indifference, just because they are clothed in the forms of mythological thinking.

A stumbling block

A simple example will make this clear. In mythological thinking, heaven above us is looked upon as God's dwelling-place. The truth intended to be expressed by this is that God does not belong to this earthly world: he is superior to it, beyond it, he is transcendent. Mythological thinking assumes that it is possible to express God's transcendence by using spatial thought-forms of infinite distance, of a place high above us. The question arises whether it is not necessary to express the truth contained in the thought of God's transcendence in other thought-forms for modern man, because he has ceased to think mythologically. So he may not be able to understand what is really meant when the Bible speaks about God in heaven, and about Christ's ascension and sitting at the right hand of God. And just as we must demythologize the image of the ascension, in order to preserve its truth, so, too, with the image of the descent into hell. For the mythological concept of hell aims similarly at expressing the transcendent power of evil and the transcendence of man's lost state when he is without God. It does this with the aid of an inadequate spatial image, in which the transcendence which is hostile to God is localized in the depths. But who really believes today that hell is in the depths, underneath the ground we tread? The image of above and below can no longer be applied to the contemporary picture of the universe. And is the stumbling block, which the Christian message is meant to provide to men, to consist in its asking them to accept an out-of-date picture of the world?

It is sometimes said that the mythological forms of the Bible are after all just pictures, and as a matter of fact the Bible does make use of mythological forms as pictures. But we must be clear that when this does happen, then demythologizing has already begun. And we must be consistent, and above all we must be quite responsible in our choice of images and concepts. to formulate properly the truth which is contained in the mythological pictures.

The illustrations of heaven and hell make clear to us the characteristic element in mythological thinking. Thus it is not sufficient to oppose mythological to rational thinking. For a myth always contains a point of rational thinking, as well—otherwise it would not be thinking at all. And there are myths which can be described as primitive science—for example, those which try to explain striking natural phenomena such as eclipses of the sun and moon. The distinction between myth and science is that myth deals with a different reality from science. The real purpose of myth—at least in the sphere of religion—is to speak of the powers, or the power, which sets a limit to man's thinking, willing, and doing, that is, the power on which man's existence depends, by whose favour or grace he lives, before whose wrath or judgement he trembles; the power, in short, which is not a part of the world managed by man, or at least managed by his knowledge, but is supernatural, beyond this world. But myth speaks of this power beyond the world in an insufficient way, when it presents transcendence as distant in space, above or beneath the earth, and when it thinks of the transcendent other-worldly power as a this-worldly power raised to enormous magnitude. This way of thinking, contrary to the intention of the myth, turns the other-worldly into something in this world; it turns the gods into a kind of super-men. Even when myth speaks of God's omnipotence and omniscience, it speaks mythologically since it makes only a quantitative and not a qualitative distinction between God's omnipotence and omniscience and human power and knowledge.

You can say that mythological thinking turns God and transcendence into this-worldly objects, and as far as it does this it is akin to scientific thinking as far as scientific thinking objectifies the world and its phenomena, that is, tries to grasp their real nature. Demythologizing is against this objectifying thought which claims that it can understand divine existence in terms of this world. Demythologizing rests upon the insight that we are unable to speak of transcendence and God as they really are, since any attempt to do so would turn them into a phenomenon of this world. Demythologizing proceeds in accordance with the words of Melanchthon when he said: 'To know Christ is to know His benefits, not to look upon His nature.' Or, as Wilhelm Hermann, a theologian of the last generation, has put it: 'We cannot say what God is like in Himself, but only what He does to us.' So the aim of demythologizing is to understand the truth of the biblical utterances as a reality which meets our existence, and to express that truth in a way which is comprehensible to modern man. You can describe this demythologizing interpretation of the Bible as existential; but the name is not important. The important thing is that the words of the Bible, which in their mythological form have become incomprehensible to the man of today, should be made comprehensible. And this can be done by showing how the truth of the words meets our existence, how it discloses our existence to us, how it radically deepens the questions which consciously or unconsciously are stirring our existence, and how, lastly, it lays bare our illusions and our flight from God.

Do I need, after this, to defend demythologizing from the reproach that it tries to make the Gospel acceptable to science? Its aim is not in the least to make God and His actions into objects, into phenomena of this world. But its aim is to make the Gospel comprehensible as a call addressed to us, and comprehensible not for rational thinking but for existential self-understanding. Can it then be said that it assesses the Gospel in terms of the scientific picture of the world—and worse, the science of the last century? Not at all: at most we can say that the biblical picture of the world, but not the truth of the Gospel itself, is assessed in terms of the modern picture of the world. For the truth of the Gospel is independent of any picture of the world.

A truth independent of pictures

When I demythologize the Bible I reckon with the fact that the thinking of modern man has ceased to be mythological and is determined by science. For modern man lives in a world in which life makes constant use of technical means which have been created by science. When we are ill we have recourse to medical science; in economics and politics we make sensible use of the findings of psychology, sociology, economic science, and so on. We no longer reckon with the direct break-in of transcendent powers. In urging that the Bible be demythologized, I am well aware that modern science is very different from nineteenth-century science; nor do I deceive myself about the findings of science, all of which are relative and productive neither today nor in earlier generations of any final scientific picture of the world. But it is equally clear that the method of scientific thought and research is the same today as it has always been, at least since the rise of science in ancient Greece. In the course of Western history this method of thought has pushed mythological thinking to one side; and it would be illusory to try to revive it. Such a revival would not in the least help us to know the truth of the Gospel; for this truth is independent of every picture of the world.

If demythologizing tries to make comprehensible the biblical truth which has become incomprehensible in its mythological garments, does that mean that the truth is rationalized in the sense of being reduced to a product of rational thought? Certainly not. But the Christian truth and the mystery of God are meant to be understood; and understanding is not identical with rational explanation. A comparison may make clear what I mean. I can understand what friendship and love and loyalty mean; but that does not mean that the friendship and love and loyalty that I meet with—that I am given—in the course of my life do not remain a gratefully accepted mystery. I do not know these things by means of rational thought, but in the existential openness of my person. Again, I can understand what the grace of God means, otherwise I could not speak about it as I do. But the fact that this grace meets me is a mystery which has no rational explanation. Unless I understand the Word of God's grace in Christ I cannot believe in that Word; and demythologizing is concerned to make this Word understandable.

One of the biblical concepts which has become largely incomprehensible to modern man is the concept of sin. Perhaps it escapes a superficial study how strongly coloured this concept is by mythological thought, as, for example, when the devil is spoken of as the creator of sin, or when sin is represented as a power brought upon mankind by the fall of Adam. Demythologizing is concerned to make clear the depths of sin as our own guilt and at the same time as a power to which we are subservient and against which we are defenceless. Demythologizing is further concerned to make clear that freedom from sin means freedom for the future. If you think it is too meagre a definition of Christian faith to call it free openness for the future, then you must reflect what this definition includes. Is not the freedom which is given to us by the forgiveness of our sins the freedom from our past which weighs upon us and enslaves us? And is not the most certain thing in our future the certainty of death? Then openness for the future means the same as Paul did in his triumphant cry: 'Death is swallowed up in victory !'

(FROM: *The Listener*, 5 February 1953, pp. 217–18.)

(*b*) *Demythologizing the Event of Christ*

. . . Now, it is beyond question that the New Testament presents the event of Jesus Christ in mythical terms. The problem is whether that is the only possible presentation. Or does the New Testament itself demand a restatement of the event of Jesus Christ in nonmythological terms? Now, it is clear from the outset that the event of Christ is of a wholly different order from the cultmyths of Greek or Hellenistic religion. Jesus Christ is certainly presented as the Son of God, a pre-existent divine being, and therefore to that extent a mythical figure. But he is also a concrete figure of history—Jesus of Nazareth. His life is more than a mythical event; it is a human life which ended in the tragedy of crucifixion. We have here a unique combination of history and myth. The New Testament claims that this Jesus of history, whose father and mother were well known to his contemporaries (John 6 : 42) is at the same time the pre-existent Son of God, and side by side with the historical event of the crucifixion it sets the definitely non-historical event of the resurrection. This combination of myth and history presents a number of difficulties, as can be seen from certain inconsistencies in the New Testament material. The doctrine of Christ's pre-existence as given by St Paul and St John is difficult to reconcile with the legend of the Virgin birth in St Matthew and St Luke. On the one hand we hear that 'he emptied himself, taking the form of a servant, being made in the likeness of men: and being found in fashion as a man . . .' (Phil. 2:7), and on the other hand we have the gospel portraits of a Jesus who manifests his divinity in his miracles, omniscience, and mysterious elusiveness, and the similar description of him in Acts as 'Jesus of Nazareth, a man approved of God unto you by mighty works and wonders and signs' (Acts 2:22). On the one hand we have the resurrection as the exaltation of Jesus from the cross or grave, and on the other the legends of the empty tomb and the ascension.

We are compelled to ask whether all this mythological language is not simply an attempt to express the meaning of the historical figure of Jesus and the events of his life; in other words, the significance of these as a figure and event of salvation. If that be so, we can dispense with the objective form in which they are cast.

It is easy enough to deal with the doctrine of Christ's pre-existence and the legend of the Virgin birth in this way. They are clearly attempts to explain the meaning of the Person of Jesus for faith. The facts which historical criticism can verify cannot exhaust, indeed they cannot adequately indicate, all that Jesus means to me. How he actually originated matters little, indeed we can appreciate his significance only when we cease to worry about such questions. Our interests in the events of his life, and above all in the cross, is more than an acedemic concern with the history of the past. We can see meaning in them only when we ask what God is trying to say to each one of us through them. Again, the figure of Jesus cannot be understood simply from his context in human evolution or history. In mythological language, this means that he stems from eternity, his origin transcends both history and nature.

We shall not, however, pursue the examination of the particular incidents of his life any further. In the end the crux of the matter lies in the cross and resurrection.

The Cross

Is the cross, understood as the event of redemption, exclusively mythical in character, or can it retain its value for salvation without forefeiting its character as history?

It certainly has a mythical character as far as its objective setting is concerned. The Jesus who was crucified was the pre-existent, incarnate Son of God, and as such he was without sin. He is the victim whose blood atones for our sins. He bears vicariously the sin of the world, and by enduring the punishment for sin on our behalf he delivers us from death. This mythological interpretation is a hotch-potch of sacrificial and juridical analogies, which have ceased to be tenable for us today. And in any case they fail to do justice to what the New Testament is trying to say. For the most they can convey is that the cross effects the forgiveness of all the past and future sins of man, in the sense that the punishment they deserved has been remitted. But the New Testament means more than this. The cross releases men not only from the guilt, but also from the power of sin. That is why, when the author of Colossians says 'He (God) . . . having forgiven us all our trespasses, having blotted out the bond written in ordinances that was against us, which was contrary to us; and he hath taken it out of the way, nailing it to the cross' he hastens to add: 'having put off from himself the principalities and powers, he made a show of them openly, triumphing over them in it' (Col. 2:13–15).

The historical event of the cross acquires cosmic dimensions and so its full significance is brought into sharper relief. For if we see in the cross the judgement of the world and the defeat of the rulers of this world (1 Cor. 2:6 ff.), the cross becomes the judgement of ourselves as fallen creatures enslaved to the powers of the 'world'.

By giving up Jesus to be crucified, God has set up the cross for us. To believe in the cross of Christ does not mean to concern ourselves with a mythical process wrought outside of us and our world, or with an objective event turned by God to our advantage, but rather to make the cross of Christ our own, to undergo crucifixion with him. The cross in its redemptive aspect is not an isolated incident which befell a mythical personage, but an event of 'cosmic' importance. Its decisive, revolutionary significance is brought out by the eschatological framework in which it is set. In other words, the cross is not just an event of the past which can be contemplated in detachment, but the eschatological event in and beyond time, for as far as its meaning—that is, its meaning for faith—is concerned, it is an ever-present reality.

The cross becomes a present reality in the sacraments. In baptism men and women are baptized into Christ's death (Rom. 6:3) and crucified with him (Rom. 6:6). At every celebration of the Lord's Supper the death of Christ is proclaimed (1 Cor. 11:26); The communicants thereby partake of his crucified body and his blood outpoured (1 Cor. 10:16).

Again, the cross of Christ is an ever-present reality in the everyday life of the Christians. 'They that are of Christ Jesus have crucified the flesh with the passions and the lusts thereof' (Gal. 5:24). That is why St Paul can speak of 'the cross of our Lord Jesus Christ, through which the world hath been crucified unto me, and I unto the world' (Gal. 6:14). That is why he seeks to know 'the fellowship of his sufferings', as one who is 'conformed to his death' (Phil. 3:10).

The crucifying of the affections and lusts includes the overcoming of our natural dread of suffering and the perfection of our detachment from the world. Hence the willing acceptance of sufferings in which death is already at work in man means: 'always bearing about in our body the dying of Jesus' and 'always being delivered unto death for Jesus' sake' (2 Cor. 4:10 f.).

Thus the cross and passion are ever-present realities. How little they are confined to the events of the first Good Friday is amply illustrated by the words which a disciple of St Paul puts into his master's mouth: 'Now I rejoice in my sufferings for your sake, and fill up on my part that which is lacking of the afflictions of Christ in my flesh for his body's sake, which is the Church' (Col. 1:24).

In its redemptive aspect the cross of Christ is no mere mythical event, but a permanent historical fact originating in the past historical event which is the crucifixion of Jesus. The abiding significance of the cross is that it is the judgement of the world, the judgement and the deliverance of man. In this sense Christ is crucified 'for us', a phrase which does not necessarily imply any theory of sacrifice or satisfaction. This interpretation of the cross as a permanent fact rather than a mythological event does far more justice to the redemptive significance of the event of the past than any of the traditional interpretations. In the last resort mythological language is only a medium for conveying the meanings of the past event. The real meaning of the cross is that it has created a new and permanent situation in history. The preaching of the cross as the event of redemption challenges all who hear it to appropriate this significance for themselves, to be willing to be crucified with Christ.

But, it will be asked, is this significance to be discerned in the actual event of past history? Can it, so to speak, be read off from that event? Or does the cross bear this significance because it is the cross of Christ? In other words, must we first be convinced of the significance of Christ and believe in him in order to discern the real meaning of the cross? If we are to perceive the real meaning of the cross, must we understand it as the cross of Jesus as a figure of past history? Must we go back to the Jesus of history?

As far as the first preachers of the gospel are concerned this will certainly be the case. For them the cross was the cross of him with whom they had lived in personal intercourse. The cross was an experience of their own lives. It presented them with a question and it disclosed to them its meaning. But for us this personal connexion cannot be reproduced. For us the cross cannot disclose its own meaning: it is an event of the past. We can never recover it as an event in our own lives. All we know of it is derived from historical report. But the New Testament does not proclaim Jesus Christ in this way. The meaning of the cross is not disclosed from the life of Jesus as a figure of past history, a life which needs to be reproduced by historical research. On the contrary, Jesus is not proclaimed merely as the crucified; he is also risen from the dead. The cross and the resurrection form an inseparable unity.

The Resurrection

But what of the resurrection? Is it not a mythical event pure and simple? Obviously it is not an event of past history with a self-evident meaning. Can the resurrection narrative and every other mention of the resurrection in the New Testament be understood simply as an attempt to convey the meaning of the cross? Does the New Testament, in asserting that Jesus is risen from the dead, mean that his death is not just an ordinary human death, but the judgement and salvation of the world, depriving death of its power? Does it not express this truth in the affirmation that the Crucified was not holden of death, but rose from the dead?

Yes indeed: the cross and the resurrection form a single, indivisible cosmic event. 'He was delivered up for our trespasses, and was raised for our justification' (Rom. 4:25). The cross is not an isolated event, as though it were the end of

Jesus, which needed the resurrection subsequently to reverse it When he suffered death, Jesus was already the Son of God, and his death by itself was the victory over the power of death. St John brings this out most clearly by describing the passion of Jesus as the 'hour' in which he is glorified, and by the double meaning he gives to the phrase 'lifted up', applying it both to the cross and to Christ's exaltation into glory.

Cross and resurrection form a single, indivisible cosmic event which brings judgement to the world and opens up for men the possibility of authentic life. But if that be so, the resurrection cannot be a miraculous proof capable of demonstration and sufficient to convince the sceptic that the cross really has the cosmic and eschatological significance ascribed to it.

Yet it cannot be denied that the resurrection of Jesus is often used in the New Testament as a miraculous proof. Take for instance Acts 17:31. Here we are actually told that God substantiated the claims of Christ by raising him from the dead. Then again the resurrection narratives: both the legend of the empty tomb and the appearances insist on the physical reality of the risen body of the Lord (see especially Luke 24:39–43). But these are most certainly later embellishments of the primitive tradition. St Paul knows nothing about them. There is, however, one passage where St Paul tries to prove the miracle of the resurrection by adducing a list of eye-witnesses (1 Cor. 15:3–8). But this is a dangerous procedure, as Karl Barth has involuntarily shown. Barth seeks to explain away the real meaning of 1 Cor. 15 by contending that the list of eye-witnesses was put in not to prove the fact of the resurrection, but to prove that the preaching of the apostle was, like the preaching of the first Christians, the preaching of Jesus as the risen Lord. The eye-witnesses therefore guarantee St Paul's preaching, not the fact of the resurrection. An historical fact which involves a resurrection from the dead is utterly inconceivable!

Yes indeed: the resurrection of Jesus cannot be a miraculous proof by which the sceptic might be compelled to believe in Christ. The difficulty is not simply the incredibility of a mythical event like the resuscitation of a corpse—for that is what the resurrection means, as is shown by the fact that the risen Lord is apprehended by the physical senses. Nor is it merely the difficulty of establishing the objective historicity of the resurrection no matter how many witnesses are cited, as though once it was established it might be believed beyond all question and faith might have its unimpeachable guarantee. No; the real difficulty is that the resurrection is itself an article of faith, and you cannot establish one article of faith by invoking another. You cannot prove the redemptive efficacy of the cross by invoking the resurrection. For the resurrection is an article of faith because it is far more than the resuscitation of a corpse—it is the eschatological event. And so it cannot be a miraculous proof. For, quite apart from its credibility, the bare miracle tells us nothing about the eschatological fact of the destruction of death. Moreover, such a miracle is not otherwise unknown to mythology.

It is however abundantly clear that the New Testament is interested in the resurrection of Christ simply and solely because it is the eschatological event par excellence. By it Christ abolished death and brought life and immortality to light (2 Tim. 1:10). This explains why St Paul borrows Gnostic language to clarify the meaning of the resurrection. As in the death of Jesus all have died (2 Cor. 5:14 f.), so through his resurrection all have been raised from the dead, though naturally this event is spread over a long period of time (1 Cor. 15:21 f.). But St Paul does not only say: 'In Christ shall all be made alive'; he can also speak of rising again with Christ in the present tense, just as he speaks of our dying with him. Through the sacrament of baptism Christians participate not only in the death of Christ but also in his resurrection. It is not simply that we shall walk with him in newness of life and be united with him in his resurrection (Rom. 6:4 f.); we are doing so already here and now. 'Even so reckon ye yourselves to be dead indeed unto sin, but alive unto God in Jesus Christ' (Rom. 6:11).

Once again, in everyday life the Christians participate not only in the death of Christ but also in his resurrection. In this resurrection-life they enjoy a freedom, albeit a struggling freedom, from sin (Rom. 6:11 ff.). They are able to 'cast off the works of darkness', so that the approaching day when the darkness shall vanish is already experienced here and now. 'Let us walk honestly as in the day' (Rom. 13:12 f.): 'we are not of the night, nor of the darkness . . . Let us, since we are of the day, be sober . . .' (1 Thess. 5:5–8). St Paul seeks to share not only the sufferings of Christ but also 'the power of his resurrection' (Phil. 3:10). So he bears about in his body the dying of Jesus, 'that the life also of Jesus may be manifested in our body' (2 Cor. 4:10 f.). Similarly, when the Corinthians demand a proof of his apostolic authority, he solemnly warns them: 'Christ is not weak, but is powerful in you: for he was crucified in weakness, yet he liveth in the power of God. For we also are weak in him, but we shall live with him through the power of God toward you' (2 Cor. 13:3 f.).

In this way the resurrection is not a mythological event adduced in order to prove the saving efficacy of the cross, but an article of faith just as much as the meaning of the cross itself. Indeed, faith in the resurrection is really the same thing as faith in the saving efficacy of the cross, faith in the cross as the cross of Christ. Hence you cannot first believe in Christ and then in the strength of that faith believe in the cross. To believe in Christ means to believe in the cross as the cross of Christ. The saving efficacy of the cross is not derived from the fact that it is the cross of Christ: it is the cross of Christ because it has this saving efficacy. Without that efficacy it is the tragic end of a great man.

We are back again at the old question. How do we come to believe in the cross as the cross of Christ and as the eschatological event par excellence? How do we come to believe in the saving efficacy of the cross?

There is only one answer. This is the way in which the cross is proclaimed. It is always proclaimed together with the resurrection. Christ meets us in the preaching as one crucified and risen. He meets us in the word of preaching and nowhere else. The faith of Easter is just this—faith in the word of preaching.

It would be wrong at this point to raise again the problem of how this preaching arose historically, as though that could vindicate its truth. That would be to tie our faith in the word of God to the results of historical research. The word of preaching confronts us as the word of God. It is not for us to question its credentials. It is we who are questioned, we who are asked whether we will believe the word or reject it. But answering this question, in accepting the word of preaching as the word of God and the death and resurrection of Christ as the eschatological event, we are given an opportunity of understanding ourselves. Faith and unbelief are never blind, arbitrary decisions. They offer us the alternative between accepting or rejecting that which alone can illuminate our understanding of ourselves.

The real Easter faith is faith in the word of preaching which brings illumination. If the event of Easter Day is in any sense an historical event additional to the event of the cross, it is nothing else than the rise of faith in the risen Lord, since it was this faith which led to the apostolic preaching. The resurrection itself is not an event of past history. All that historical criticism can establish is the fact that the first disciples came to believe in the resurrection. The historian can perhaps to some extent account for that faith from the personal intimacy which the disciples had enjoyed with Jesus during his earthly life, and so reduce the resurrection appearances to a series of subjective visions. But the historical problem is scarcely relevant to Christian belief in the resurrection. For the historical event of the rise of the Easter faith means for us what it meant for the first disciples—namely, the self-manifestation of the risen Lord, the act of God in which the redemptive event of the cross is completed.[1]

We cannot buttress our own faith in the resurrection by that of the first disciples and so eliminate the element of risk which faith in the resurrection always involves. For the first disciples' faith in the resurrection is itself part and parcel of the eschatological event which is the article of faith.

In other words, apostolic preaching which originated in the event of Easter Day is itself a part of the eschatological event of redemption. The death of Christ, which is both the judgement and the salvation of the world, inaugurates the 'ministry of reconciliation' or 'word of reconciliation' (2 Cor. 5:18 f.). This word supplements the cross and makes its saving efficacy

[1] This and the following paragraphs are also intended as an answer to the doubts and suspicions which Paul Althaus has raised against me in *Die Wahrheit des kirchlichen Osterglaubens*, 1941. Cp. also my discussion of Emanuel Hirsch's 'Die Auferstehungsgeschichten und der christliche Glaube', 1940, in *Theol. Lit.-Ztg.*, 1940, pp. 242–6.

intelligible by demanding faith and confronting men with the question whether they are willing to understand themselves as men who are crucified and risen with Christ. Through the word of preaching the cross and the resurrection are made present: the eschatological 'now' is here, and the promise of Isaiah 49:8 is fulfilled: 'Behold, now is the acceptable time; behold, now is the day of salvation' (2 Cor. 6:2). That is why the apostolic preaching brings judgement. For some the apostle is 'a savour from death unto death' and for others 'a savour from life unto life' (2 Cor. 2:16). St Paul is the agent through whom the resurrection life becomes effective in the faithful (2 Cor. 4:12). The promise of Jesus in the Fourth Gospel is eminently applicable to the preaching in which he is proclaimed: 'Verily I say unto you, He that heareth my words and believeth on him that sent me, hath eternal life, and cometh not unto judgement, but hath passed out of death into life . . . The hour cometh and now is, when the dead shall hear the voice of the Son of God; and they that hear shall live' (John 5:24 f.). In the word of preaching and there alone we meet the risen Lord. 'So belief cometh of hearing, and hearing by word of Christ' (Rom. 10:17).

Like the word itself and the apostle who proclaims it, so the Church where the preaching of the word is continued and where the believers or 'saints' (i.e., those who have been transferred to eschatological existence) are gathered is part of the eschatological event. The word 'Church' (ἐκκλησία) is an eschatological term, while its designation as the Body of Christ emphasizes its cosmic significance. For the Church is not just a phenomenon of secular history, it is a phenomenon of significant history, in the sense that it realizes itself in history.

(FROM: *Kerygma and Myth* I, edited by H.-W. Bartsch, London 1957, pp. 34–43.)

4 The Idea of God and Modern Man

[In this extract we have Bultmann's reaction to the debate started by the Bishop of Woolwich's *Honest to God.* This centred on the use of metaphor in religious language, and the meaning to be attached to the 'transcendence' of God. Bultmann also touches on the 'death of God' theology in the United States (William Hamilton, Thomas J. J. Altizer and others, see introduction pp. 31 ff.) and in doing so provides an illuminating pedigree of contemporary atheism.]

At the beginning of 1963 there appeared the book of the Anglican bishop, John A. T. Robinson, *Honest to God* (honest to and about God).[1] In both England and Germany (as well as in America) it has provoked a somewhat heated debate. Articles appeared in the Hamburg newspaper, *Die Zeit,* with captions 'Is God a metaphor?', 'Is our image of God dated?', 'Is faith in God finished?'—questions evoked by Robinson's book. Some theologians rightly observed that the ideas advanced by Robinson were not new in contemporary theology. Now Robinson had not made this claim at all. He calls repeatedly on Paul Tillich, Dietrich Bonhoeffer and others.[2] But in the process of assimilating their thought, he sees that they add up to the following sum, so to speak: *a revolution is necessary.* For, since the traditional ecclesiastical image of God is no longer credible to contemporary men, *a new image of God* is required; the old one is obsolete.

It is understandable that for many readers—especially for readers among the laity to whom the book is directed—this thesis is frightening. With the disposal of the old image of God, is not faith in God and thereby also God himself finished? That this question forces itself upon men today is not signalized by Robinson's book alone. As early as 1961 there appeared

[1] SCM Press (England), Westminster Press (U.S.A.), 1963.

[2] Professor Bultmann's modesty prevents him from mentioning that Robinson also calls frequently on him. (Trs.)

the book, *The Death of God*,[1] by the American theologian, Gabriel Vahanian, which is a peculiar and admittedly theologically independent parallel to Robinson's book. The title of Vahanian's book comes from the famous pronouncement of Nietzsche[2]: 'God is dead.'

The note 'God is dead' was struck almost a hundred years before Nietzsche by Jean Paul[3] in his *Siebenkäs,* which appeared in 1796–7, and there is a ghastly vision: 'Discourse of the dead Christ from atop the cosmos: there is no God.'[4] This discourse is not a philosophical discussion of atheism. The import of the vision consists rather in showing that atheism is nihilism (in this respect also a precursor of Nietzsche): 'The whole universe is burst asunder by the hand of atheism and fragmented into innumerable quick-silver particles of I's, which twinkle, roll about, wander, flee together and from each other without unity and stability. No one is so very much alone in the universe as the one who denies God . . . Alas, if every I is its own father and creator, why can it not also be its own angel of destruction?'

Nietzsche permits the 'madman' to proclaim the message of the death of God in his work *Die fröhiche Wissenschaft* (1881). Martin Heidegger says in his essay 'Nietzsches Wort "God ist tot" '[5]: 'Nietzsche's word spells the destiny of two thousand years of Western history.' This remarkable assertion rests on

[1] G. Vahanian, *The Death of God.* The Culture of our Post-Christian Era, New York, George Braziller, 1961. By the same author, *Beyond the Death of God:* The Need of Cultural Revolution, Dialog 1, 4, 1962, pp. 18–21.

[2] Friedrich Nietzsche (1844–1900). German philosopher and poet. The phrase 'God is dead' comes in his *The Gay Science.* (Ed.)

[3] 'Jean Paul' the pseudonym of Johann Paul Friedrich Richter (1763–1825), German novelist. (Ed.)

[4] G. Bornkamm has reprinted the speech as an appendix to the second volume of his collected essays: *Studien zu Antike und Urchristentum,* Gesammelte Aufsätze II. (Beiträge zur evangelischen Theologie, Band 287, 1959, pp. 345–50.) Hegel had also said that God was dead, namely the God of Church dogmatics. On this point cf. W. Anz, 'Tod und Unsterblichkeit' (in: *Einsichten.* Festschrift für G. Krüger, 1962, 11–35), p. 25. The 'atheism' of Hegel, however, is not nihilism in the sense of Jean Paul and Nietzsche.

[5] Heidegger, *Holzwege,* Frankfurt: Klostermann, 1950, 103–247. Cf. also Löwith, 'Nietzches antichristliche Bergpredigt', *Heidelberger Jahrbücher* 6, 1962, pp. 39–50.

the conviction that Western history has been determined for two thousand years by Greek metaphysics, through which the secularization of the world, brought to completion in modern times, has finally been established. We may here suspend judgement about the correctness of this assertion. Explicit atheism, in any case, is a phenomenon of the modern period, and Gerhard Ebeling has rightly said that this atheism is a counter-movement against Christianity.[1] It is also clear that the death of God for Nietzsche means the death of the Christian God. 'But', Heidegger adds, 'it is equally certain and is to be borne in mind in advance that the names of God and the Christian God are used to designate the supersensory world in general. God is the name for the realm of ideas and ideals.'[2]

The 'madman' cries: 'What did we do when we unchained this earth from its sun?', and continues: 'Where is it moving to now? Where are we moving to? Away from all suns? Do we not stumble all the time? Backwards, sidewards, forward, and in every direction? Is there an above and a below any more? Are we not wandering as through an endless nothingness?' The consequence of the death of God is therefore nihilism, as Jean Paul had pictured it.

We must guard against viewing *atheism* merely or even basically as a consequence of natural science and its world-view. To be sure, modern natural science has found the hypothesis 'God' unnecessary, according to the well-known dictum of La Place,[3] and the atheism of natural science has without doubt been widely influential, leading even to absurdities in Russia, where as the result of a space-flight it is given out that there was no trace of God in the space above the earth. Nevertheless, even when there are natural scientists today who again hold the hypothesis 'God' to be possible and appropriate, atheism is not thereby contradicted. For it has far deeper roots.

Atheism, as Jean Paul and Nietzsche understood it, is indeed nihilism, and this is not necessarily a consequence of the way in which natural science understands the world. In this respect the loss of the supernatural could be and was replaced

[1] G. Ebeling, *The Nature of Faith*, London, 1961, pp. 80 ff.; *Word and Faith*, London 1963, pp. 135 ff., 343.

[2] Heidegger, *Holzwege*, p. 199.

[3] Cf. Ebeling, *The Nature of Faith*, p. 81 f.

in the eighteenth and nineteenth centuries by the belief in progress and its accompanying optimism. The atheism of the natural sciences is a methodological procedure in so far as it subjects the world to an objectivizing way of viewing things. It must necessarily disregard God, because God, as the supersensory, cannot be the object of an objectivizing way of seeing.[1]

Atheism which ends in nihilism is rather the consequence of the *secularization of the world*, of which the objectivizing way of viewing nature is only a partial symptom. Secularization can be characterized simply as the world being conceived by man as an object[2] and thus delivered over to technology as its object.[3] This secularization takes place in every sphere of life, in morality, in law, in politics. For the relation of man to a transcendental power has been abandoned in all spheres of life. Heidegger calls this epoch in which the world has become an object the epoch of *subjectity*.[4] i.e., the era in which the world conceived as object is subjected to the planning of man as subject, a planning which is controlled by the values which man himself establishes.

And religion? One must first of all reflect that *Christianity itself was a decisive factor in the development of the secularization of the world* in that it de-divinized the world.[5] The Christian faith, by de-divinizing the world, allowed it to appear in its pure worldliness. It disclosed and evoked the *freedom*

[1] Op. cit.

[2] Cf. Heidegger, *Holzwege*, p. 236.

[3] Cf. Bonhoeffer, *Letters and Papers from Prison* (Fontana), p. 106 f.: 'Man has learned to cope with all questions of importance without recourse to God as a working hypothesis.' Also on the process of secularization, cf. Ebeling, *Word and Faith*, pp. 128 ff.; R. G. Smith, A Theological Perspective of the Secular, *The Christian Scholar*, 43, 1960, pp. 11–24, p. 18 f.

[4] Heidegger, *Holzwege*, p. 237. Subjectity, of course, is to be distinguished from subjectivity. The latter refers to the subjective mode of the individual in his judgements (e.g., judgements of taste); the former refers to the disposition of an entire epoch to the world and history, a disposition which has achieved the status of self-evidentness. [The reader will perhaps excuse the neologism subjectity, which represents Subjektität; the form is drawn by analogy: Subjektität—Subjektivität: subjectity—subjectivity. Trs.]

[5] Cf. Ebeling, *Word and Faith*, pp. 135 f., 344; *The Nature of Faith*, p. 80 f. Also especially F. Gogarten, *Verhängnis und Hoffnung der Neuzeit*, 1952; R. G. Smith, *A Theological Perspective*, p. 21.

of man from the world, freedom from all powers which can encounter man from out of the world.[1] It is the freedom of which Luther said: 'A Christian is a free master over all things and subject to no one.' This consciousness of freedom is the presupposition of the secularization of the world; the latter follows, however, only when the continuation of Luther's remark is forgotten: 'A Christian is a servant in the service of all things and subject to every one,' or, to put it differently, when it is forgotten that *freedom* from the world is at the same time *responsibility* for the world.[2] This forgetfulness increases the more man becomes conscious of the possibility, in pure objectivizing thought, of dominating the world through science and technology, of making it serve his purposes, values and plans.

This process plays the rôle, so to speak, which reason plays in life. Freedom from the world is at the same time responsibility for the world; that means, the world is delivered over to the reason of man.[3] For in order to be able to act responsibly, to come to decisions as they are required again and again, man must recognize the causal connexion of events in the world, must gain insight into causes and effects, and arrive at judgements about what serves the purpose and what does not. It is precisely for this purpose that he has his reason. Indeed, in the power of his reason he grasps the laws under which man's actions universally stand, i.e., the moral laws,

[1] Cf. Gogarten, op. cit., p. 8 (the most remarkable thing transpires in secularization) 'that the autonomy of man gains the radical sense which it has in the modern world only through the perceptions and experiences disclosed in the Christian faith'. Ibid., p. 12: Secularization is the 'legitimate consequence' of the Christian faith, and in so far as it 'is grounded in the Christian faith', it 'makes the world the world (Verweltichung de Welt)'. Cf. ibid., pp. 93 ff.

[2] On the interdependence of freedom from the world and responsibility for the world, cf. Gogarten, op. cit., pp. 19, 24 ff. Vahanian makes the same point, *The Death of God*, p. 61: 'Biblical thought considers the world as man's sphere of action and pre-eminence. Man's responsibility to God and his involvement in the world emerge as polar elements attesting to the original goodness of creation.' It is significant that both Gogarten and Vahanian make the distinction between a legitimate secularization (secularity) and a denegerate secularism (secularism). Cf. Gogarten, p. 129 ff.; Vahanian, p. 60 ff. Cf. R. G. Smith, *A Theological Perspective*, p. 21.

[3] Cf. Gogarten, op. cit., p. 88.

whose force alone keeps the human community sound and whole. According to the myth of Protagoras in Plato,[1] Zeus sent reverence and justice to the earth by Hermes in order that political community might be possible. But rational judgements and plans, without which human work and community are not possible, are threatened by the danger that they will be placed in the service of self-seeking and that the authority of the moral laws will thereby wane.

The more reason is conscious of itself, the more the laws which regulate the community will no longer be simply derived from tradition, but will be understood as the moral laws which reason sanctions. And thus out of heteronomy arises *autonomy*. Autonomy is equivocal. In the genuine sense autonomy means self-legislation in the sense that the individual affirms the moral law as that in which he himself comes to win his authenticity.[2] But from the recognition that the rational man is a lawgiver in this sense, there arises the delusion that the individual as subject arbitrarily determines what is good and evil, as was the case already in the 'Greek Enlightenment' among the Sophists.[3] And so today autonomy is unfortunately often spoken of as a self-legislation of the individual, and that determines value and valuelessness of itself. The outcome is nihilism.[4]

[1] Plato, *Protagoras*, 322a–c.

[2] Cf. Kant, 'In this manner the moral law leads through the conception of the summum bonum, as the object and final end of pure practical reason, to religion, that is, to the recognition of all duties as divine commands, not as sanctions, that is to say, arbitrary ordinances of a foreign will and contingent in themselves, but as essential laws of every free will in itself, which, however, must be regarded as commands of the supreme being . . .' (Kant's *Critique of Practical Reason*, tr. T. K. Abbott, London: Longmans, 1923, p. 226.)

[3] Wandering Teachers who came to Athens in the 5th century B.C. (Ed.)

[4] On autonomy cf. also R. G. Smith, *A Theological Perspective*, p. 18. Ebeling puts it well in *Word and Faith*, p. 113 f.: 'But now, to the reality that concerns modern man there belongs . . . the discovery of the autonomy of the reason and accordingly the inescapable duty to make use of the autonomous reason—not, be it noted, to make autonomous use of the reason; for it is not man himself but reason which, rightly understood, is autonomous, whereas to confuse the autonomy of the reason with the autonomy of man results precisely in a new heteronomy of the reason . . .'

Religion was also drawn into the wake of 'subjectity'. That Christianity appears as a particular example of religion and is classified within the continuity of the history of religions (which, of course, is possible in any case) indicates that the decline has already set in. Moreover, if Christianity is acknowledged as the highest religion, then the capitulation to subjectity becomes evident at just that point. For the judgement about lower and higher religions can only be a judgement of the subject which evaluates. It is by no means the case that religion necessarily disappears in subjectity. If we consider the Western world, which has been a 'Christian' world for centuries, that world today is in general not anti-Christian, but a-Christian, partly in the sense that Christianity appears to it to be antiquated, and the questions to which Christianity proposes to give answers irrelevant; but partly in the sense that while the questions as such remain live issues, modern man himself now gives the answers. Thus ideologies arise, which assert that they are able to reveal the meaning of the world and history[1]; or doctrines of salvation are propagated, often from exotic religions, with the choice left to the subjectity of the individual; or again—especially in the U.S.A.—the biblical hope of a millennium is secularized, that is, converted into optimism which seeks to renew the world through the 'social gospel'.[2] But above all, there arises a religiosity to which men flee from the claims as well as from the bitterness or tediousness of secular everyday life.

'In the last analysis, religiosity is an expression of sublimated loneliness.'[3] The pressing problem for man in a world which has been cut loose from ties to the beyond is to find himself, to become certain of his own being. For with the loss of reference to the transcendent, man's certainty of knowledge concerning himself has also been lost.[4] The question of God does

[1] Cf. R. G. Smith, *A Theological Perspective*, p. 19.

[2] Cf. Vahanian, op. cit., p. 28 ff.

[3] Vahanian, op. cit., p. 4. Cf. also R. G. Smith, *A Theological Perspective*, p. 20 f.; *The New Man*, London, 1956, p. 62 f.

[4] Cf. Vahanian, op. cit., p. 183. Also, Bonhoeffer, LPP, p. 164: 'Man (scil. who is threatened by today's organization) is thrown back upon himself. He is ready to cope with everything, but not with himself. He is able to secure himself against everything, but not against man. In the last analysis, however, everything depends on man.' LPP., p. 178. Also, R. G. Smith, 'A Theological Perspective', p. 12.

not therefore die away; but the form of the question suggests 'that the deity is a missing link in man's unsuccessful attempts to grasp the meaning of his self and of the world'.[1]

The question by no means completely dies away in decided atheism either, provided that it draws back from the abyss of nihilism and does not risk laying hold of the ideas of the transcendent God and his revelation, but would still like to speak in some way of the divine as somehow immanent in the world, whether it be as the world's creative ground or as the spiritual life which lives and evolves in the world.[2] Indeed, one can say that such 'atheism' stands nearer the Christian understanding of faith than some institutional Christians who understand the transcendent God as the beyond which has retired from the world.[3]

Religiosity abandons precisely—at least according to the Christian faith—that upon which genuine religion is based: the relation of man to the transcendent God as that which stands over against him. Religiosity thinks from the point of view of the subjectivity of man. In this sense Karl Barth once fought against Schleiermacher and the theology of experience inaugurated by him, in which religion is understood as a province of the human spirit, as the feeling of absolute dependence. To what extent Barth's criticism of Schleiermacher was justified, I leave open.[4] In any case, it was justified to the extent that the relation to God was reduced to feeling. Vahanian takes up this battle against religiosity from the standpoint of the Christian faith with renewed vigour, as did Bonhoeffer before him. And they are followed by John Robinson.

Gone is *the relation of man to the transcendent* as that which stands over against man and the world and is not at their

[1] Vahanian, op. cit., p. 78.

[2] Cf., for example, what Robinson, op. cit., pp. 127–9, says about Julian Huxley and Albert Camus.

[3] It is therefore understandable when Robinson, p. 127, produces a variation on Paul's formulation for 1 Corinthians 9:20 f.: 'I am prepared to be an agnostic with the agnostic, even an atheist with the atheists.' Likewise, cf. R. G. Smith, *The New Man*, p. 109, on Feuerbach.

[4] On this point cf. C. Senft, *Wahrhaftigkeit und Wahrheit.* Die Theologie des 19. Jahrhunderts zwischen Orthodoxie und Aufklärung (Beiträge zur historischen Theologie, 22), 1956, pp. 1–46.

disposal, which is manifested only through encounter, only as gift, and cannot be reached by turning away from the world in a religious flight into a beyond. Now the word transcendence is ambiguous. It can be said that rational thought transcends all unmethodical and random thought. Reason is transcendent with respect to primitive-innocent opinions as well as arbitrary individual judgements and evaluations. But reason remains in the sphere of subjectivity, while religion, particularly the Christian faith, abandons this sphere.[1] The Christian faith speaks of a revelation, by which it understands God's act as an event which is not visible to the objectivizing thought of reason, an event which does not communicate doctrines, but concerns the existence of man[2] and teaches him, or better, enables him to understand himself as sustained by the transcendent power of God.[3]

In this, theologians like Tillich, Bonhoeffer, Ebeling, Vahanian, R. G. Smith and Robinson are one. But they are also agreed that *the transcendent* is to be sought and can be found not above or beyond the world, but *in the midst of this world*.[4]

[1] I leave it open here whether and to what extent it can be said that the existential life (e.g., in personal relationships) transcends the sphere of subjectity.

[2] Here I disregard the paradox, which involves the revelatory event being at once an historical as well as an eschatological event, both with respect to its origin, Jesus Christ, and with respect to its constant renewal in the church's proclamation.

[3] If one is persuaded that every man is basically moved by the question of God and that therefore the Christian proclamation may reckon with a pre-understanding, then one can ask whether this pre-understanding is not also concealed precisely in religiosity. Now H. G. Gadamer, in his book, *Wahrheit und Methode* (Tübingen: Siebeck, 1960), which is of greatest significance for theologians, has contested (in the context of the hermeneutical problem, p. 313 f.) whether one can speak of a pre-understanding for the understanding of the biblical texts, namely, a pre-understanding that is given with the question of God that drives human existence. I am of the opinion that the pre-understanding is given precisely in that experience which Gadamer designates as the 'authentic experience', namely, the experience in which 'man becomes conscious of his finiteness' (p. 339 f.). This experience is certainly not always realized, but it surely persists as an ever-present possibility.

[4] For R. G. Smith cf. *A Theological Perspective*, p. 15; *The New Man*, pp. 65–70, and especially pp. 94–112: 'This-Worldly Transcendance'. Ebeling, *The Nature of Faith*, p. 160 f.

Allow me to quote some sentences of Bonhoeffer: 'The "beyond" of God is not the beyond of our cognitive faculties. Epistemological transcendence has nothing to do with the transcendence of God. God is transcendent in the midst of our life.' The transcendent is not the infinitely remote, but the nearest at hand."[1] The 'death of God', according to Vahanian, takes place precisely in that the transcendent presence of God is lost if transcendence is conceived as purely other-worldly—just as in religiosity.' Or, to quote another formulation of Vahanian: 'Religious authority does not entail the eradication of personal autonomy for the sake of blind assent to a system of beliefs claiming sanction of absolute or divine authority. But religious authority . . . symbolizes a synthesis of subjective truth and objective reality . . . Faith is an attempt to reconcile subject and object, subjective truth and objective reality, without overwhelming either one of the terms.'[3]

Faith permits the world to be the world; indeed, it gives back to the world its authentic worldliness; faith 'recognizes the hidden unconditional ground even in the most autonomous of human pursuits. It needs to welcome those pursuits not for the hope that they may be violently "baptized" into Christ, but for their own sake'.[4] Dietrich Bonhoeffer formulates the discernment of faithful relation to the world very pointedly: 'And we cannot be honest without recognizing that we must live in the world—*etsi deus non daretur*. And this is just what we

[1] LPP, pp. 165, 163. On Bonhoeffer cf. especially R. G. Smith, *The New Man*, pp. 96–106; Ebeling, 'The Non-religious Interpretation of Biblical Concepts', in *Word and Faith*, pp. 98–161.

[2] Vahanian, op. cit., p. 44.

[3] Op. cit., p. 164 f. Cf. II; 'Now, as then, today and always, the Christian problem is to correlate the truth of Christianity with the empirical truths men live by, without confusing them: man cannot live by one or the other kind of truth alone,' p. 169: 'On the contrary, even as the meaning of existence lies outside existence, in the dialectical relatedness implied by the polarity between Creator and creature, so also the meaning of history lies above and beyond history.' The formulation of Tillich, quoted also by Vahanian, is in substantial agreement: 'Theology moves back and forth between two poles, the eternal truth of its foundation and the temporal situation in which the eternal truth must be received' (*Systematic Theology*, Vol. I, Chicago University Press, 1951, p. 3).

[4] R. G. Smith, *The New Man*, p. 69.

do recognize—before God! God himself drives us to this recognition.'[1] This is precisely what Robinson designates as the necessary revolution: the God above the world having become the God beyond the world, today it is a question of finding God in the midst of the world, in the present. The contrast between here and beyond, and thus the contrast between naturalism and supernaturalism, must be overcome. God must be recognized as the unconditional in the conditional.

It is surprising how such theological perceptions are also taken up by sociologists. Eckart Schleth says in his book, *Der profane Weltchrist*: 'The unity of Christ and world is found in the "nevertheless" of the believer for the world, in his imperceptible eschatological existence here and now, in his freedom from the world, in the world and for the world.' Also 'Life in faith, the character of which is to be permanently in process of fulfilment, is life in the "ultimate reality", which is always here and now and identical with everyday things.'[2]

The relation of faith and worldliness is a dialectical relationship, as R. G. Smith especially has emphasized.[3] I will try to make the meaning of this dialectical relation clear by means of an analogy. The loving look into an eye which is loved and loving is fundamentally different from the objectivizing look with which an ophthalmologist examines the eye of a patient. But when the doctor who has to treat the diseased eye is also the one who loves, the two ways of seeing stand in a dialectical relationship; he has to examine the eye of the other in an objectivizing way precisely in his love. The objectivizing way of seeing enters into the service of the one who loves. Robinson endeavours, following Tillich, to make clear the relation between faith and worldliness in the dialectical relation between engagement with the world and withdrawal from the world. To this dialectic corresponds the dialectic in the relation of man to God, namely, as the relation between

[1] *Letters and Papers from Prison*, pp. 121 ff. (see Book 5, pp. 341ff.).

[2] E. Schleth, *Der profane Weltchrist*. Neubau der Lebensform für den Industrietmenschen, 1957, pp. 114, 159. Cf. p. 8: The author is of the opinion 'that the church as "eschatological phenomenon" occurs where Christians without reservation take the profane world seriously, because only in the "solidarity of faith and unfaith" can the new creation in Christ be recognized and the world served by it'.

[3] *The New Man*, pp. 106 ff., also pp. 58–70.

personal freedom and utter dependence, between ultimacy and intimacy.[1]

He who has understood the dialectic of the relationship between worldliness and faith in relation to the transcendent God, also sees that the recognition of God as the nearest at hand, as he who is in the midst of worldly life, does not imply pantheism.[2] For the dialectic is missing in pantheism, and it avoids the paradox that is given to man to conquer by grasping the unconditional in the conditional in every now: that means, not in a theory, but in existential comportment, in the conscious or unconscious decisions of life.

The contrast can be made clear by saying that faith in the transcendent presence of God can be expressed in the phrase 'transformations of God'. Ernst Barlach chose this phrase in order to say that the paradox of the presence of God in the world takes shape in ever new form, just as God himself wishes to give expression to the supra-real and infinite in his works perpetually in new forms.

Ernst Troeltsch once also spoke of the 'transformations of God', since he sought to hold on to the idea of God in his philosophy of history in view of the 'pluralism of reality and its movement' *vis-à-vis* changes in the knowledge of truth and ideals.[3] These changes depend upon an 'inner life-knowledge of the All or the Divinity', upon a 'life-process of the Absolute', a 'becoming of the divine Spirit'.

Troeltsch saw the problem, but he sought to solve it not on the basis of the historicity (*Geschichtlichkeit*) of human existence, but from a standpoint which views history from the outside and speculatively postulates a transcendent deity, which always has its life beyond my historicity.[4]

Hans Jonas represents the opposite extreme in his essay 'Immortality and the Modern Temper',[5] in which he projects,

[1] Robinson, op. cit., pp. 100, 130 f.

[2] R. G. Smith, *A Theological Perspective*, p. 16, also emphasizes this point.

[3] E. Troeltsch, *Der Historismus und seine Probleme*, 1922. The formulations in question, to which reference is made above, are collected by Gogarten, *Verhängnis und Hoffnung der Neuzeit*, pp. 112–14.

[4] For criticism of Troeltsch, see Gogarten, op. cit., pp. 114–16.

[5] *Harvard Theological Review*, 55, 1962, pp. 1–20.

so to speak, the historicity of man into God himself and speaks of the destiny of the deity for which man is responsible.[1] We men are experiments of eternity, as it were, and God's own destiny is at stake in our decisions, in the universe to which he has given himself up. God's being at the mercy of the world does not mean his immanence in the sense of pantheism. Rather, there is the paradox that the deity has chosen a destiny which consists in the continuous elevation out of immanence into transcendence, for which we men are responsible. In such a process, in the succession of surrender and deliverance, the deity becomes itself.

Schubert M. Ogden understands God's being as historical being in another way.[2] God's eternity is not to be conceived as his timelessness following the metaphysical tradition, but rather as his eminent temporality, his historicity.[3] God is a God who acts, as he is known in the Bible; his self must therefore be conceived in strict analogy with the human self, and anthropological language about God is entirely appropriate. Just as man is not an isolated I, neither is God. Without the universe, without the world, his creation, God is not. To this extent he not only stands in relation to the world, but is dependent upon it. But this dependence is actual, i.e., it is actualized in his own free decisions as well as in the free decisions, which correspond to his own, of the creatures that constitute his world. Decisions arising from the unbounded love as answer to God themselves contribute to God's self-creation.

This all certainly sounds astonishing at first hearing. For is not God, as we learned from Psalm 90, he who was there before the mountains were brought forth and the earth and the world created, God from everlasting to everlasting? Indeed he is ! But we understand Ogden when we comprehend

[1] Jonas, of course, also sees the dialectic between the relation to the world and the relation to God, and says that we encounter the eternal in the temporal, especially in the decisions in which eternity and nothingness meet in one in that the now of the decision is always to be understood as the final moment of time granted us. That means in fact to understand the end in a light from beyond time.

[2] *Journal of Religion*, 43, 1963, pp. 1–19.

[3] Cf. M. Heidegger, *Being and Time*, tr. J. Macquarrie and E. Robinson, London, 1962, 499, n. xiii: 'If God's eternity can be "construed" philosophically, then it may be understood only as a more primordial temporality which is "infinite".'

how he endeavours to free the idea of the eternity of God from the metaphysical conception of God as the unmoved mover, the *causa sui*,[1] and to conceive the eternity of God as historical without giving up thinking of God as creator. If, according to the biblical tradition, God is a person, so is he historical. In support of the view that God is not, apart from the world, the creator is not, apart from the creation, Ogden is able to invoke John 1 : 1–3, that remarkable assertion that in the beginning was the word, and the word of creation at that, through which everything came into being. This word in the beginning was with God, indeed the word was God. That is no different from what Ogden intends to say. And when we reflect on the word 'before' in the psalm, it is to be said that already for the psalmist the meaning of 'before' is not exhausted in the chronological sense, but that it means the creative superiority, the creative origin. This origin did not occur once as *prima causa*, out of which world history then unfolded in time; on the contrary, the origin is always present.

With this we come back to the assertion that for modern man the idea of God above or beyond the world is either no longer viable or is distorted into a religiosity which would like to escape from the world. By no means ! Only the idea of God which finds, which can seek and find, the unconditional in the conditional, the beyond in the here, the transcendent in the present at hand, as possibility of encounter, is possible for modern man.

It then remains to keep oneself open at any time for the *encounter with God in the world, in time.* It is not the acknowledgement of an image of God, be it ever so correct, that is real faith in God; rather, it is the readiness for the eternal to encounter us at any time in the present—at any time in the varying situations of our life. Readiness consists in openness in allowing something really to encounter us that does not leave the I alone, the I that is encapsulated in its purposes and plans, but whose encounter transforms us, permits us to become new selves again and again. The situation can be heartening just as well as disheartening, can be challenging as

[1] Cf. M. Heidegger, *Identität und Differenz*, 1957, p. 70 f. (Essays in Metaphysics: Identity and Difference, tr. Kurt F. Leidecker, New York: Philosophical Library, 1960, p. 64 f.)

well as requiring endurance. What is demanded is selflessness, not as a pattern of moral behaviour, but as the readiness not to cling to our old selves, but to receive our authentic selves ever anew. This can be a questioning readiness, but it can also be completely unconscious. For, suprisingly, God can encounter us where we do not expect it.[1]

We have thus perhaps come to an understanding of what is meant by the 'transformations of God'. All of us are probably acquainted with sagas and legends, pagan as well as Christian, in which the profound idea of the transformation of God has been concealed in the mythological representation of the metamorphosis of the deity or of gods, who visit a mortal incognito and unrecognized. How the one visited receives the god determines his destiny.

The New Testament contains the most striking proclama-

[1] That is evidently also the intention of Herbert Braun, whose avoidance of the word 'God' in his delineation of what the New Testament has to say to me (*Gesammelte Studien zum Neuen Testament und seiner Umwelt*, Tübingen: Siebeck, 1962, p. 297) has offended and evoked criticism (cf. especially H. Gollwitzer, *Die Existenz Gottes im Bekenntnis des Glaubens*, 1963, pp. 26–9). Braun's purpose is to emphasize, over against atheism with a world-view, that God is not 'the one who exists for himself', but rather is 'the whence of my being driven around' (op. cit., p. 341). This being driven about is understood by Braun as determined by the 'I may' and 'I ought'. It might be asked how this dialectic (if it may be called that) relates to the dialectic between worldliness and a believing relation to transcendence. But, in any case, the relation to transcendence is understood in the New Testament, according to Braun, as an event, and indeed, as he formulates it, as an 'unexpectable' event (p. 275). The believing self-understanding awakened in such an event is not theoretical knowledge, but 'an event which occurs again and again' (p. 277). The truth of the relation to transcendence understood in this sense is 'bound to its being perpetually proclaimed anew' (p. 277) and to its being heeded (p. 297), to its being heard (p. 298), respectively. The self-understanding awakened by such hearing is actualized in concrete human community. Braun is thus able to put it very sharply: 'Man as man, man in his community with man, implies God.'—R. G. Smith also emphasizes the importance of the community, *A Theological Perspective*, p. 22: 'Man is (scil. man) in so far as he receives. He is (scil. man) only so far as he is whole. And this wholeness is found only in relation to others. Man's being is being in relation. This simply cannot be arranged or planned. It happens, it is an event in which man's being is disclosed in the presence of the other.' The problem of the relation of law and gospel also belongs here; see, e.g., Ebeling, *Word and Faith*, p. 143 f.

tions of the 'transformations' of God, and oddly enough in the picture which Jesus sketches of the last judgement (Matt. 25: 31–46). The Judge of the world assembles all men before his throne, some to the right, some to the left. To those on the right he says: 'I was hungry and you gave me food, I was thirsty and you gave me drink, I was a stranger and you welcomed me...' And when those so addressed inquire in astonishment, 'When did we do all this?', the Lord will answer, 'What you did to one of the least of these my brethren you did to me!' The dialogue with those on the left runs correspondingly 'I was hungry and you me no food, I was thirsty and you gave me no drink...' And when they ask, 'Lord, when did we see thee hungry or thirsty... and did not minister to thee?', then they must face the answer, 'What you did not do to the least of these, you did not do to me either!' This picture thus contains the two doctrines which belong together, of the 'transformations' of God and of the presence of eternity in time.

(FROM: *World Come of Age*, A symposium on Dietrich Bonhoeffer, edited by R. Gregor Smith, London 1967, pp. 256–73.)

FOR FURTHER STUDY AND DISCUSSION

1 The debate about the results of form-criticism and its bearing on the question of the historical Jesus continues. A volume of essays critical of Bultmann's handling of form-criticism and suggesting a number of questions for further study is *Vindications* (edited by Anthony Hanson) 1966. Professor Dennis Nineham has replied to some of the criticisms made there in an essay published in *Christian History and Interpretation* (Essays presented to John Knox) edited by W. R. Farmer, C. F. D. Moule and R. R. Niebuhr, 1968.

2 Is the 'demythologizing' enterprise necessary and worth-

while? Some critical questions raised by Bultmann's work will be found in an appendix on 'demythologizing' in Hugo Meynell's *Sense, nonsense and Christianity* 1964 and also in his *The New Theology and Modern Theologians* 1967.

FOR FURTHER READING

Principal Works of Rudolf Bultmann (in English translation)

'The Study of the Synoptic Gospels' in *Form Criticism* edited by F. C. Grant, 1962, New York (Harper Torchbooks).

Jesus and the Word (translated by L. P. Smith and E. Huntress), London (Fontana Books), 1962.

Theology of the New Testament (translated by Kendrick Grobel), Vol. I, 1952; Vol. II, 1955, London.

'New Testament and Mythology', 'A reply to the theses of Julius Schniewind', 'Bultmann replies to his critics' in *Kerygma and Myth*, Vol. I (edited by H.-W. Bartsch), London, 1953.

Jesus Christ and Mythology, London, 1960.

History and Eschatology, New York (Harper Torchbooks), 1962.

Existence and Faith (shorter writings selected, translated and introduced by Schubert M. Ogden), Fontana Books, London, 1964.

Some Books about Rudolf Bultmann

L. Malevez, *The Christian Message and Myth*: the theology of Rudolf Bultmann, London, 1958. (A very valuable critique of Bultmann by a Roman Catholic theologian.)

Paul Althaus, *The so-called kerygma and the historical Jesus*, Edinburgh, 1959. (An excellent discussion of the place of history and the historical Jesus in Bultmann's theology.)

David Cairns, *A gospel without myth?* London, 1960.

John Macquarrie, *The scope of demythologizing*, London, 1960.
H. A. Meynell, *The New Theology and Modern Theologians*, London, 1967. (A stimulating volume of essays containing some shrewd comments on Bultmann's theological method.)

FOR GENERAL BACKGROUND READING

John Macquarrie, *Twentieth-century Religious Thought*, 1963.
——, *God-talk*, 1967.
——, *God and Secularity*, 1968.
Frederick Ferré, *Language, Logic and God*, 1962.
——, *Basic Modern Philosophy of Religion*, 1968.
David E. Jenkins, *Guide to the Debate about God*, 1966.
Colin Williams, *Faith in a Secular Age*, 1966.
E. L. Mascall, *The Secularisation of Christianity*, 1965.
H. Gollwitzer, *The Existence of God as confessed by faith*, 1964.
A. M. Ramsey, *God, Christ and the World*, 1969.
T. W. Ogletree, *The Death of God Controversy*, 1966.

3. Paul Tillich

1886–1965

BIOGRAPHICAL INTRODUCTION

Tillich has written his own autobiographical reflections in *The Protestant Era*, *The Interpretation of History* and in an essay at the beginning of *The Theology of Paul Tillich* (edited by Kegley and Bretall).

He was an exact contemporary of Karl Barth, being born in 1886 at Starzeddel in the German province of Brandenburg. Like Barth also, and indeed all the writers in this series, he came of clerical stock, his father being the village pastor. Tillich retained vivid memories of conversations with his father about philosophy and spoke of them in later life as 'the most happy instance of a positive relation to my father'. In common with Bultmann he had a country upbringing, but this seems to have made a much deeper impression on Tillich who speaks of his mystical feeling towards nature, the land and the soil. He had also the same feeling for the sea. He obviously reacted sensitively to his home life and says that the influence of life in a parish house with Lutheran school on one side and Gothic church on the other gave him his 'idea of the holy'. All this influenced profoundly the kind of theology which was to come later. He could see himself later as something of a nineteenth-century romantic with a deep sense of man's 'mystical' participation in nature and profound belief that man, finite and limited creature though he be, is able to experience the infinite.

In spite of his attachment to the country, he was greatly excited by his first visit to Berlin and says he felt 'extreme joy' when the family moved there in 1900. Tillich studied theology at the universities of Berlin, Tübingen and Halle, taking his doctorate in 1910 at Breslau. In 1912 he was ordained pastor and worked in the province of Brandenburg. During the 1914–18 war he served as an army chaplain. Important for his later development were his studies in art at this period, particularly early Christian mosaics. Tillich was to remain specially interested in religion and the arts and is the only thinker in the group represented in this series who attempted to construct a theology of culture.

In 1919 Tillich began his university teaching career in

Berlin, moving in 1924 to Marburg where he held the chair of theology. In 1925 he became professor of the philosophy of religion and social philosophy at Dresden. He also taught in Leipzig at this period. Then in 1929 he was appointed professor of philosophy at Frankfurt.

Tillich had become opposed to the Nazi movement long before 1933 when Hitler came to power. He was dismissed from his chair at Frankfurt. Reinhold Niebuhr happened to be in America that year, and arranged for Tillich to go to Union Theological Seminary, New York. He was appointed professor of philosophical theology. This was the beginning of Tillich's American period which proved to be specially happy and fruitful. He spoke warmly of what he owed to Union, especially its community life after the 'extreme individualism of one's academic existence in Germany'. Here also he developed his interests in religious socialism which went back to his student days.

After his retirement in 1955 he was invited to become professor at Harvard University. He taught also in the University of Chicago. Tillich died on 27 October 1965.

SELECTIONS

1 Theology and Theological Method

(a) The Method of Correlation

[Tillich suggests that the 'method of correlation' best expresses the relation between theology and philosophy. Unlike Barth, Tillich believed that theology can only be done in close association with philosophy. For him man is such a kind of being that a full analysis of himself would raise questions about the relation between finite and infinite, time and eternity, etc. Such an analysis is the task of philosophy, especially existentialist philosophy. It is to these basic questions raised by such a philosophical analysis that theology addresses itself.]

This method tries to overcome the conflict between the naturalistic and supernaturalistic methods which imperils not only any real progress in the work of systematic theology but also any possible effect of theology on the secular world. The method of correlation shows, at every point of Christian thought, the interdependence between the ultimate questions to which philosophy (as well as pre-philosophical thinking) is driven and the answers given in the Christian message.

Philosophy cannot answer ultimate or existential questions *qua* philosophy. If the philosopher tries to answer them (and all creative philosophers have tried to do so), he becomes a theologian. And, conversely, theology cannot answer those questions without accepting their presuppositions and implications. Question and answer determine each other; if they are separated, the traditional answers become unintelligible, and the actual questions remain unanswered. The method of correlation aims to overcome this situation. In the chapter on 'Philosophy and Theology' (as well as in all my work in systematic theology) the method is explained and applied. Such a method is truly dialectical and therefore opposed to the supernaturalism of later Barthianism as well as to any other type of orthodoxy and fundamentalism. Philosophy and theology are not separated, and they are not identical, but they are correlated, and their correlation is the methodological problem of a Protestant theology . . .

(FROM: *The Protestant Principle*, p. xlii.)

. . . Theology formulates the questions implied in human existence, and theology formulates the answers implied in divine self-manifestation under the guidance of the questions implied in human existence. This is a circle which drives man to a point where question and answer are not separated. This point, however, is not a moment in time. It belongs to man's essential being, to the unity of his finitude with the infinity in which he was created and from which he is separated. A symptom of both the essential unity and the existential separation of finite man from his infinity is his ability to ask about the infinite to which he belongs: the fact that he must ask about it indicates that he is separated from it.

The answers implied in the event of revelation are meaningful only in so far as they are in correlation with questions concerning the whole of our existence, with existential questions. Only those who have experienced the shock of transitoriness, the anxiety in which they are aware of their finitude, the threat of non-being, can understand what the notion of God means. Only those who have experienced the tragic ambiguities of our historical existence and have totally questioned the meaning of existence can understand what the symbol of the Kingdom of God means. Revelation answers questions which have been asked and always will be asked because they are 'we ourselves'. Man is the question he asks about himself, before any qustion has been formulated. It is, therefore, not surprising that the basic questions were formulated very early in the history of mankind. Every analysis of the mythological material shows this.[1] Nor is it surprising that the same questions appear in early childhood as every observation of children shows. Being human means asking the question of one's own being and living under the impact of the answers given to this question. And, conversely, being human means

[1] Cf. H. Gunkel, *The Legends of Genesis* (Chicago: Open Court Pub. Co., 1901).

receiving answers to the question of one's own being and asking questions under the impact of the answers.

In using the method of correlation, systematic theology proceeds in the following way: it makes an analysis of the human situation out of which the existential questions arise. and it demonstrates that the symbols used in the Christian message are the answers to these questions. The analysis of the human situation is done in terms which today are called 'existential'. Such analyses are much older than existentialism; they are, indeed, as old as man's thinking about himself, and they have been expressed in various kinds of conceptualization since the beginning of philosophy. Whenever man has looked at his world he has found himself in it as a part of it. But he also has realized that he is a stranger in the world of objects, unable to penetrate it beyond a certain level of scientific analysis. And then he has become aware of the fact that he himself is the door to the deeper levels of reality, that in his own existence he has the only possible approach to existence itself.[1] This does not mean that man is more approachable than other objects as material for scientific research. The opposite is the case! It does mean that the immediate experience of one's own existing reveals something of the nature of existence generally. Whoever has penetrated into the nature of his own finitude can find the traces of finitude in everything that exists. And he can ask the question implied in his finitude as the question implied in finitude universally. In doing so he does not formulate a doctrine of man; he expresses a doctrine of existence as experienced in him as man. When Calvin in the opening sentences of the *Institutes* correlates our knowledge of God with our knowledge of man, he does not speak of the doctrine of man as such and of the doctrine of God as such. He speaks of man's misery, which gives the existential basis for his understanding of God's glory, and of God's glory, which gives the essential basis for man's understanding of his

[1] Cf. Augustine's doctrine of truth dwelling in the soul and transcending it at the same time; the mystical identification of the ground of being with the ground of self; the use of psychological categories for ontological purposes in Paracelsus, Böhme, Schelling, and in the 'philosophy of life' from Schopenhauer to Bergson; Heidegger's notion of 'Dasein' (being there) as the form of human existence and the entrance to ontology.

misery. Man as existing, representing existence generally and asking the question implied in his existence, is one side of the cognitive correlation to which Calvin points, the other side being the divine majesty. In the initial sentences of his theological system Calvin expresses the essence of the method of correlation.[1]

The analysis of the human situation employs materials made available by man's creative self-interpretation in all realms of culture. Philosophy contributes, but so do poetry, drama, the novel, therapeutic psychology, and sociology. The theologian organizes these materials in relation to the answer given by the Christian message. In the light of this message he may make an analysis of existence which is more penetrating than that of most philosophers. Nevertheless, it remains a philosophical analysis. The analysis of existence, including the development of the questions implicit in existence, is a philosophical task, even if it is performed by a theologian, and even if the theologian is a reformer like Calvin. The difference between the philosopher who is not a theologian and the theologian who works as a philosopher in analysing human existence is only that the former tries to give an analysis which will be part of a broader philosophical work while the latter tries to correlate the material of his analysis with the theological concepts he derives from the Christian faith. This does not make the philosophical work of the theologian heteronomous. As a theologian he does not tell himself what is philosophically true. As a philosopher he does not tell himself what is theologically true. But he cannot help seeing human existence and existence generally in such a way that the Christian symbols appear meaningful and understandable to him. His eyes are partially focused by his ultimate concern, which is true of every philosopher. Nevertheless, his act of seeing is autonomous, for it is determined only by the object as it is given in his experience. If he sees something he did not expect to see in the light of his theological answer, he

[1] 'The knowledge of ourselves is not only an incitement to seek after God, but likewise a considerable assistance towards finding him. On the other hand, it is plain that no man can arrive at the true knowledge of himself, without having first contemplated the divine character, and then descended to the consideration of his own' (John Calvin, *Institutes*, I, 48).

holds fast to what he has seen and reformulates the theological answer. He is certain that nothing he sees can change the substance of his answer, because this substance is the *logos* of being, manifest in Jesus as the Christ. If this were not his presupposition, he would have to sacrifice either his philosophical honesty or his theological concern.

The Christian message provides the answers to the questions implied in human existence. These answers are contained in the revelatory events on which Christianity is based and are taken by systematic theology *from* the sources, *through* the medium, *under* the norm. Their content cannot be derived from the questions, that is, from an analysis of human existence. They are 'spoken' *to* human existence from beyond it. Otherwise they would not be answers, for the question is human existence itself. But the relation is more involved than this, since it is correlation. There is a mutual dependence between question and answer. In respect to content the Christian answers are dependent on the revelatory events in which they appear; in respect to form they are dependent on the structure of the questions which they answer. God is the answer to the question implied in human finitude. This answer cannot be derived from the analysis of existence. However, if the notion of God appears in systematic theology in correlation with the threat of non-being which is implied in existence, God must be called the infinite power of being which resists the threat of non-being. In classical theology this is being-itself. If anxiety is defined as the awareness of being finite, God must be called the infinite ground of courage. In classical theology this is universal providence. If the notion of the Kingdom of God appears in correlation with the riddle of our historical existence, it must be called the meaning, fulfilment, and unity of history. In this way an interpretation of the traditional symbols of Christianity is achieved which preserves the power of these symbols and which opens them to the questions elaborated by our present analysis of human existence.

(FROM: *Systematic Theology*, I, pp. 69–72.)

. . . The term 'philosophical theology' points to a theology that has a philosophical character. What does this mean?

First of all, it implies that there is a theology that has *not* a philosophical but some other character. This, indeed, is the case. As long as theological thought has existed, there have been two types of theology, a philosophical one and—let me call it—a 'kerygmatic' one. Kerygmatic is derived from the New Testament word *kerygma*, 'message'. It is a theology that tries to reproduce the content of the Christian message in an ordered and systematic way, without referring to philosophy. In contrast to it, philosophical, theology, although based on the same *kerygma*, tries to explain the contents of the *kerygma*, in close interrelation with philosophy. The tension and mutual fertilization between these two types is a main event and a fortunate one in all history of Christian thought. The fight of the traditionalists of the early church against the rising logos-Christology, the struggle between the mystics and dialecticians in the early Middle Ages, between Biblicism and scholasticism in the later Middle Ages, between the Reformers and the Aristotelian scholastics, the attack of the Ritschlians on speculative theology, and of the Barthians on a philosophy of religion—all this and much more was the consequence of the existence of a philosophical and a kerygmatic theology. The duality is natural. It is implied in the very word 'theology', the syllable 'theo' pointing to the *kerygma*, in which God is revealed, and the syllable 'logy' pointing to the endeavour of human reason to receive the message. This implies further that kerygmatic and philosophical theology demand each other and are wrong in the moment in which they become exclusive. No kerygmatic theology ever existed which did not use philosophical terms and methods. And no philosophical theology ever existed—deserving the name 'theology' —which did not try to explain the content of the message. Therefore, the theological ideal is the complete unity of both types, an ideal which is reached only by the greatest theologians and even by them only approximately. The fact that every human creativity has its typological limitations makes it desirable that theological faculties should include a representative of kerygmatic and one of philosophical theology, whether the latter is called apologetics, speculative theology, Christian philosophy of religion, or philosophical theology. The church cannot do without this type, just as, of course, it cannot dispense with the kerygmatic type.

(FROM: *The Protestant Principle*, pp. 93–4.)

(*b*) *Faith and Doubt in the Theologian*

[In this passage Tillich touches on the question of the relationship of theology to religion, and in particular the matter of the theologian's own faith. The 'philosopher of religion' is more detached from his subject than the 'theologian', argues Tillich, since the latter, as one who participates in the particular beliefs of a specific religious community, stands inside 'the theological circle'. But the theologian also needs to be 'distanced' from religion, to know what it is like to be outside this circle.]

But the circle within which the theologian works is narrower than that of the philosopher of religion. He adds to the 'mystical *a priori*' the criterion of the Christian message. While the philosopher of religion tries to remain general and abstract in his concepts, as the concept 'religion' itself indicates, the theologian is consciously and by intention specific and concrete. The difference, of course, is not absolute. Since the experiential basis of every philosophy of religion is partly determined by the cultural tradition to which it belongs—even mysticism is culturally conditioned—it inescapably includes concrete and special elements. The philosopher as philosopher, however, tries to abstract from these elements and to create generally valid concepts concerning religion. The theologian, on the other hand, claims the universal validity of the Christian message in spite of its concrete and special character. He does not justify this claim by abstracting from the concreteness of the message but by stressing its unrepeatable uniqueness. He enters the theological circle with a concrete commitment. He enters it as a member of the Christian Church to perform one of the essential functions of the Church—its theological self-interpretation.

The 'scientific' theologian wants to be more than a philosopher of religion. He wants to interpret the Christian message generally with the help of his method. This puts before him two alternatives. He may subsume the Christian message under his concept of religion. Then Christianity is considered to be one example of religious life beside other examples, certainly the highest religion, but not the final one and not unique. Such a theology does not enter the theological circle. It keeps itself within the religious-philosophical circle and its indefinite horizons—horizons which beckon towards a future which is open for new and perhaps higher examples of religion. The scientific theologian, in spite of his desire to be a theologian, remains a philosopher of religion. Or he becomes really a theologian, an interpreter of his Church and its claim to uniqueness and universal validity. Then he enters the theological circle and should admit that he has done so and stop speaking of himself as a scientific theologian in the ordinary sense of 'scientific'.

But even the man who has entered the theological circle consciously and openly faces another serious problem. Being inside the circle, he must have made an existential decision; he must be in the situation of faith. But no one can say of himself that he is in the situation of faith. No one can call himself a theologian, even if he is called to be a teacher of theology. Every theologian is committed *and* alienated; he is always in faith *and* in doubt; he is inside *and* outside the theological circle. Sometimes the one side prevails, sometimes the other; and he is never certain which side really prevails. Therefore, one criterion alone can be applied: a person can be a theologian as long as he acknowledges the content of the theological circle as his ultimate concern. Whether this is true does not depend on his intellectual or moral or emotional state; it does not depend on the intensity and certitude of faith; it does not depend on the power of regeneration or the grade of sanctification. Rather it depends on his being ultimately concerned with the Christian message even if he is sometimes inclined to attack and to reject it.

(FROM: *Systematic Theology*, I, pp. 12–13.)

(*c*) *Paradox, logic and symbols in religious language*

[In these two passages Tillich deals first with the difficult question of the relation between the language of paradox and the language of logic. Paradoxical language, as a matter of words, looks logically self-contradictory, but it makes sense, Tillich implies, in experience. Paradoxical language is used, not to defy the rules of logic, but to indicate a reality which, while it goes beyond human rationality, does not contradict it.

In the second extract Tillich turns to the meaning and use of symbols, whether in words or in art. One of the gains of modern linguistic philosophy has been to show that there is a wide variety in the uses of language: scientific, poetic, moral etc. Scientific language prefers to use words which mean one thing at a time whereas poetic language depends upon words meaning several things simultaneously.

Tillich distinguishes 'symbols' from 'signs'. Signs indicate what they stand for in a conventional way and have a limited suggestiveness. New signs are easily invented and being conventional may be changed without difficulty. For instance red as a traffic sign for 'stop' could be changed to purple. Symbols are much more potent. They open up new levels of meaning and enhance human powers of perception. They are irreplaceable. This has an important bearing on the 'demythologizing' controversy (see Bk 2, pp. 132ff.) Symbols, says Tillich, participate in the reality to which they point. By this he seems to mean that when one is truly reacting to an effective symbol one has the experience of responding at the same time to another reality. This makes it inevitable, especially perhaps in religion, that people will identify the symbol with this reality. That however would be to turn the symbol into an idol.]

. . . Theological dialectics does not violate the principle of logical rationality. The same is true of paradoxical statements in religion and theology. When Paul points to his situation as an apostle and to that of Christians generally in a series of *paradoxa* (2 Corinthians), he does not intend to say something illogical; he intends to give the adequate, understandable, and therefore logical expression of the infinite tensions of Christian existence. When he speaks about the paradox of the justification of the sinner (in Luther's formula, *simul peccator et iustus*),[1] and when John speaks about the Logos becoming flesh (later expressed in the *paradoxa* of the creed of Chalcedon),[2] neither of them wishes to indulge in logical contradictions.[3] They want to express the conviction that God's acting transcends all possible human expectations and all necessary human preparations. It transcends, but it does not destroy, finite reason; for God acts through the Logos which is the transcendent and transcending source of the *logos* structure of thought and being. God does not annihilate the expressions of his own Logos. The term 'paradox' should be defined carefully, and paradoxical language should be used with discrimination. Paradoxical means 'against the opinion', namely, the opinion of finite reason. Paradox points to the fact that in God's acting finite reason is superseded but not annihilated; it expresses this fact in terms which are not logically contradictory but which are supposed to point beyond the realm in which finite reason is applicable. This is indicated by the ecstatic state in which all biblical and classical theological *paradoxa* appear. The confusion begins when these *paradoxa* are brought down to the level of genuine logical contradictions and people are asked to sacrifice reason in order to accept senseless combinations of words as divine wisdom. But Christianity does not demand such intellectual 'good words' from anyone, just as it does not ask artificial 'works' of practical asceticism. There is, in the last analysis, only *one* genuine paradox in the Christian message—the appearance of that which conquers existence under the conditions of existence. Incarnation, redemption, justification, etc., are implied in this paradoxical event. It is not a logical contradiction which makes it a paradox but the fact that it transcends all human expectations and possibilities. It breaks into the context of experience or reality, but it cannot be derived from it. The acceptance of this paradox is not the acceptance of the absurd, but it is the state of being grasped by the power of that which breaks into our experience

[1] 'Sinner and righteous at one and the same time' (Ed.).

[2] Council of Chalcedon A.D. 451. The definition of this Council spoke of Christ paradoxically as 'truly God and truly man' (Ed.).

[3] It is the mistake of Brunner in *The Mediator* that he makes the offence of logical rationality the criterion of Christian truth. This 'offence' is neither that of Kierkegaard nor that of the New Testament.

from above it. Paradox in religion and theology does not conflict with the principle of logical rationality. Paradox has its logical place . . .

(FROM: *Systematic Theology*, I, pp. 63–4.)

. . . The fact that there is so much discussion about the meaning of symbols going on in this country as well as in Europe is a symptom of something deeper, something both negative and positive in its import. It is a symptom of the fact that we are in a confusion of language in theology and philosophy and related subjects which has hardly been surpassed at any time in history. Words do not communicate to us any more what they originally did and what they were invented to communicate. This has something to do with the fact that our present culture has no clearing house such as medieval scholasticism was, Protestant scholasticism in the seventeenth century at least tried to be, and philosophers like Kant tried to renew. We have no such clearing house, and this is the one point at which we might be in sympathy with the present day so-called logical positivists or symbolic logicians or logicians generally. They at least try to produce a clearing house. The only criticism is that this clearing house is a very small room, perhaps only a corner of a house, and not a real house. It excludes most of life. But it could become useful if it increased in reach and acceptance of realities beyond the mere logical calculus.

The positive point is that we are in a process in which a very important thing is being rediscovered: namely, that there are levels of reality of great difference, and that these different levels demand different approaches and different languages; not everything in reality can be grasped by the language which is most adequate for mathematical sciences. The insight into this situation is the most positive side of the fact that the problem of symbols is again taken seriously.

Let us proceed with the intention of clearing concepts as much as we are able, and let us take five steps, the first of which is the discussion of 'symbols and signs'. Symbols are similar to signs in one decisive respect: both symbols and signs point beyond themselves to something else. The typical sign, for instance the red light at the corner of the street, does not point to itself but it points to the necessity of cars stopping. And every symbol points beyond itself to a reality for which it stands. In this, symbols and signs have an essential identity—they point beyond themselves. And this is the reason that the confusion of language mentioned above has also conquered the discussion about symbols for centuries and has produced confusion between signs and symbols. The first step in any clearing up of the meaning of symbols is to distinguish it from the meaning of signs.

The difference, which is a fundamental difference between them, is that signs do not participate in any way in the reality and power of that to which they point. Symbols, although they are not the same as that which they symbolize, participate in its meaning and power. The difference between symbol and sign is the participation in the symbolized reality which characterizes the symbols, and the non-participation in the 'pointed-to' reality which characterizes a sign. For example, letters of the alphabet as they are written, an 'A' or an 'R' do not participate in the sound to which they point; on the other hand, the flag participates in the power of the king or the nation for which it stands and which it symbolizes. There has, therefore, been a fight since the days of William Tell as to how to behave in the presence of the flag. This would be meaningless if the flag did not participate as a symbol in the power of that which it symbolizes. The whole monarchic idea is itself entirely incomprehensible, if you do not understand that the king always is both: on the one hand, a symbol of the power of the group of which he is the king and on the other hand, he who exercises partly (never fully, of course) this power.

But something has happened which is very dangerous for all our attempts to find a clearing house for the concepts of symbols and signs. The mathematician has usurped the term 'symbol' for mathematical 'sign', and this makes a disentaglement of the confusion almost impossible. The only thing we can do is to distinguish different groups, signs which are called symbols, and genuine symbols. The mathematical signs are signs which are wrongly called symbols.

Language is a very good example of the difference between

signs and symbols. Words in a language are signs for a meaning which they express. The word 'desk' is a sign which points to something quite different—namely, the thing on which a paper is lying and at which we might be looking. This has nothing to do with the word 'desk', with these four letters. But there are words in every language which are more than this, and in the moment in which they get connotations which go beyond something to which they point as signs, then they can become symbols; and this is a very important distinction for any speaker. He can speak almost completely in signs, reducing the meaning of his words almost to mathematical signs, and this is the absolute ideal of the logical positivist. The other pole of this is liturgical or poetic language where words have a power through centuries, or more than centuries. They have connotations in situations in which they appear so that they cannot be replaced. They have become not only signs pointing to a meaning which is defined, but also symbols standing for a reality in the power of which they participate.

Now we come to a second consideration dealing with the functions of symbols. The first function is implied in what has already been said—namely, the representative function. The symbol represents something which is not itself, for which it stands and in the power and meaning of which it participates. This is a basic function of every symbol, and therefore, if that word had not been used in so many other ways, one could perhaps even translate 'symbolic' as 'representative', but for some reason that is not possible. If the symbols stand for something which they are not, then the question is, 'Why do we not have that for which they stand directly? Why do we need symbols at all?' And now we come to something which is perhaps the main function of the symbol—namely, the opening up of levels of reality which otherwise are hidden and cannot be grasped in any other way.

Every symbol opens up a level of reality for which non-symbolic speaking is inadequate. Let us interpret this, or explain this, in terms of artistic symbols. The more we try to enter into the meaning of symbols, the more we become aware that it is a function of art to open up levels of reality;

in poetry, in visual art, and in music, levels of reality are opened up which can be opened up in no other way. Now if this is the function of art then certainly artistic creations have symbolic character. You can take that which a landscape of Rubens, for instance, mediates to you. You cannot have this experience in any other way than through this painting made by Rubens. This landscape has some heroic character; it has character of balance, of colours, of weights, of values, and so on. All this is very external. What this mediates to you cannot be expressed in any other way than through the painting itself. The same is true also in the relationship of poetry and philosophy. The temptation may often be to confuse the issue by bringing too many philosophical concepts into a poem. Now this is really the problem; one cannot do this. If one uses philosophical language or scientific language, it does not mediate the same thing which is mediated in the use of really poetic language without a mixture of any other language.

This example may show what is meant by the phrase 'opening up of levels of reality'. But in order to do this, something else must be opened up—namely, levels of the soul, levels of our interior reality. And they must correspond to the levels in exterior reality which are opened up by a symbol. So every symbol is two-edged. It opens up reality and it opens up the soul. There are, of course, people who are not opened up by music or who are not opened up by poetry, or more of them (especially in Protestant America) who are not opened up at all by visual arts. The 'opening up' is a two-sided function—namely, reality in deeper levels and the human soul in special levels.

If this is the function of symbols then it is obvious that symbols cannot be replaced by other symbols. Every symbol has a special function which is just *it* and cannot be replaced by more or less adequate symbols. This is different from signs, for signs can always be replaced. If one finds that a green light is not so expedient as perhaps a blue light (this is not true, but could be true), then we simply put on a blue light, and nothing is changed. But a symbolic word (such as the word 'God') cannot be replaced. No symbol can be replaced when used in its special function. So one asks rightly, 'How do symbols arise, and how do they come to an end?' As different from signs, symbols are born and die. Signs are consciously invented and removed. This is a fundamental difference.

'Out of what womb are symbols born?' Out of the womb which is usually called today the 'group unconscious' or 'collective unconscious', or whatever you want to call it—out of a group which acknowledges, in this thing, this word, this flag, or whatever it may be, its own being. It is not invented intentionally; and even if somebody would try to invent a symbol, as sometimes happens, then it becomes a symbol only if the unconscious of a group says 'yes' to it. It means that something is opened up by it in the sense which I have just described. Now this implies further that in the moment in which this inner situation of the human group to a symbol has ceased to exist, then the symbol dies. The symbol does not 'say' anything any more. In this way, all of the polytheistic gods have died; the situation in which they were born, has changed or does not exist any more, and so the symbols died. But there are events which cannot be described in terms of intention and invention.

Now we come to a third consideration—namely, the nature of religious symbols. Religious symbols do exactly the same thing as all symbols do—namely, they open up a level of reality, which otherwise is not opened at all, which is hidden. We can call this the depth dimension of reality itself, the dimension of reality which is the ground of every other dimension and every other depth, and which therefore, is not one level beside the others but is the fundamental level, the level below all other levels, the level of being itself, or the ultimate power of being. Religious symbols open up the experience of the dimension of this depth in the human soul. If a religious symbol has ceased to have this function, then it dies. And if new symbols are born, they are born out of a changed relationship to the ultimate ground of being, i.e., to the Holy.

The dimension of ultimate reality is the dimension of the Holy. And so we can also say, religious symbols are symbols of the Holy. As such they participate in the holiness of the

Holy according to our basic definition of a symbol. But participation is not identity; they are not themselves *the* Holy. The wholly transcendent transcends every symbol of the Holy. Religious symbols are taken from the infinity of material which the experienced reality gives us. Everything in time and space has become at some time in the history of religion a symbol for the Holy. And this is naturally so, because everything that is in the world we encounter rests on the ultimate ground of being. This is the key to the otherwise extremely confusing history of religion. Those of you who have looked into this seeming chaos of the history of religion in all periods of history from the earliest primitive to the latest developments, will be extremely confused about the chaotic character of this development. They key which makes order out of this chaos is comparatively simple. It is that everything in reality can impress itself as a symbol for a special relationship of the human mind to its own ultimate ground and meaning. So in order to open up the seemingly closed door to this chaos of religious symbols, one simply has to ask, 'What is the relationship to the ultimate which is symbolized in these symbols?' And then they cease to be meaningless; and they become, on the contrary, the most revealing creations of the human mind, the most genuine ones, the most powerful ones, those who control the human consciousness, and perhaps even more the unconsciousness, and have therefore this tremendous tenacity which is characteristic of all religious symbols in the history of religion.

Religion, as everything in life, stands under the law of ambiguity, 'ambiguity' meaning that it is creative and destructive at the same time. Religion has its holiness and its unholiness, and the reason for this is obvious from what has been said about religious symbolism. Religious symbols point symbolically to that which transcends all of them. But since, as symbols, they participate in that to which they point, they always have the tendency (in the human mind, of course) to replace that to which they are supposed to point, and to become ultimate in themselves. And in the moment in which they do this, they become idols. All idolatry is nothing else than the absolutizing of symbols of the Holy, and making them identical with the Holy itself. In this way, for instance, holy persons can become a god. Ritual acts can take on unconditional validity, although they are only expressions of a special situation. In all sacramental activities of religion, in all holy objects, holy books, holy doctrines, holy rites, you find this danger which we will call 'demonization'. They become demonic at the moment in which they become elevated to the unconditional and ultimate character of the Holy itself.

Now we turn to a fourth consideration—namely, the levels of religious symbols. There are two fundamental levels in all religious symbols: the transcendent level, the level which goes *beyond* the empirical reality we encounter, and the immanent level, the level which we find *within* the encounter with reality. Let us look at the first level, the transcendent level. The basic symbol on the transcendent level would be God himself. But we cannot simply say that God is a symbol. We must always say two things about him: we must say that there is a non-symbolic element in our image of God—namely, that he is ultimate reality, being itself, ground of being, power of being; and the other, that he is the highest being in which everything that we have does exist in the most perfect way. If we say this we have in our mind the image of a highest being, a being with the characteristics of highest perfection. That means we have a symbol for that which is not symbolic in the idea of God—namely, 'Being Itself'.

It is important to distinguish these two elements in the idea of God. Thus all of these discussions going on about God being a person or not a person, God being similar to other beings or not similar, these discussions which have a great impact on the destruction of the religious experience through false interpretations of it, could be overcome if we would say, 'Certainly the awareness of something unconditional is in itself what it is, is not symbolic'. We can call it '*Being Itself*', *esse qua esse, esse ipsum*, as the scholastics did. But in our relationship to this ultimate we symbolize and must symbolize. We could not be in communication with God if he were only 'ultimate being'. But in our relationship to him we encounter him with the highest of what we ourselves are, *person*. And so in the symbolic form of speaking about him, we have both that which transcends infinitely our experience of ourselves as persons, and that which is so adequate to our being persons that we can say, 'Thou' to God, and can pray to him. And these two elements must be preserved. If we preserve only the element of the unconditional, then no relationship to God is possible. If we preserve only the element of the ego-thou relationship, as it is called today, we lose the element of the divine—namely, the unconditional which transcends subject and object and all other polarities. This is the first point on the transcendent level.

The second is the qualities, the attributes of God, whatever you say about him: that he is love, that he is mercy, that he is power, that he is omniscient, that he is omnipresent, that he is almighty. These attributes of God are taken from experienced qualities we have ourselves. They cannot be applied to God in the literal sense. If this is done, it leads to an infinite amount of absurdities. This again is one of the reasons for the destruction of religion through wrong communicative interpretation of it. And again the symbolic character of these qualities must be maintained consistently. Otherwise, every speaking about the divine becomes absurd.

A third element on the transcendent level is the acts of God, for example, when we say, 'He has created the world', 'He has sent his son', 'He will fulfill the world'. In all these temporal, causal, and other expressions we speak symbolically of God. As an example, look at the one small sentence: '*God has sent his son.*' Here we have in the word 'has' temporality. But God is beyond *our* temporality, though not beyond every temporality. Here is space; 'sending somebody' means moving him from one place to another place. This certainly is speaking symbolically, although spatiality is in God as an element in his creative ground. We say that he 'has sent'—that means that he has caused something. In this way God is subject to the category of causality. And when we speak of him and his Son, we have two different substances and apply the category of substance to him. Now all this, if taken literally, is absurd. If it is taken symbolically, it is a profound expression, the ultimate Christian expression, of the relationship between God and man in the Christian experience. But to distinguish these two kinds of speech, the non-symbolic and the symbolic, in such a point is so important that if we are not able to make understandable to our contemporaries that we speak symbolically when we use such language, they will rightly turn away from us, as from people who still live in absurdities and superstitions.

Now consider the immanent level, the level of the appearances of the divine in time and space. Here we have first of all the incarnations of the divine, different beings in time and space, divine beings transmuted into animals or men or any kinds of other beings as they appear in time and space. This is often forgotten by those within Christianity who like to use in every second theological proposition the word 'incarnation'. They forget that this is not an especially Christian characteristic, because incarnation is something which happens in paganism all the time. The divine beings always incarnate in different forms. That is very easy in paganism. This is not the real distinction between Christianity and other religions.

Here we must say something about the relationships of the transcendent to the immanent level just in connection with the incarnation idea. Historically, one must say that preceding both of them was the situation in which the transcendent and immanent were not distinguished. In the Indonesian doctrine of 'Mana', that divine mystical power which permeates all reality, we have some divine presence which is both immanent in everything as a hidden power, and at the same time transcendent, something which can be grasped only through very difficult ritual activities known to the priest.

Out of this identity of the immanent and the transcendent, the gods of the great mythologies have developed in Greece and in the Semitic nations and in India. There we find incarnations as the immanent element of the divine. The more transcendent the gods become, the more incarnations of personal or sacramental character are needed in order to overcome the remoteness of the divine which develops with the strengthening of the transcendent element.

And from this follows the second element in the immanent religious symbolism, namely, the sacramental. The sacramental is nothing else than some reality becoming the bearer of the Holy in a special way and under special circumstances. In this sense, the Lord's Supper, or better the materials in the Lord's Supper, are symbolic. Now you will ask perhaps, 'only symbolic?' That sounds as if there were something more than symbolic, namely, 'literal'. But the literal is not more but less than symbolic. If we speak of those dimensions of reality which we cannot approach in any other way than by symbols, then symbols are not used in terms of 'only' but in terms of that which is necessary, of that which we *must* apply. Sometimes, because of nothing more than the confusion of signs with symbols, the phrase 'only a symbol' means 'only a sign'. And then the question is justified. 'Only a sign?' 'No.' The sacrament is not only a sign. In the famous discussion between Luther and Zwingli, in Marburg in 1529, it was just this point on which the discussion was held. Luther wanted to maintain the genuinely symbolic character of the elements, but Zwingli said that the sacramental materials, bread and wine, are 'only symbolic'. Thus Zwingli meant that they are only signs pointing to a story of the past. Even in that period there was semantic confusion. And let us not be misled by this. In the real sense of symbol, the sacramental materials are symbols. But if the symbol is used as *only* symbol (i.e., only signs), then of course the sacramental materials are more than this.

Then there is the third element on the immanent level. Many things—like special parts of the church building, like the candles, like the water at the entrance of the Roman Church, like the cross in all churches, especially Protestant churches—were originally only signs, but in use became symbols; call them sign-symbols, signs which have become symbols.

And now a last consideration—namely, the truth of religious symbols. Here we must distinguish a negative, a positive, and an absolute statement. First the negative statement. Symbols are independent of any empirical criticism. You cannot kill a symbol by criticism in terms of natural sciences or in terms of historical research. As was said, symbols can only die if the situation in which they have been created has passed. They are not on a level on which empirical criticism can dismiss them. Here are two examples, both connected with Mary, the mother of Jesus, as Holy Virgin. First of all you have here a symbol which has died in Protestantism by the changed situation of the relation to God. The special, direct, immediate relationship to God, makes any mediating power impossible. Another reason which has made this symbol disappear is the negation of the ascetic element which is implied in the glorification of virginity. And as long as the Protestant religious situation lasts it cannot be re-established. It has not died because Protestant scholars have said, 'Now there is no empirical reason for saying all this about the Holy Virgin'. There certainly is not, but this the Roman Church also knows. But the Roman Church sticks to it on the basis of its tremendous symbolic power which step by step brings her nearer to Trinity itself, especially in the development of the last decade. If this should ever be completed as is now discussed in groups of the Roman Church, Mary would become co-Saviour with Jesus. Then, whether this is admitted or not, she is actually taken into the divinity itself.

Another example is the story of the virginal birth of Jesus. This is from the point of view of historical research a most obviously legendary story, unknown to Paul and to John. It is a late creation, trying to make understandable the full possession of the divine Spirit of Jesus of Nazareth. But again its legendary character is not the reason why this symbol will die or has died in many groups of people, in even quite conservative groups within the Protestant churches. The reason is different. The reason is that it is theologically quasi-heretical. It takes away one of the fundamental doctrines of Chalcedon, viz., the classical Christian doctrine that the full humanity of Jesus must be maintained beside his whole divinity. A human being who has no human father has no full humanity. This story then has to be criticized on inner-symbolic grounds, but not on historical grounds. This is the negative statement about the truth of religious symbols. Their truth is their adequacy to the religious situation in which they are created, and their inadequacy to another situation is their untruth. In the last sentence both the positive and the negative statement about symbols are contained.

Religion is ambiguous and every religious symbol may become idolatrous, may be demonized, may elevate itself to ultimate validity although nothing is ultimate but the ultimate itself; no religious doctrine and no religious ritual may be. If Christianity claims to have a truth superior to any other truth in its symbolism, then it is the symbol of the cross in which this is expressed, the cross of the Christ. He who himself embodies the fullness of the divine's presence sacrifices himself in order not to become an idol, another god beside God, a god into whom the disciples wanted to make him. And therefore the decisive story is the story in which he accepts the title 'Christ' when Peter offers it to him. He accepts it under the one condition that he has to go to Jerusalem to suffer and to die, which means to deny the idolatrous tendency even with respect to himself. This is at the same time the criterion of all other symbols, and it is the criterion to which every Christian church should subject itself.

[FROM: *Theology of Culture*, pp. 53–67.]

(*d*) *The Bible as a Source for Christian Theology*

[It is instructive to compare Tillich's attitude to the use of the Bible in Christian theology with Barth's (see Book 1, pp. 71ff.). The Bible is a *normative* source for Christian theology, certainly, but this does not mean that one can read off theology deductively from the Bible. For one thing the Bible does not provide the terms for an inclusive systematized theology. For another theology has to take account of the experience of a believing community like the Church. On the shelf, the Bible is not a witness to anything; it only functions in the life of the Church. Furthermore the theologian's use of the Bible needs to be related to his use of culture in general.]

If the task of systematic theology is to explain the contents of the Christian faith, three questions immediately arise: What are the sources of systematic theology? What is the medium of their reception? What is the norm determining the use of the sources? The first answer to these questions might be the Bible. The Bible is the original document about the events on which Christianity is based. Although this cannot be denied, the answer is insufficient. In dealing with the question of the sources of systematic theology, we must reject the assertion of neo-orthodox biblicism[1] that the Bible is the *only* source. The biblical message cannot be understood and could not have been received had there been no preparation for it in human religion and culture. And the biblical message would not have become a message for anyone, including the theologian himself, without the experiencing participation of the Church and of every Christian. If the 'Word of God' or the 'act of revelation' is called the source of systematic theology, it must be emphasized that the 'Word of God' is not limited to the words of a book and that the act of revelation is not the 'inspiring' of a 'book of revelations', even if the book is the document of the final 'Word of God', the fulfilment and criterion of all revelations. The biblical message embraces more (and less) than the biblical books. Systematic theology, therefore, has additional sources beyond the Bible.

The Bible, however, is the basic source of systematic theology because it is the original document about the events on which the Christian Church is founded. If we use the word 'document' for the Bible, we must exclude legal connotations. The Bible is not a legally conceived, formulated, and sealed record about a divine 'deed' on the basis of which claims can be decided. The documentary character of the Bible is identical with the fact that it contains the original witness of those who participated in the revealing events. Their participation was their response to the happenings which became revealing events through this response. The inspiration of the biblical writers is their receptive and creative response to potentially revelatory facts. The inspiration of the writers of the New Testament is their acceptance of Jesus as the Christ, and with him, of the New Being, of which they became witnesses. Since there is no revelation unless there is someone who receives it as revelation, the act of reception is a part of the event itself.

[1] Tillich here has Barth in mind (Ed.).

The Bible is both original event and original document; it witnesses to that of which it is a part.

The biblical material as a source of systematic theology is presented in a methodological way by the historical theologian. Biblical theology, in co-operation with the other disciplines of historical theology, opens the Bible as the basic source of systematic theology. But how it does this is by no means obvious. The biblical theologian, to the degree to which he is a theologian (which includes a systematic point of view), does not present pure facts to us; he gives us theologically interpreted facts. His exegesis is pneumatic (spiritual) or, as we should call it today, 'existential'. He speaks of the results of his philosophical and detached interpretation as matters of ultimate concern to him. He unites philology and devotion in dealing with the biblical texts. It is not easy to do this with fairness to both points of view. A comparison of any recent scientific commentary on Romans (e.g., C. H. Dodd or Sanday and Headlam[1]) with Barth's pneumatic-existential interpretation of it lays bare the unbridged gap between both methods. All theologians, and especially the students of systematic theology, suffer because of this situation. Systematic theology needs a biblical theology which is historical-critical without any restrictions and, at the same time, devotional-interpretative, taking account of the fact that it deals with matters of ultimate concern. It is possible to fulfil this demand, for that which concerns us ultimately is not linked with any special conclusion of historical and philological research. A theology which is dependent on predetermined results of the historical approach is bound to something conditional which claims to be unconditional, that is, with something demonic. And the demonic character of any demand imposed on the historian for definite results becomes visible in the fact that it destroys his honesty. Being ultimately concerned about what is really ultimate liberates the theologian from all 'sacred dishonesty'. It makes conservative as well as revolutionary historical criticism open to him. Only such free historical work, united with the attitude

[1] C. H. Dodd, *The Epistle to the Romans* (Fontana Books); W. Sanday and A. C. Headlam, *A Critical and Exegetical Commentary on the Epistle to the Romans*, 1895, International Critical Commentary (Ed.).

of ultimate concern, can open the Bible to the systematic theologian as his basic source.

The genesis of the Bible is an event in Church history—an event in a comparatively late stage of early Church history. The systematic theologian, therefore, in using the Bible as a source, implicitly uses Church history as a source. He must do this explicitly. Systematic theology has a direct and definite relation to Church history. On this point there is a real difference between the Catholic and the Protestant attitude, and no systematic theologian can escape a decision about it. The decision is easy for those who are bound by the authority of the Roman Church. It is also easy for those who believe that Protestantism means a radical biblicism and who assume that radical biblicism is a possible theological position. But most theologians in the non-Roman Churches are not willing to accept this alternative. It is obvious to them that the radical biblicistic attitude is a self-deception. No one is able to leap over two thousand years of Church history and become contemporaneous with the writers of the New Testament, except in the Spiritual sense of accepting Jesus as the Christ. Every person who encounters a biblical text is guided in his religious understanding of it by the understanding of all previous generations. Even the Reformers were dependent on the Roman tradition against which they protested. They directed special elements of the ecclesiastical tradition against others in order to fight the distortion which had affected the whole tradition, but they did not and could not jump out of the tradition into the situation of Matthew and Paul. The Reformers were aware of this situation, and their orthodox systematisers were still aware of it. Evangelical biblicism, both past and present, is unaware of it, and produces a 'biblical' theology which actually is dependent on definite dogmatic developments of the post-Reformation period. Through historical scholarship the difference between the dogmatic teaching of most American evangelical churches and the original meaning of the biblical texts can easily be shown. Church history cannot be evaded; therefore, it is a religious as well as a scholarly necessity that the relationship of systematic theology to the ecclesiastical tradition be stated frankly and pointedly.

Another approach which is not acceptable to most non-Roman theologians is the subjection of systematic theology to the decisions of councils and popes. Roman Catholic dogmatics uses those doctrinal traditions which have gained legal standing (*de fide*) as the real source of systematic theology. It presupposes dogmatically, with or without *a posteriori* proofs, that those doctrines whose validity is guaranteed by canon law agree essentially with the biblical message. The work of the systematic theologian is an exact and, at the same time, polemic interpretation of the statements *de fide*. This is the reason for the dogmatic sterility of Roman Catholic theology, in contrast to its liturgical and ethical creativity and the great scholarship it develops in areas of Church history which are free from dogmatic prohibitions. It is important for the ecumenical character of systematic theology that Greek Orthodox theologians, although they accept the authority of tradition, deny the legalization of tradition by papal authority. This gives the Greek Orthodox theologian creative possibilities from which Roman theologians are excluded. Protestant theology protests in the name of the Protestant principle against the identification of our ultimate concern with any creation of the Church, including the biblical writings in so far as their witness to what is really ultimate concern is also a conditioned expression of their own spirituality. Therefore, it is able to use all the materials provided by Church history. It can make use of Greek and Roman and German and modern concepts in interpreting the biblical message; it can make use of the decisions of sectarian protests against official theology; but it is not bound to any of these concepts and decisions.

A special problem arises from the fact that no one is actually able to handle all these materials, because the denominational structures operate as an unconscious and conscious principle of selection. This cannot be avoided, and it has a creative side. The ecclesiastical and theological climate in which the theologian grows up or for which he has later made a personal decision produces understanding through familiarity. Without such familiarity no existential use of the Church-historical material is possible. The systematic theologian encounters in the concrete life of his denomination in its liturgy and hymns, its sermons and sacraments, that which concerns him ultimately—the New Being in Jesus as the Christ. Therefore, the denominational tradition is a decisive source for the systematic theologian, however ecumenically he may use it.

The biblical source is made available to the systematic theologian through a critical and ultimately concerned biblical theology. In the same way Church history is made available to the systematic theologian through a historically critical and ultimately concerned history of Christian thought, formerly called 'history of dogma'. The traditional term 'dogmatics' implies a concern which the more recent term does not express. The 'history of Christian thought' can mean a detached description of the ideas of theological thinkers through the centuries. Some of the critical histories of Christian thought are not far removed from such an attitude. The historical theologian must show that in all periods Christian thought has dealt with matters of ultimate concern and that therefore it is itself a matter ol ultimate concern. Systematic theology needs a history of Christian thought written from a point of view which is radically critical and, at the same time, existentially concerned.

A broader source of systematic theology than all those mentioned so far is the material presented by the history of religion and culture. Its impact on the systematic theologian begins with the language he uses and the cultural education he has received. His spiritual life is shaped by his social and individual encounter with reality. This is expressed in the language, poetry, philosophy, religion, etc., of the cultural tradition in which he has grown up and from which he takes some content in every moment of his life, in his theological work and also outside it. Beyond this immediate and unavoidable contact with his culture and religion, the systematic theologian deals with them directly in many ways. He uses culture and religion intentionally as his means of expression, he points to them for confirmation of his statements, he fights against them as contradictions of the Christian message, and, above all, he formulates the existential questions implied in them, to which his theology intends to be the answer.

This continuous and never ending use of cultural and religious contents as a source of systematic theology raises the question: How are these contents made available for use in a way parallel to the method by which the biblical theologian makes the biblical materials available and the historian of Christian thought makes the doctrinal materials available? There is no established answer to this question, since neither a theological history of religion nor a theological history of culture has been theoretically conceived and practically established.

A theological history of religion should interpret theologically the material produced by the investigation and analysis of the pre-religious and religious life of mankind. It should elaborate the motives and types of religious expression, showing how they follow from the nature of the religious concern and therefore necessarily appear in all religions, including Christianity in so far as it is a religion. A theological history of religion also should point out demonic distortions and new tendencies in the religions of the world, pointing to the Christian solution and preparing the way for the acceptance of the Christian message by the adherents of non-Christian religions. One could say that a theological history of religion should be carried through in the light of the missionary principle that the New Being in Jesus as the Christ is the answer to the question asked implicitly and explicitly by the religions of mankind. Some materials taken from a theological history of religion appear in the present theological system.

A theological history of culture cannot be a continuous historical report (this is also true of the theological history of religion). It can only be what I like to call a 'theology of culture',[1] which is the attempt to analyse the theology behind all cultural expressions, to discover the ultimate concern in the ground of a philosophy, a political system, an artistic style, a set of ethical or social principles. This task is analytic rather than synthetic, historical rather than systematic. It is a preparation for the work of the systematic theologian. At the present time a theology of culture is continuously being constructed from the non-theological, and, less vigorously, from the theological side. It has become an important part of the many critical analyses of the present world situation, of the cultural

[1] Paul Tillich, 'Uber die Idee einer Theologie der Kultur', in *Kanstudien* (Berlin: Pan-Verlag, Rolf Heise, 1920); see also my *The Religious Situation* (New York: Henry Holt and Co., 1932).

decline of the West, of developments in special realms. Theological analysis has been carried on in connection with the history of modern thought, art, science, social movements (called in German *Geistesgeschichte,* 'the history or spiritual life'). It should, however, be worked out in a more organized way by theologians. It should be taught as 'the theology of culture' in all institutions of theological learning; for instance, as theological history of philosophy, the arts, etc. Concerning the method of such a theological analysis of culture the following might be said. The key to the theological understanding of a cultural creation is its style. Style is a term derived from the realm of the arts, but it can be applied to all realms of culture. There is a style of thought, of politics, of social life, etc. The style of a period expresses itself in its cultural forms, in its choice of objects, in the attitudes of its creative personalities, in its institutions and customs. It is an art as much as a science to 'read styles', and it requires religious intuition, on the basis of an ultimate concern, to look into the depth of a style, to penetrate to the level where an ultimate concern exercises its driving power. This, however, is what is demanded of the theological historian of culture, and in performing this function he opens up a creative source for systematic theology.

(FROM: *Systematic Theology*, I, pp. 39–45.)

2 The Existence of God

[Tillich here discuses belief in the existence of God and uses the term 'being' to do it. We can start from our ordinary use of the phrase 'human beings' for ourselves, by which we refer to our existence as separate individuals. By analogy theology has made use of the phrase 'divine being' of God, and this has often given the impression that God is to be thought of as also a separate Being, however perfect, over against finite human beings. Tillich is anxious to emphasize that God exists in a way so incommensurate with our being that strictly speaking one has to say that God does not exist—in the way human beings exist. Nevertheless their existence as 'beings' is derived from God's 'Being'—he is the cause of their effect—so that it might be better for us to think of our being, our existence, in God. We all participate in being, and it is this fact which gives their peculiar potency and effectiveness to symbols.]

The being of God is being-itself. The being of God cannot be understood as the existence of a being alongside others or above others. If God is *a* being he is subject to the categories of finitude, especially to space and substance. Even if he is called the 'highest being' in the sense of the 'most perfect' and the 'most powerful' being, this situation is not changed. When applied to God, superlatives become diminutives. They place him on the level of other beings while elevating him above all of them. Many theologians who have used the term 'highest being' have known better. Actually they have described the highest as the absolute, as that which is on a level qualitatively different from the level of any being—even the highest being. Whenever infinite or unconditional power and meaning are attributed to the highest being, it has ceased to be *a* being and has become being-itself. Many confusions in the doctrine of God and many apologetic weaknesses could be avoided if God were understood first of all as being-itself or as the ground of being. The power of being is another way of expressing the same thing in a circumscribing phrase. Ever since the time of Plato it has been known—although it often has been disregarded, especially by the nominalists[1] and their modern followers—that the concept of being as being, or being-itself, points to the power inherent in everything, the power of resisting non-being. Therefore, instead of saying that God is first of all being-itself, it is possible to say that he is the power of being in everything and above everything, the infinite power of being. A theology which does not dare to identify God and the power of being as the first step toward a doctrine of God relapses into monarchic monotheism, for if God is not being-itself he is subordinate to it, just as Zeus is subordinate to fate in Greek religion. The structure of being-itself is his fate, as it is the fate of all other beings. But God is his own fate; he is 'by himself'; he possesses 'aseity'.[2] This can be said of him only if he is the power of being, if he is being-itself.

As being-itself God is beyond the contrast of essential and existential being. We have spoken of the transition of being into existence, which involves the possibility that being will contradict and lose itself. This transition is excluded from being-itself (except in terms of the Christological paradox), for being-itself does not participate in non-being. In this it stands in contrast to every being. As classical theology has emphasized, God is beyond essence and existence. Logically, being-itself is 'before', 'prior to', the split which characterizes finite being.

For this reason it is as wrong to speak of God as the universal essence as it is to speak of him as existing. If God is understood as universal essence, as the form of all forms, he is identified with the unity and totality of finite potentialities; but he has ceased to be the power of the ground in all of them, and therefore he has ceased to transcend them. He has poured all his creative power into a system of forms, and he is bound to these forms. This is what pantheism means.

On the other hand, grave difficulties attend the attempt to speak of God as existing. In order to maintain the truth that

[1] From Latin *nominalis* ('belonging to a name'). The nominalists taught that abstract terms, like 'Being' as Tillich uses it, did not relate to anything that really existed but were mere words. (Ed.)

[2] Self-sufficient being in himself, in no way dependent on anything outside himself. (Ed.)

God is beyond essence and existence while simultaneously arguing for the existence of God, Thomas Aquinas is forced to distinguish between two kinds of divine existence: that which is identical with essence and that which is not. But an existence of God which is not united with its essence is a contradiction in terms. It makes God a being whose existence does not fulfil his essential potentialities; being and not-yet-being are 'mixed' in him, as they are in everything finite. God ceases to be God, the ground of being and meaning. What really has happened is that Thomas has had to unite two different traditions: the Augustinian, in which the divine existence is included in his essence, and the Aristotelian, which derives the existence of God from the existence of the world and which then asserts, in a second step, that his existence is identical with his essence. Thus the question of the existence of God can be neither asked nor answered. If asked, it is a question about that which by its very nature is above existence, and therefore the answer—whether negative or affirmative—implicitly denies the nature of God. It is as atheistic to affirm the existence of God as to deny it. God is being-itself, not *a* being. On this basis a first step can be taken toward the solution of the problem which usually is discussed as the immanence and the transcendence of God. As the power of being, God transcends every being and also the totality of being—the world. Being-itself is beyond finitude and infinity; otherwise it would be conditioned by something other than itself, and the real power of being would lie beyond both it and that which conditioned it. Being-itself infinitely transcends every finite being. There is no proportion or gradation between the finite and the infinite. There is an absolute break, an infinite 'jump'. On the other hand, everything finite participates in being-itself and in its infinity. Otherwise it would not have the power of being. It would be swallowed by non-being, or it never would have emerged out of non-being. This double relation of all beings to being-itself gives being-itself a double characteristic. In calling it creative we point to the fact that everything participates in the infinite power of being. In calling it abysmal we point to the fact that everything participates in the power of being in a finite way, that all beings are infinitely transcended by their creative ground.

Man is bound to the categories of finitude. He uses the two categories of relation—causality and substance—to express the relation of being-itself to finite beings. The 'ground' can be interpreted in both ways, as the cause of finite beings and as their substance. The former has been elaborated by Leibniz[1] in the line of the Thomistic tradition, and the latter has been elaborated by Spinoza[2] in the line of the mystical tradition. Both ways are impossible. Spinoza establishes a naturalistic pantheism, in contrast to the idealistic type which identifies God with the universal essence of being, which denies finite freedom and in so doing denies the freedom of God. By necessity God is merged into the finite beings, and their being is his being. Here again it must be emphasized that pantheism does not say that God is everything. It says that God is the substance of everything and that there is no substantial independence and freedom in anything finite.

Therefore, Christianity, which asserts finite freedom in man and spontaneity in the non-human realm, has rejected the category of substance in favour of the category of causality in attempting to express the relation of the power of being to the beings who participate in it. Causality seems to make the world dependent on God, and, at the same time, to separate God from the world in the way a cause is separated from its effect. But the category of causality cannot 'fill the bill', for cause and effect are not separate; they include each other and form a series which is endless in both directions. What is cause at one point in this series is effect at another point and conversely. God as cause is drawn into this series, which drives even him beyond himself. In order to disengage the divine cause from the series of causes and effects, it is called the first cause, the absolute beginning. What this means is that the category of causality is being denied while it is being used. In other words, causality is being used not as a category but as a symbol. And if this is done and is understood the difference between substance and causality disappears, for if God is the cause of the entire series of causes and effects, he is the substance underlying the whole process of becoming. But this 'underlying' does not have the character of a substance

[1] Gottfried Wilhelm Leibniz (1646–1716), German philosopher. (Ed.)
[2] Baruch Spinoza (1632–77), Dutch Jewish philosopher. (Ed.)

which underlies its accidents and which is completely expressed by them. It is an underlying in which substance and accidents preserve their freedom. In other words, it is substance not as a category but as a symbol. And, if taken symbolically there is no difference between *prima causa* and *ultima substantia*. Both mean what can be called in a more directly symbolic term 'the creative and abysmal ground of being'. In this term both naturalistic pantheism, based on the category of substance, and rationalistic theism, based on the category of causality, are overcome.

Since God is the ground of being, he is the ground of the structure of being. He is not subject to this structure; the structure is grounded in him. He *is* this structure, and it is impossible to speak about him except in terms of this structure. God must be approached cognitively through the structural elements of being-itself. These elements make him a living God, a God who can be man's concrete concern. They enable us to use symbols which we are certain point to the ground of reality.

(FROM: *Systematic Theology*, I, pp. 261–4.)

3 Faith as Ultimate Concern

[In this passage Tillich makes his famous definition of religious faith as 'ultimate concern'. When asked by a student to clarify the meaning of this term he said 'taking something with ultimate seriousness' (*Ultimate Concern,* p. 7). Tillich means by the term more than that which may be, as we say, a matter of life and death to us. It is more too than deciding what to us is most important in life. It has this subjective quality but it is also objective in that it involves the sense of being shown, being made aware, that nature or the arts or science or moral endeavour point coercively to an abiding reality.]

We have used the term 'ultimate concern' without explanation. Ultimate concern is the abstract translation of the great commandment: 'The God, our God, the Lord is one; and you shall love the Lord your God with all your heart, and with all your soul, and with all your mind, and with all your strength' (Mark 12:29 R.S.V.). The religious concern is ultimate; it excludes all other concerns from ultimate significance; it makes them preliminary. The ultimate concern is unconditional, independent of any conditions of character, desire, or circumstance. The unconditional concern is total: no part of ourselves or of our world is excluded from it; there is no 'place' to flee from it (Psalm 139). The total concern is infinite: no moment of relaxation and rest is possible in the face of a religious concern which is ultimate, unconditional, total and infinite.

The word 'concern' points to the 'existential' character of religious experience. We cannot speak adequately of the 'object of religion' without simultaneously removing its character as an object. That which is ultimate gives itself only to the attitude of ultimate concern. It is the correlate of an unconditional concern but not a 'highest thing' called 'the absolute' or 'the unconditioned', about which we could argue in detached objectivity. It is the object of total surrender, demanding also the surrender of our subjectivity while we look at it. It is a matter of infinite passion and interest (Kierkegaard), making us its object whenever we try to make it our object. For this reason we have avoided terms like '*the* ultimate', '*the* unconditioned', '*the* universal', '*the* infinite' and have spoken of ultimate, unconditional, total, infinite concern. Of course, in every concern there is *something* about which one is concerned; but this something should not appear as a separated object which could be known and handled without concern. This, then, is the first formal criterion of theology: *The object of theology is what concerns us ultimately. Only those propositions are theological which deal with their object in so far as it can become a matter of ultimate concern for us.*

The negative meaning of this proposition is obvious. Theology should never leave the situation of ultimate concern and try to play a role within the arena of preliminary concerns. Theology cannot and should not give judgements about the aesthetic value of an artistic creation, about the scientific value of a physical theory or a historical conjecture, about the best methods of medical healing or social reconstruction, about the solution of political or international conflicts. The theologian *as* theologian is no expert in any matters of preliminary concern. And, conversely, those who are experts in these matters should not *as such* claim to be experts in theology. The first formal principle of theology, guarding the boundary line between ultimate concern and preliminary concerns, protests theology as well as the cultural realms on the other side of the line.

But this is not its entire meaning. Although it does not indicate the content of the ultimate concern and its relation to the preliminary concerns, it has implications in both respects. There are three possible relations of the preliminary concerns to that which concerns us ultimately. The first is mutual indifference, the second is a relation in which a preliminary concern is elevated to ultimacy, and the third is one in which a preliminary concern becomes the vehicle of the ultimate concern without claiming ultimacy for itself. The first relation is predominant in ordinary life with its oscillation between conditional, partial, finite situations and experiences and moments when the question of the ultimate meaning of existence takes hold of us. Such a division, however, contradicts the unconditional, total and infinite character of the religious concern. It places our ultimate concern beside other concerns and deprives it of its ultimacy. This attitude sidesteps the ultimacy of the biblical commandments and that of the first theological criterion. The second relation is idolatrous in its very nature. Idolatry is the elevation of a preliminary concern to ultimacy. Something essentially conditioned is taken as unconditional, something essentially partial is boosted into universality, and something essentially finite is given infinite significance (the best example is the contemporary idolatry of religious nationalism). The conflict between the finite basis of such a concern and its infinite claim leads to a conflict of ultimates; it radically contradicts the biblical commandments and the first theological criterion. The third relation between the ultimate concern and the preliminary concerns makes the latter bearers and vehicles of the former. That which is a finite concern is not elevated to infinite significance, nor is it put beside the infinite, but in and through it the infinite becomes real. Nothing is excluded from this function. In and through every preliminary concern the ultimate concern can actualize itself. Whenever this happens, the preliminary concern becomes a possible object of theology. But theology deals with it only in so far as it is a medium, a vehicle, pointing beyond itself.

Pictures, poems, and music can become objects of theology, not from the point of view of their aesthetic form, but from the point of view of their power of expressing some aspects of that which concerns us ultimately, in and through their aesthetic form. Physical or historical or psychological insights can become objects of theology, not from the point of view of their cognitive form, but from the point of view of their power of revealing some aspects of that which concerns us ultimately in and through their cognitive form. Social ideas and actions, legal projects and procedures, political programmes and decisions, can become objects of theology, not from the point of view of their social, legal, and political form, but from the point of view of their power of actualizing some aspects of that which concerns us ultimately in and through their social, legal, and political forms. Personality problems and developments, educational aims and methods, bodily and mental healing, can become objects of theology, not from the point of view of their ethical and technical form, but from the point of view of their power of mediating some aspects of that which concerns us ultimately in and through their ethical and technical form.

The question now arises: What is the content of our ultimate concern? What *does* concern us conditionally? The answer, obviously, cannot be a special object, not even God, for the first criterion of theology must remain formal and general. If more is to be said about the nature of our ultimate concern, it must be derived from an analysis of the concept 'ultimate concern'. *Our ultimate concern is that which determines our being or non-being. Only those statements are theological which deal with their object in so far as it can become a matter of being or non-being for us.* This is the second formal criterion of theology.

Nothing can be of ultimate concern for us which does not have the power of threatening and saving our being. The term 'being' in this context does not designate existence in time and space. Existence is continuously threatened and saved by things and events which have no ultimate concern for us. But the term 'being' means the whole of human reality, the structure, the meaning, and the aim of existence. All this is threatened; it can be lost or saved. Man is ultimately concerned about his being and meaning. 'To be or not to be' in *this* sense is a matter of ultimate unconditional total, and infinite concern. Man is infinitely concerned about the infinity to which he belongs, from which he is separated, and for which he is longing. Man is totally concerned about the totality which is his true being and which is disrupted in time and space. Man is unconditionally concerned about that which conditions his being beyond all the conditions in him and around him. Man is ultimately concerned about that which determines his ultimate destiny beyond all preliminary necessities and accidents.

The second formal criterion of theology does not point to any special content, symbol, or doctrine. It remains formal and, consequently, open for contents which are able to express 'that which determines our being or non-being'. At the same time it excludes contents which do not have this power from entering the theological realm. Whether it is a god who is a being beside others (even a highest being) or an angel who inhabits a celestial realm (called the realm of 'spirits') or a man who possesses supernatural powers (even if he is called a god-man)—none of these is an object of theology if it fails to withstand the criticism of the second formal criterion of theology, that is, if it is not a matter of being or non-being for us.

(FROM: *Systematic Theology*, I, pp. 14–18.)

4 The historical Jesus and belief in Christ

[Tillich is here concerned with the crucial problem of the place of the historical Jesus in Christian belief. To what extent does the historical Jesus matter? Tillich sketches the problems of reconstructing, on the base of the findings of historical criticism, a 'Life of Jesus'. He then criticizes two common reactions to the inconclusive results of 'The quest of the historical Jesus'. One is to say that what really matters is the ethical teaching of Jesus and this can be separated from the question of belief about his person. This is the approach of the 'liberal protestantism' of people like Adolf von Harnack. The other reaction is to say that the essence of the teaching of Jesus, his 'message', is about the necessity for 'decision'. Here Tillich has in mind existentialist theologians like Bultmann. Tillich then hints generally at his own approach which would be to say that the teaching of Jesus is inseparable from his person and that everything turns on what one believes he was and did (including his teaching on this): 'The cross is the symbol of a gift before it is the symbol of a demand'.]

From the moment that the scientific method of historical research was applied to biblical literature, theological problems which were never completely absent became intensified in a way unknown to former periods of Church history. The historical method unites analytical-critical and constructive-conjectural elements. For the average Christian consciousness shaped by the orthodox doctrine of verbal inspiration, the first element was much more impressive than the second. One felt only the negative element in the term 'criticism' and called the whole enterprise 'historical criticism' or 'higher criticism', or, with reference to a recent method, 'form criticism'. In itself the term 'historical criticism' means nothing more than historical research. Every historical research criticizes its sources, separating what has more probability from that which has less or is altogether improbable. Nobody doubts the validity of this method, since it is confirmed continuously by its success; and nobody seriously protests if it destroys beautiful legends and deeply rooted prejudices. But biblical research became suspect from its very beginning. It seemed to criticize not only the historical sources but the revelation contained in these sources. Historical research and rejection of biblical authority were identified. Revelation, it was implied, covered not only the revelatory content but also the historical form in which it had appeared. This seemed to be especially true of the facts concerning the 'historical Jesus'. Since the biblical revelation is essentially historical, it appeared to be impossible to separate the revelatory content from the historical reports as they are given in the biblical records. Historical criticism seemed to undercut faith itself.

But the critical part of historical research into biblical literature is the less important part. More important is the constructive-conjectural part, which was the driving force in the whole enterprise. The facts behind the records, especially the facts about Jesus, were sought. There was an urgent desire to discover the reality of this man, Jesus of Nazareth, behind the colouring and covering traditions which are almost as old as the reality itself. So the research for the so-called 'historical Jesus' started. Its motives were religious and scientific at the same time. The attempt was courageous, noble and extremely significant in many respects. Its theological consequences are numerous and rather important. But, seen in the light of its basic intention, the attempt of historical criticism to find the empirical truth about Jesus of Nazareth was a failure. The historical Jesus, namely, the Jesus behind the symbols of his reception as the Christ, not only did not appear but receded farther and farther with every new step. The history of the attempts to write a 'life of Jesus' elaborated by Albert Schweitzer in his early work, *The Quest of the Historical Jesus*, is still valid. His own constructive attempt has been corrected. Scholars, whether conservative or radical, have become more cautious, but the methodological situation has not changed. This became manifest when R. Bultmann's bold programme of a 'demythologization of the New Testament'[1] aroused a storm in all theological camps and the slumber of Barthianism with respect to the historical problem was followed by an

[1] See Book 2, pp. 132ff.

astonished awakening. But the result of the new (and very old) questioning is not a picture of the so-called historical Jesus but the insight that there is no picture behind the biblical one which could be made scientifically probable.

This situation is not a matter of a preliminary shortcoming of historical research which will some day be overcome. It is caused by the nature of the sources itself. The reports about Jesus of Nazareth are those of Jesus as the Christ, given by persons who had received him as the Christ. Therefore, if one tries to find the real Jesus behind the picture of Jesus as the Christ, it is necessary critically to separate the elements which belong to the factual side of the event from the elements which belong to the receiving side. In doing so, one sketches a 'Life of Jesus'; and innumerable such sketches have been made. In many of them scientific honesty, loving devotion, and theological interest have worked together. In others critical detachment and even malevolent rejection are visible. But none can claim to be a probable picture which is the result of the tremendous scientific toil dedicated to this task for two hundred years. At best, they are more or less probable results, able to be the basis neither of an acceptance nor of a rejection of the Christian faith.

In view of this situation, there have been attempts to reduce the picture of the historical Jesus to the 'essentials', to elaborate a *Gestalt*[1] while leaving the particulars open to doubt. But this is not a way out. Historical research cannot paint an essential picture after all the particular traits have been eliminated because they are questionable. It remains dependent on the particulars. Consequently, the pictures of the historical Jesus in which the forms of a 'Life of Jesus' is wisely avoided still differ from one another as much as those in which such self-restriction is not applied.

The dependence of the *Gestalt* on the valuation of the particulars is evident in an example taken from the complex of what Jesus thought about himself. In order to elaborate this point, one must know, besides many other things, whether he applied the title 'Son of Man' to himself and, if so, in what sense. Every answer given to this question is a more or less probable hypothesis, but the character of the 'essential' picture

[1] *Gestalt*: general picture. (Ed.)

of the historical Jesus depends decisively on this hypothesis. Such an example clearly shows the impossibility of replacing the attempt to portray a 'Life of Jesus' by trying to paint the '*Gestalt* of Jesus'.

At the same time, this example shows another important point. People who are not familiar with the methodological side of historical research and are afraid of its consequences for Christian doctrine like to attack historical research generally and the research in the biblical literature especially, as being theologically prejudiced. If they are consistent, they will not deny that their own interpretation is also prejudiced or, as they would say, dependent on the truth of their faith. But they deny that the historical method has objective scientific criteria. Such an assertion, however, cannot be maintained in view of the immense historical material which has been discovered and often empirically verified by a universally used method of research. It is characteristic of this method that it tries to maintain a permanent self-criticism in order to liberate itself from any conscious or unconscious prejudice. This is never completely successful, but it is a powerful weapon and necessary for achieving historical knowledge.

One of the examples often given in this context is the treatment of the New Testament miracles. The historical method approaches the miracle stories neither with the assumption that they have happened because they are attributed to him who is called the Christ nor with the assumption that they have not happened because such events would contradict the laws of nature. The historical method asks how trustworthy the records are in every particular case, how dependent they are on older sources, how much they might be influenced by the credulity of a period, how well confirmed they are by other independent sources, in what style they are written, and for what purpose they are used in the whole context. All these questions can be answered in an 'objective' way without necessary interference of negative or positive prejudices. The historian never can reach certainty in this way, but he can reach high degrees of probability. It would, however, be a leap to another level if he transformed historical probability into positive or negative historical certainty by a judgement of faith (as will be shown at a later point). This clear distinction is often confused by the obvious fact that the understanding of the meaning of a text is partly dependent on the categories of understanding used in the encounter with texts and records. But it is not wholly dependent on them, since there are philological as well as other aspects which are open to an objective approach. Understanding demands one's participation in what one understands, and we can participate only in terms of what we are, including our own categories of understanding. But this 'existential' understanding should never prejudice the judgement of the historian concerning facts and relations. The person whose ultimate concern is the content of the biblical message is in the same position as the one who is indifferent to it if such questions are discussed as the development of the Synoptic tradition, or the mythological and legendary elements of the New Testament. Both have the same criteria of historical probability and must use them with the same rigour, although doing so may affect their own religious or philosophical convictions or prejudices. In this process, it may happen that prejudices which close the eyes to particular facts open them to others. But this 'opening of the eyes' is a personal experience which cannot be made into a methodological principle. There is only one methodological procedure, and that is to look at the subject matter and not at one's own looking at the subject matter. Actually, such looking is determined by many psychological, sociological, and historical factors. These aspects must be neglected intentionally by everyone who approaches a fact objectively. One must not formulate a judgement about the self-consciousness of Jesus from the fact that one is a Christian—or an anti-Christian. It must be derived from a degree of plausibility based on records and their probable historical validity. This, of course, presupposes that the content of the Christian faith is independent of this judgement.

The search for the historical Jesus was an attempt to discover a minimum of reliable facts about the man Jesus of Nazareth, in order to provide a safe foundation for the Christian faith. This attempt was a failure. Historical research provided probabilities about Jesus of a higher or lower degree. On the basis of these probabilities, it sketched 'Lives of Jesus'. But they were more like novels than biographies, they certainly could not provide a safe foundation for the Christian faith. Christianity is not based on the acceptance of a historical novel; it is based on the witness to the messianic character of Jesus by people who were not interested at all in a biography of the Messiah.

The insight into this situation induced some theologians to give up any attempt to construct a 'life' or a *Gestalt* of the historical Jesus and to restrict themselves to an interpretation of the 'words of Jesus'. Most of these words (though not all of them) do not refer to himself and can be separated from any biographical context. Therefore, their meaning is independent of the fact that he may or may not have said them. On that basis the insoluble biographical problem has no bearing on the truth of the words rightly or wrongly recorded as the words of Jesus. That most of the words of Jesus have parallels in contemporaneous Jewish literature is not an argument against their validity. This is not even an argument against their uniqueness and power as they appear in collections like the Sermon on the Mount, the parables, and the discussions with foes and followers alike.[1]

A theology which tries to make the words of Jesus into the historical foundation of the Christian faith can do so in two ways. It can treat the words of Jesus as the 'teachings of Jesus' or as the 'message of Jesus'. As the teachings of Jesus, they are understood as refined interpretations of the natural law or as original insights into the nature of man. They have no relation to the concrete situation in which they are spoken. As such, they belong to the law, prophecy, or Wisdom literature such as is found in the Old Testament. They may transcend all three categories in terms of depth and power; but they do not transcend them in terms of character. The retreat in historical research to the 'teachings of Jesus' reduces Jesus to the level of the Old Testament and implicitly denies his claim to have overcome the Old Testament context.

The second way in which historical research restricts itself to the words of Jesus is more profound than the first. It denies

[1] This refers also to the discovery of the Dead Sea Scrolls, which—in spite of much sensationalism in the publicity given to it—has opened the eyes of many people to the problem of biblical research but which has not changed the theological situation at all.

that the words of Jesus are general rules of human behaviour, that they are rules to which one has to subject one's self, or that they are universal and can therefore be abstracted from the situation in which they were spoken. Instead, they emphasize Jesus' message that the Kingdom of God is 'at hand' and that those who want to enter it must decide for or against the Kingdom of God. These words of Jesus are not general rules but concrete demands. This interpretation of the historical Jesus, suggested especially by Rudolf Bultmann, identifies the meaning of Jesus with that of his message. He calls for a decision, namely, the decision for God. And this decision includes the acceptance of the Cross, by his own acceptance of the Cross. The historically impossible, namely, to sketch a 'life' of a *Gestalt* of Jesus, is ingeniously avoided by using the immediately given—namely, his message about the Kingdom of God and its conditions—and by keeping as nearly as possible to the 'paradox of the Cross of Christ'. But even this method of restricted historical judgement cannot give a foundation to the Christian faith. It does not show how the requirement of deciding for the Kingdom of God can be fulfilled. The situation of having to decide remains one of being under the law. It does not transcend the Old Testament situation, the situation of the quest for the Christ. One could call this theology 'existentialist liberalism' in contrast to the 'legalist liberalism' of the first. But neither method can answer the question of wherein lies the power to obey the teachings of Jesus or to make the decision for the Kingdom of God. This these methods cannot do because the answer must come from a new reality, which, according to the Christian message, is the New Being in Jesus as the Christ. The Cross is the symbol of a gift before it is the symbol of a demand. But, if this is accepted, it is impossible to retreat from the being of the Christ to his words. The last avenue of the search for the historical Jesus is barred, and the failure of the attempt to give a foundation to the Christian faith through historical research becomes obvious.

This result would probably have been more easily acknowledged if it had not been for the semantic confusion about the meaning of the term 'historical Jesus'. The term was predominantly used for the results of historical research into the character and life of the person who stands behind the Gospel reports. Like all historical knowledge, our knowledge of this person is fragmentary and hypothetical. Historical research subjects this knowledge to methodological scepticism and to continuous change in particulars as well as essentials. Its ideal is to reach a high degree of probability, but in many cases this is impossible.

The term 'historical Jesus' is also used to mean that the event 'Jesus as the Christ' has a factual element. The term in this sense raises the question of faith and not the question of historical research. If the factual element in the Christian event were denied, the foundation of Christianity would be denied. Methodological scepticism about the work of historical research does not deny this element. Faith cannot even guarantee the name 'Jesus' in respect to him who was the Christ. It must leave that to the incertitudes of our historical knowledge. But faith does guarantee the factual transformation of reality in that personal life which the New Testament expresses in its picture of Jesus as the Christ. No fruitful and honest discussion is possible if these two meanings of the term 'historical Jesus' are not clearly distinguished.

(FROM: *Systematic Theology*, II, pp. 116–23.)

5 The Cross and Resurrection of Christ

[The crucifixion and the resurrection of Christ test the realism of the Christian's belief. Because the Incarnation was real it meant participating in the whole reach of the human tragic experience including death. As genuine history the crucifixion can be mistaken for 'one more tragic event'. Similarly the resurrection is a real conquest of life over death, although it can be taken as only a vulgar wonder-story.

The resurrection is an ambiguous sign to faith and not an indisputable event that can be established by some historical reconstruction. There have been attempts at the latter like the stories of the empty tomb, or the suggestion that the resurrection means the survival of the soul of Jesus, or finally the idea that it relates only to some interior experience of the disciples. Tillich then presents his own 'restitution-theory'. His meaning is very elusive, and readers will find it useful to ponder whether this presentation of the resurrection as the continuing power of the Christ as the New Being is essentially any different from Bultmann's treatment (see Book 2, pp. 141ff.).]

The 'Cross of the Christ' and the 'Resurrection of the Christ' are interdependent symbols; they cannot be separated without losing their meaning. The Cross of the Christ is the Cross of the one who has conquered the death of existential estrangement. Otherwise it would only be one more tragic event (which it *also* is) in the long history of the tragedy of man. And the Resurrection of the Christ is the Resurrection of the one who, as the Christ, subjected himself to the death of existential estrangement. Otherwise it would be only one more questionable miracle story (which it also is in the records).

If Cross and Resurrection are interdependent, they must be both reality and symbol. In both cases something happened within existence. Otherwise the Christ would not have entered existence and could not have conquered it. But there is a qualitative difference. While the stories of the Cross probably point to an event that took place in the full light of historical observation, the stories of the Resurrection spread a veil of deep mystery over the event. The one is a highly probable fact; the other a mysterious experience of a few. One can ask whether this qualitative difference does not make a real interdependence impossible? Is it perhaps wiser to follow the suggestion of those scholars who understand the Resurrection as a symbolic interpretation of the Cross without any kind of objective reality?[1]

The New Testament lays tremendous significance on the objective side of the Resurrection; at the same time, it elevates the objective event indicated in the stories of the Crucifixion to universal symbolic significance. One could say that in the minds of the disciples and of the writers of the New Testament the Cross is both an event and a symbol and that the Resurrection is both a symbol and an event. Certainly, the Cross of Jesus is seen as an event that happened in time and space. But, as the Cross of the Jesus who is the Christ, it is a symbol and a part of a myth. It is the myth of the bearer of the new eon who suffers the death of a convict and slave under the powers of that old eon which he is to conquer. This Cross, whatever the historical circumstances may have been, is a symbol based on a fact.

But the same is true of the Resurrection. The resurrection of gods and half-gods is a familiar mythological symbol. It plays a major role in some mystery cults in which mystical participation in the death and the resurrection of the god on the part of the initiated is the ritual centre. A belief in the future resurrection of the martyrs grew up in later Judaism. In the moment in which Jesus was called the Christ and the combination of his messianic dignity with an ignominious death was asserted—whether in expectation or in retrospection—the application of the idea of resurrection to the Christ was almost unavoidable. The disciples' assertion that the symbol had become an event was dependent in part upon their belief in Jesus, who, as the Christ, became the Messiah. But it was affirmed in a way which transcended the mythological symbolism of the mystery cults, just as the concrete picture of Jesus as the Christ transcended the mythical pictures of the

[1] Tillich has Bultmann in mind, see Book 2, pp. 141ff. (Ed.)

mystery gods. The character of this event remains in darkness, even in the poetic rationalization of the Easter story. But one thing is obvious. In the days in which the certainty of his Resurrection grasped the small, dispersed, and despairing group of his followers, the Church was born, and, since the Christ is not the Christ without the Church, he has become the Christ. The certainty that he who is the bringer of the new eon cannot finally have succumbed to the powers of the old eon made the experience of the Resurrection the decisive test of the Christ-character of Jesus of Nazareth. A real experience made it possible for the disciples to apply the known symbol of resurrection to Jesus, thus acknowledging him definitely as the Christ. They called this experienced event the 'Resurrection of the Christ', and it was a combination of event and symbol.

The attempt has been made to describe both events, the Cross and the Resurrection, as factual events separated from their symbolic meaning. This is justified, in so far as the significance of both symbols rests on the combination of symbol and fact. Without the factual element, the Christ would not have participated in existence and consequently not have been the Christ. But the desire to isolate the factual from the symbolic element is, as has been shown before, not a primary interest of faith. The results of the research for the purely factual element can never be on the basis of faith or theology.

With this in mind, one can say that the historical event underlying the Crucifixion story shines with comparative clarity through the different and often contradictory legendary reports. Those who regard the passion story as cult-legend, which is told in various ways, simply agree with the thesis presented about the symbolic character of the Cross of the Jesus who is the Christ. The only factual element in it having the immediate certainty of faith is the surrender of him who is called the Christ to the ultimate consequence of existence, namely, death under the conditions of estrangement. Everything else is a matter of historical probability, elaborated out of legendary interpretation.

The event which underlies the symbol of the Resurrection must be treated in an analogous way. The factual element is a necessary implication of the symbol of the Resurrection (as it is of the symbol of the Cross). Historical research is justified in trying to elaborate this factual element on the basis of the legendary and mythological material which surrounds it. But historical research can never give more than a probable answer. The faith in the Resurrection of the Christ is neither positively nor negatively dependent on it. Faith can give certainty only to the victory of the Christ over the ultimate consequence of the existential estrangement to which he subjected himself. And faith can give this certainty because it is itself based on it. Faith is based on the experience of being grasped by the power of the New Being through which the destructive consequences of estrangement are conquered.

It is the certainty of one's own victory over the death of existential estrangement which creates the certainty of the Resurrection of the Christ as event and symbol; but it is not historical conviction or the acceptance of biblical authority which creates this certainty. Beyond this point there is no certainty but only probability, often very low, sometimes rather high.

There are three theories which try to make the event of the Resurrection probable. The most primitive theory, and at the same time most beautifully expressed, is the physical one. It is told in the story of the tomb which the women found empty on Easter morning. The sources of this story are rather late and questionable, and there is no indication of it in the earliest tradition concerning the event of the Resurrection, namely, 1 Corinthians, chapter 15. Theologically speaking, it is a rationalization of the event, interpreting it with physical categories that identify resurrection with the presence or absence of a physical body. Then the absurd question arises as to what happened to the molecules which comprise the corpse of Jesus of Nazareth. Then absurdity becomes compounded into blasphemy.

A second attempt to penetrate into the factual side of the Resurrection event is the spiritualistic one. It uses, above all, the appearances of the Resurrected as recorded by Paul. It explains them as manifestations of the soul of the man Jesus to his followers, in analogy to the self-manifestations of the souls of the dead in spiritualistic experiences. Obviously, this is not the Resurrection of the Christ but an attempt to prove the general immortality of the soul and the claim that it has the general ability after death to manifest itself to the living. Spiritualistic experiences may or may not be valid. But, even if valid, they cannot explain the factual side of the Resurrection of the Christ symbolized as the reapparance of the total personality, which includes the bodily expression of his being. This is so much the case that he can be recognized in a way which is more than the manifestation of a bodiless 'spirit'.

The third attempt to approach the factual side of the Resurrection is the psychological one. It is the easiest and most accepted way of describing the factual element in the Resurrection. Resurrection is an inner event in the minds of Jesus' adherents. Paul's description of the Resurrection experiences (including his own) lends itself to the psychological interpretation. And—if we exclude the physical interpretation—Paul's words, like the story of his conversion, point to something which happened in the minds of those who had the experiences. This does not imply that the event itself was 'merely' psychological, namely, wholly dependent on psychological factors in the minds of those whom Paul enumerates (e.g., an intensification of the memory of Jesus). But the psychological theory misses the reality of the event which is presupposed in the symbol—the event of the Resurrection of the Christ.

The preceding theory concerning the event which underlies the symbol of Resurrection dismisses physical as well as spiritualistic literalism. It replaces both by a description which keeps nearer to the oldest source (1 Cor., chap. 15) and which places at the centre of its analysis the religious meaning of the Resurrection for the disciples (and all their followers), in contrast to their previous state of negativity and despair. This view is the ecstatic confirmation of the indestructible unity of the New Being and its bearer, Jesus of Nazareth. In eternity they belong together. In contrast to the physical, the spiritualistic, and the psychological theories concerning the Resurrection event, one could call this the 'restitution theory'. According to it, the Resurrection is the restitution of Jesus as the Christ, a restitution which is rooted in the personal unity between Jesus and God and in the impact of this unity on the minds of the apostles. Historically, it may well be that the restitution of Jèsus to the dignity of the Christ in the minds of the disciples may precede the story of the acceptance of Jesus as the Christ by Peter. The latter may be a reflex of the former; but, even if this is the case, the experience of the New Being in Jesus must precede the experience of the Resurrected.

Although it is my conviction that the restitution theory is most adequate to the facts, it must also be considered a theory. It remains in the realm of probability and does not have the certainty of faith. Faith provides the certainty that the picture of the Christ in the Gospels is a personal life in which the New Being has appeared in its fullness and that the death of Jesus of Nazareth was not able to separate the New Being from the picture of its bearer. If physical or spiritualistic literalists are not satisfied with this solution, they cannot be forced to accept it in the name of faith. But they can perhaps grant that the attitude of the New Testament and especially of the non-literalistic Apostle Paul justifies the theory of restitution.

(FROM: *Systematic Theology*, II, pp. 176–82.)

FOR FURTHER STUDY AND DISCUSSION

1 Theology and religion are often taken to be the same thing. How would you distinguish them? Is religious belief necessary for the study of theology?
2 Is the use of paradox, metaphor and symbol necessary in religious language? How would you distinguish poetic language from religious language?
3 What are the advantages and disadvantages of thinking of God in terms of 'Being'? Can you suggest a better category?
4 How does Tillich's approach to the Bible compare with Barth's?
5 Compare Tillich and Bultmann on the meaning of the resurrection of Christ.
6 'One is tempted to say that for Tillich the meaning of Christian belief is exhausted in the present attitude and experience of the believer' (H. A. Meynell). Is it true to say that Tillich tends to dissolve the content of faith into our subjective attitudes to it?

FOR FURTHER READING

Principal Works of Paul Tillich

The Protestant Era, London, 1957.

The Courage to be, London (Fontana Books), 1962.

The New Being, London, 1956.

The Shaking of the Foundations, London (Pelican Books), 1962.

The Eternal Now, Sermons, London, 1963.

Morality and Beyond, London, 1964.

Systematic Theology, London, Vol. I 1953, Vol. II 1957, Vol. III 1964.

Theology of Culture, New York (Galaxy Books), 1964.

Ultimate Concern: Tillich in dialogue, London, 1965 (useful for Tillich's clarifications of some of the obscurities in his *Systematic Theology*).

Some Books about Paul Tillich

Charles W. Kegley and Robert W. Bretall (Eds.), *The theology of Paul Tillich*, London, 1952. (A volume of essays by theologians and philosophers on various aspects of Tillich's thought, with a chapter of autobiography and replies to criticisms by Tillich himself.)

Walter Leibrecht (Ed.), *Religion and culture*: essays in honour of Paul Tillich, London, 1959.

G. H. Tavard, *Paul Tillich and the Christian message*, London, 1962. (An examination of Tillich's theology by a Roman Catholic theologian.)

J. Heywood Thomas, *Paul Tillich*: an appraisal, London, 1963.

A. J. McElway, *The Systematic Theology of Paul Tillich*: a review and analysis, London, 1964 (an exposition of the contents of the three volumes of Tillich's *Systematic Theology*).

FOR GENERAL BACKGROUND READING

John Macquarrie, *Twentieth-century Religious Thought*, 1963.
——, *God-talk*, 1967.
——, *God and Secularity*, 1968.
Frederick Ferré, *Language, Logic and God*, 1962.
——, *Basic Modern Philosophy of Religion*, 1968.
David E. Jenkins, *Guide to the Debate about God*, 1966.
Colin Williams, *Faith in a Secular Age*, 1966.
E. L. Mascall, *The Secularisation of Christianity*, 1965.
H. Gollwitzer, *The Existence of God as confessed by faith*, 1964.
A. M. Ramsey, *God, Christ and the World*, 1969.
T. W. Ogletree, *The Death of God Controversy*, 1966.

4. Reinhold Niebuhr

1892–1971

BIOGRAPHICAL INTRODUCTION

Reinhold Niebuhr was born in 1892 in Wright City, Missouri, where his father Gustav Niebuhr was the German pastor. Like Tillich he paid warm tribute in later life to the influence of his father: 'The first formative religious influence on my life was my father, who combined a vital personal piety with a complete freedom in his theological studies.'

Niebuhr began his theological studies at Elmhurst College and theological seminary, and then graduated at the University of Yale. He was appointed pastor in Detroit in 1915 just at the time when the Ford Motor Company was beginning its spectacular expansion. His experiences at Detroit influenced him, Niebuhr said later, more than any of the books he had hitherto read. He became vividly aware 'of the irrelevance of the mild moralistic idealism, which I had identified with the Christian faith, to the power realities of our modern technical society'. His youthful optimism was undermined by the 'social realities of Detroit' and 'the moral pretensions of Henry Ford'. An entry in his journal for 1927 explains what he meant by this phrase:

> The new Ford car is out. The town is full of talk about it. Newspaper reports reveal that it is the topic of the day in all world centers. Crowds storm every exhibit to get the first glimpse of this new creation. Mr. Ford has given out an interview saying that the car has cost him about a hundred million dollars and that after finishing it he still has about a quarter of a billion dollars in the bank.
>
> I have been doing a little arithmetic and have come to the conclusion that the car cost Ford workers at least fifty million in lost wages during the past year. No one knows how many hundreds lost their homes in the period of unemployment, and how many children were taken out of school to help fill the depleted family exchequer, and how many more children lived on short rations during this period. Mr. Ford refuses to concede that he made a mistake in bringing the car out so late. He has a way of impressing the

public even with his mistakes. We are now asked to believe that the whole idea of waiting a year after the old car stopped selling before bringing out a new one was a great advertising scheme which reveals the perspicacity of this industrial genius. But no one asks about the toll in human lives.

What a civilization is this ! Naïve gentlemen with a genius for mechanics suddenly become the arbiters over the lives and fortunes of hundreds of thousands. Their moral pretensions are credulously accepted at full value. No one bothers to ask whether an industry which can maintain a cash reserve of a quarter of a billion ought not to make some provision for its unemployed. It is enough that the new car is a good one. Here is a work of art in the only realm of art which we can understand. We will therefore refrain from making undue ethical demands upon the artist. Artists of all the ages have been notoriously unamenable to moral discipline. The cry of the hungry is drowned in the song, 'Henry has made a lady out of Lizzy'.[1]

Out of this experience came such books as *Moral Man and Immoral Society* (1932) and *The Nature and Destiny of Man* (1941). In 1928 Niebuhr was appointed Professor of Christian Ethics at Union Theological Seminary, New York, remaining there until his retirement in 1960. Niebuhr both as writer and speaker exercised great influence on social and religious thinking in both America and Britain especially during and after the Second World War. The poet W. H. Auden owed much in the development of his religious beliefs, especially about its social implications, to Reinhold Niebuhr and his wife Ursula to whom the volume *Nones* (1942) is dedicated.

Niebuhr died on 31 May 1971.

[1] *Leaves from the notebook of a tamed cynic* (entry for 1927), pp. 180–1.

SELECTIONS

1 Man as a Problem to Himself

[One of the most memorable features of Niebuhr's writing is his exposition of the Christian concept of man. He is particularly skilful in striking a fine balance between those contradictory elements in man which make him as Pascal put it 'ni ange ni bête' (neither angel nor animal). This extract shows how the commonly accepted view of man in the West has been a blend of classical (especially Greek) and Judaeo-Christian traditions. He then characterizes these two traditions: the classical view, where man as made in the image of God is interpreted in terms of his rational capacity, and the Christian where the image of God is not a possession (like reason) but a relationship to God in which he may (or may not) wish to stand.]

Man has always been his own most vexing problem. How shall he think of himself? Every affirmation which he may make about his stature, virtue, or place in the cosmos becomes involved in contradictions when fully analysed. The analysis reveals some presupposition or implication which seems to deny what the proposition intended to affirm.

If man insists that he is a child of nature and that he ought not to pretend to be more than the animal which he obviously is, he tacitly admits that he is, at any rate, a curious kind of animal who has both the inclination and the capacity to make such pretensions. If on the other hand he insists upon his unique and distinctive place in nature and points to his rational faculties as proof of his special eminence, there is usually an anxious note in his avowals of uniqueness which betrays his unconscious sense of kinship with the brutes. This note of anxiety gives a poignant significance to the heat and animus in which the Darwinian controversy[1] was conducted

[1] The controversy about the evolution of human life, especially man's 'descent from the apes', which followed the publication of Charles Darwin's *The Origin of Species* (1859) and *The Descent of Man* (1871). (Ed.)

and the Darwinian thesis was resisted by the traditionalists. Furthermore the very effort to estimate the significance of his rational faculties implies a degree of transcendence over himself which is not fully defined or explained in what is usually connoted by 'reason'. For the man who weighs the importance of his rational faculties is in some sense more than 'reason', and has capacities which transcend the ability to form general concepts.

If man takes his uniqueness for granted he is immediately involved in questions and contradictions on the problem of his virtue. If he believes himself to be essentially good and attributes the admitted evils of human history to specific social and historical causes, he involves himself in begging the question; for all these specific historical causes of evil are revealed, upon close analysis, to be no more than particular consequences and historical configurations of evil tendencies in man himself. They cannot be understood at all if a capacity for, and inclination towards, evil in man himself are not presupposed. If, on the other hand, man comes to pessimistic conclusions about himself, his capacity for such judgements would seem to negate the content of the judgements. How can man be 'essentially' evil if he knows himself to be so? What is the character of the ultimate subject, the quintessential 'I', which passes such devastating judgements upon itself as object?

If one turns to the question of the value of human life and asks whether life is worth living, the very character of the question reveals that the questioner must in some sense be able to stand outside of, and to transcend, the life which is thus Judged and estimated. Man can reveal this transcendence more explicitly not only by actually committing suicide, but by elaborating religions and philosophies which negate life and regard a 'lifeless' eternity, such as Nirvana,[1] as the only possible end of life.

Have those who inveigh so violently against otherworldliness in religion, justified as their criticisms may be, ever fully realized what the error of denying life implies in regard to the

[1] Nirvana, a sanskrit word meaning literally 'coolness' and denoting in Buddhism the state of equilibrium or non-attachment when one has learned how to be free from the clamorous demands of the self. (Ed.)

stature of man? The man who can negate 'life' must be something other than mere vitality. Every effort to dissuade him from the neglect of natural vitality and historic existence implies a vantage point in him above natural vitality and history; otherwise he could not be tempted to the error from which he is to be dissuaded.

Man's place in the universe is subject to the same antinomies. Men have been assailed periodically by qualms of conscience and fits of dizziness for pretending to occupy the centre of the universe. Every philosophy of life is touched with anthropocentric tendencies. Even theocentric religions believe that the Creator of the world is interested in saving man from his unique predicament. But periodically man is advised and advises himself to moderate his pretensions and admit that he is only a little animal living a precarious existence on a second-rate planet, attached to a second-rate sun. There are moderns who believe that this modesty is the characteristic genius of modern man and the fruit of his discovery of the vastness of interstellar spaces; but it was no modern astronomer who confessed, 'When I consider thy heavens, the work of thy fingers, the moon and the stars, which thou hast ordained; What is man, that thou art mindful of him?' (Ps. 8:3–4). Yet the vantage point from which man judges his insignificance is a rather significant vantage point. This fact has not been lost on the moderns, whose modesty before the cosmic immensity was modified considerably by pride in their discovery of this immensity. It was a modern, the poet Swinburne, who sang triumphantly:

> The seal of his knowledge is sure, the truth and his spirit are wed; . . .
>
> Glory to Man in the highest ! for man is the master of things,

thereby proving that the advance of human knowledge about the world does not abate the pride of man.

While these paradoxes of human self-knowledge are not easily reduced to simpler formulae, they all point to two facts about man: one of them obvious and the other not quite as obvious. The two are not usually appreciated with equal sympathy. The obvious fact is that man is a child of nature, subject to its vicissitudes, compelled by its necessities, driven by its impulses, and confined within the brevity of the years which nature permits its varied organic forms, allowing them some, but not too much, latitude. The other less obvious fact is that man is a spirit who stands outside of nature, life, himself, his reason and the world. This latter fact is appreciated in one or the other of its aspects by various philosophies. But it is not frequently appreciated in its total import. That man stands outside of nature in some sense is admitted even by naturalists who are intent upon keeping him as close to nature as possible. They must at least admit that he is *homo faber*, a tool-making animal. That man stands outside the world is admitted by rationalists who, with Aristotle, define man as a rational animal and interpret reason as the capacity for making general concepts. But the rationalists do not always understand that man's rational capacity involves a further ability to stand outside himself, a capacity for selftranscendence, the ability to make himself his own object, a quality of spirit which is usually not fully comprehended or connoted in '*ratio*' or '*nous*' or 'reason' or any of the concepts which philosophers usually use to describe the uniqueness of man.

How difficult it is to do justice to both the uniqueness of man and his affinities with the world of nature below him is proved by the almost unvarying tendency of those philosophies, which describe and emphasize the rational faculties of man or his capacity for self-transcendence, to forget his relation to nature and to identify him, prematurely and unqualifiedly, with the divine and the eternal; and of naturalistic philosophies to obscure the uniquesness of man.

The Classical View of Man

Though man has always been a problem to himself, modern man has aggravated that problem by his too simple and premature solutions. Modern man, whether idealist or naturalist, whether rationalist or romantic, is characterized by his simple certainties about himself. He has aggravated the problem of understanding himself because these certainties are either in contradiction with each other or in contradiction with the obvious facts of history, more particularly of contemporary history; and either they have been controverted by that history or they are held in defiance of its known facts. It is not unfair to affirm that modern culture, that is, our culture since the Renaissance, is to be credited with the greatest advances in the understanding of nature and with the greatest confusion in the understanding of man. Perhaps this credit and debit are logically related to each other.

Fully to appreciate the modern conflicts in regard to human nature it is necessary to place the characteristically modern doctrines of man in their historic relation to the traditional views of human nature which informed Western culture. All modern views of human nature are adaptations, transformations and varying compounds of primarily two distinctive views of man: (*a*) The view of classical antiquity, that is of the Graeco-Roman world, and (*b*) the Biblical view. It is important to remember that, while these two views are distinct and partly incompatible, they were actually merged in the thought of mediaeval Catholicism. (The perfect expression of this union is to be found in the Thomistic synthesis of Augustinian and Aristotelian thought.) The history of modern culture really begins with the destruction of this synthesis, foreshadowed in nominalism, and completed in the Renaissance and Reformation. In the dissolution of the synthesis, the Renaissance distilled the classical elements out of the synthesis and the Reformation sought to free the Biblical from the classical elements. Liberal Protestantism is an effort (on the whole an abortive one) to reunite the two elements. There is, in fact, little that is common between them. What was common in the two views was almost completely lost after modern thought had reinterpreted and transmitted the classical view of man in the direction of a greater naturalism. Modern culture has thus been a battleground of two opposing views of human nature. This conflict could not be resolved. It ended in the more or less complete triumph of the modernized classical view of man, a triumph which in this latter day is imperilled not by any external foe but by confusion within its own household. To validate this analysis of the matter requires at least a brief preliminary analysis of the classical and the Christian views of human nature.

The classical view of man, comprised primarily of Platonic, Aristotelian and Stoic conceptions of human nature, contains, of course, varying emphases, but it may be regarded as one in its common conviction that man is to be understood primarily from the standpoint of the uniqueness of his rational faculties. What is unique in man is his *nous*. *Nous* may be translated as 'spirit', but the primary emphasis lies upon the capacity for thought and reason. In Aristotle the *nous* is the vehicle of purely intellectual activity and is a universal and immortal principle which enters man from without. Only one element in it, the 'passive' in distinction to the 'active' *nous*, becomes involved in, and subject to, the individuality of a particular physical organism. How completely the Aristotelian *nous* is intellectual may best be understood by Aristotle's explicit denial of its capacity for self-consciousness. It does not make itself its own object except in making things known the object of consciousness: 'No mind knows itself by participation in the known; it becomes known by touching and knowing, so that the same thing is mind and object of mind.'[1] This definition is the more significant when contrasted with Aristotle's conception of divine consciousness which expresses itself only in terms of self-knowledge.

In Plato the *nous* or *logistikon* is not as sharply distinguished from the soul as in Aristotle. It is, rather, the highest element in the soul, the other two being the spirited element (θυμοειδές) and the appetitive element (ἐπιθυμητικόν). In both Plato and Aristotle 'mind' is sharply distinguished from the body. It is the unifying and ordering principle, the organ of *logos*, which brings harmony into the life of the soul, as *logos* is the creative and forming principle of the world. Greek metaphysical presuppositions are naturally determinative for the doctrine of man; and since Parmenides[2] Greek philosophy had on the one hand assumed an identity between being and reason and on the other had presupposed that reason works upon some formless or unformed stuff which is never completely tractable. In the thought of Aristotle matter is 'a remnant, the non-existent in itself unknowable and alien to reason, that remains

[1] *Physics*, 20.

[2] Parmenides, sixth to fifth century B.C., Greek philosopher. (Ed.)

after the process of clarifying the thing into form and conception. This non-existent neither is nor is not; it is "not yet", that is to say it attains reality only in so far as it becomes the vehicle of some conceptual determination.'[1]

Plato and Aristotle thus share a common rationalism, and also a common dualism which is explicit in the case of Plato and implicit and covert in the case of Aristotle.[2] The effect of this rationalism and dualism has been determinative for the classical doctrine of man and for all modern doctrines which are borrowed from it. The consequences are: (*a*) The rationalism practically identifies rational man (who is essential man) with the divine; for reason is, as the creative principle, identical with God. Individuality is no significant concept, for it rests only upon the particularity of the body. In the thought of Aristotle only the active *nous*, precisely the mind which is not involved in the soul, is immortal; and for Plato the immutability of ideas is regarded as a proof of the immortality of the spirit. (*b*) The dualism has the consequence for the doctrine of man of identifying the body with evil and of assuming the essential goodness of mind or spirit. This body-mind dualism and the value judgements passed upon both body and mind stand in sharpest contrast to the Biblical view of man, and achieve a fateful influence in all subsequent theories of human nature. The Bible knows nothing of a good mind and an evil body.

While Stoicism, as a monistic and pantheistic philosophy, sharply diverges from the Aristotelian and Platonic concepts in many respects, its view of human nature betrays more similarities than differences. The similarities are great enough, at any rate, to constitute it a part of the general 'classical' picture of man. The Stoic reason is more immanent in both the world process and in the soul and body of man than in Platonism; yet man is essentially reason. Even the dualism is not completely lacking. For while Stoicism is not always certain

[1] Cf. Werner Jaeger, *Aristotle*, Ch. VIII.

[2] Despite Aristotles naturalism, his psychology is dependent upon Plato's and it may be wrong to speak of his dualism as covert. It was fairly explicit. He believed that life without the body was the soul's normal state and that its sojourn in the body was a severe illness. Cf. Jaeger, ibid., p. 51.

whether the reason which governs man must persuade him to emulate nature as he finds it outside of his reason or whether it, being a special spark of the divine reason, must set him against the impulses of nature, it arrives on the whole at convictions which do not qualify the classical concepts essentially.[1] The emphasis upon human freedom in its psychology overcomes the pantheistic naturalism of its metaphysics; and its completely negative attitude towards the passions and the whole impulsive life of man sets reason in contrast to the impulses of the body, however much it conceives reason as basically the principle of harmony within the body.

Obviously, the Platonic, Aristotelian and Stoic conceptions which define the 'classical' view of man do not exhaust Greek speculations about human nature. Modern vitalism and romanticism have their antecedents in the earlier Dionysian religion, in Heraclitus' [2] conception of ultimate reality as Flux and Fire and more particularly in the development of the Dionysian theme in Greek tragedy.[3] Subsequent mysticism is anticipated in Orphism and Pythagoreanism.[4] Even more significant for developments in contemporary culture, Democritus

[1] The confusion in Stoic thought between the reason in man and the reason in nature, a confusion which was perpetuated constantly in eighteenth-century borrowings from Stoicism, is clearly revealed in Diogenes Laërtius' account of Zeno's thought. He writes: 'When rational animals are endowed with reason in token of a more complete superiority, life in them in accordance with nature is rightly understood to mean life in accordance with reason. For reason is like a craftsman, shaping impulses and desires. Hence Zeno's definition of the end is to live in conformity with nature, which means to live a life of virtue; for it is virtue to which nature leads. On the other hand a virtuous life is one which conforms to our experience of the course of nature, our human natures being parts of universal nature.' Diogenes Laërtius VII, 85.

[2] Heraclitus, *c.* 536–470 B.C., Greek philosopher. (Ed.)

[3] Nietzsche in his *Birth of Tragedy* claims the Greek dramatists too unreservedly for his vitalistic philosophy. The significance of the tragedies lies in the unresolved conflict between the Olympian and Dionysian, the rational and the vitalistic, principles in Greek thought. Significantly Zeus, the god of order and measure, remains the ultimate arbiter in the Greek tragedies.

[4] Orphism: one of the Greek mystery-religions, flourishing in the sixth century B.C. Pythagoreanism: the teaching of Pythagoras and his school which were influential from the sixth to the fourth century B.C. (Ed.)

and Epicurus[1] interpreted man, in accordance with their naturalism and materialism, not as standing outside of nature by the quality of his unique reason, but as wholly a part of nature. This Greek materialism was no less rationalistic than Platonism or Aristotelianism, but it reduced the immanental reason in the world to mechanical necessity and sought to understand man in terms of this mechanism. It was by combining Stoic with Democritan and Epicurean naturalism that modern culture arrived at concepts which were to express some of its most characteristic interpretations of man as primarily a child of nature.

It must be observed that, while the classical view of human virtue is optimistic when compared with the Christian view (for it finds no defect in the centre of human personality) and while it has perfect confidence in the virtue of the rational man, it does not share the confidence of the moderns in the ability of all men to be either virtuous or happy. Thus an air of melancholy hangs over Greek life which stands in sharpest contrast to the all-pervasive optimism of the now dying bourgeois culture, despite the assumption of the latter that it had merely restored the classical world view and the Greek view of man. 'There is nothing, methinks, more piteous than a man, of all things that creep and breathe upon the earth', declares Zeus in the *Iliad*, and that note runs as a consistent strain through Greek thought from Homer to the Hellenistic age. Primarily it was the brevity of life and the mortality of man which tempted the Greeks to melancholy. They were not dissuaded from this mood either by Plato's assurance of immortality nor yet by Epicurus' counsel that death need not be feared, since there was nothing on the other side of the grave.

Aristotle confessed that 'not to be born is the best thing and death is better than life', and gave it as his opinion that melancholy was a concomitant of genius. The philosophers were optimistic in their confidence that the wise man would be virtuous; but, alas, they had no confidence that the many could be wise. The Stoic Chrysippus[2] could conceive happiness

[1] Democritus (*c.* 460–360 B.C.), materialist philosopher. Epicurus (341–270 B.C.), taught that pleasure and happiness are the natural aims of life. (Ed.)

[2] Chrysippus (280–209 B.C.), one of the leaders of the Stoic School. (Ed.)

only for the wise and was certain that most men were fools. The Stoics tended on the one hand to include all men in the brotherhood of man on the ground that they all had the spark of divine reason; but on the other hand they pitied the multitude for having no obvious graces of rationality. Thus their equalitarianism rapidly degenerated into an aristocratic condescension not very different from Aristotle's contempt for the slave as a 'living tool'. Seneca,[1] despite his pious universalism, prays 'forgive the world: they are all fools'.

Neither Greek nor Roman classicists had any conception of a meaning in human history. History was a series of cycles, a realm of endless recurrences. Aristotle maintained that the arts and sciences were lost and found again not once but an infinite number of times.[2] Zeno envisaged the end of the world as a huge conflagration which would destroy the world's body. This pessimism about both man and his history is the natural consequence of the mind-body dualism which characterizes Greek thought far beyond the limits of Platonism. It culminated invariably in the conviction that the body is a tomb (σῶμασῆμα),[3] a conviction which makes neo-Platonism the logical consummation of Greek thought.

The pessimism of Greek tragedy is somewhat difierent from that of the philosophers and most nearly approaches the Christian interpretation of life. But, unlike Christian thought, it has no answer for the problem it presents. In Aeschylus and Sophocles[4] the capricious jealousy of Zeus against mortal men of Homeric legend had been transmuted into the lawlessness of human passions. But, unlike the philosophers, the dramatists see human passions as something more than mere impulses of the body. The principle of order and measure, represented by Zeus, is constantly defied by vitalities in human life which are creative as well as destructive. The tragedy of human history consists precisely in the fact that human life cannot be creative without being destructive, that biological urges are enhanced

[1] Seneca (A.D. 4–65), a Roman stoic, and tutor of Nero. (Ed.)

[2] Cf. S. H. Butcher on 'The Melancholy of the Greeks', in *Some Aspects of the Greek Genius.*

[3] Cf. E. Bevan, *Stoics and Sceptics*, p. 100.

[4] Aeschylus (525–456 B.C.) and Sophocles (496–406 B.C.), Greek dramatists. (Ed.)

and sublimated by daemonic spirit and that this spirit cannot express itself without committing the sin of pride. The heroes of Greek tragedy are always being counselled to remember their mortality and to escape νέμεσις[1] by observing a proper restraint. But the ὕβρις which offends Zeus is an inevitable concomitant of their creative action in history. The tragic heroes are heroes precisely because they disregard this prudent advice of moderation. In that sense Greek tragedy is an explication of Nietzsche's observation: 'Every doer loves his deeds much more than it deserves to be loved; and the best deeds are born out of such an excess of love that they could not be worthy of it, even though their worth be very great.'[2] The various vitalities of human history are moreover not only in conflict with Zeus but in conflict with each other. There is no simple resolution of the conflict between the state and the family, usually symbolized as a conflict between man and woman, the latter representing the community of blood and family in contrast to the political community (as in *Iphigenia at Aulis* and in *Antigone*).[3] The conflict in Greek tragedy is, in short, between Gods, between Zeus and Dionysius; and not between God and the devil, nor between spirit and matter. The spirit of man expresses itself in his vital energies as well as in the harmonizing force of mind; and while the latter, as the rational principle of order, is the more ultimate (here the dramatists remain typically Greek) there can be creativity in human affairs only at the price of disturbing this order.

Thus life is at war with itself, according to Greek tragedy. There is no solution, or only a tragic solution, for the conflict between the vitalities of life and the principle of measure. Zeus remains God. But one is prompted to both admiration and pity toward those who defy him. It is significant that this profound problem posed by Greek tragedy was never sensed by the moderns, who revived classicism and ostensibly built their view of man upon Greek thought. They may have understood or misunderstood Plato and Aristotle; but the message of

[1] Retribution. (Ed.)

[2] *Kritik und Zukunft der Kultur*, Ch. IV, Par. 13.

[3] *Iphigenia at Aulis*, play by Euripides (480–406 B.C.); *Antigone*, play by Sophocles. (Ed.)

Aeschylus and Sophocles was neither understood nor misunderstood. It was simply neglected, except as the minor romantic note in modern culture appreciated and partly misunderstood it.

The Christian View of Man

The Christian view of man, which modern culture ostensibly rejects in its entirety but by which its estimate of human nature is influenced more than it realizes, will be more fully analysed in this book. At this point we must briefly anticipate subsequent elaborations by distinguishing the Christian view from the classical doctrine of man. As the classical view is determined by Greek metaphysical presuppositions, so the Christian view is determined by the ultimate presuppositions of Christian faith. The Christian faith in God as Creator of the world transcends the canons and antinomies of rationality, particularly the antinomy between mind and matter, between consciousness and extension. God is not merely mind who forms a previously given formless stuff. God is both vitality and form and the source of all existence. He creates the world. This world is not God; but it is not evil because it is not God. Being God's creation, it is good.

The consequence of this conception of the world upon the view of human nature in Christian thought is to allow an appreciation of the unity of body and soul in human personality which idealists and naturalists have sought in vain. Furthermore it prevents the idealistic error of regarding the mind as essentially good or essentially eternal and the body as essentially evil. But it also obviates the romantic error of seeking for the good in man-as-nature and for evil in man-as-spirit or as reason. Man is, according to the Biblical view, a created and finite existence in both body and spirit. Obviously a view which depends upon an ultra-rational presupposition is immediately endangered when rationally explicated; for reason, which seeks to bring all things into terms of rational coherence, is tempted to make one known thing the principle of explanation and to derive all other things from it. Its most natural inclination is to make itself that ultimate principle, and thus in effect to declare itself God. Christian psychology and philosophy have never completely freed themselves from this fault, which explains why naturalists plausibly though erroneously regard Christian faith as the very fountain source of idealism.

This is also the reason why the Biblical view of the unity of man as body and soul has often seemed to be no more than the consequence of primitive Hebraic psychology. In Hebrew thought the soul of man resides in his blood and the concept of an immortal mind in a mortal body remains unknown to the end. It is true that certain distinctions are gradually made. At first both *ruach* and *nephesh*[1] mean little more than 'breath'; but they are gradually distinguished and *ruach* becomes roughly synonymous with spirit or *nous* and *nephesh* with soul or *psyche*. But, unlike Greek thought, this distinction does not lead to dualistic consequences. The monism of the Biblical view is something other than the failure to differentiate *physis*, *psyche* and *nous*, which characterized Greek thought before Anaxagoras[2]; nor is it merely the consequence of an undeveloped psychology. It is ultimately derived from the Biblical view of God as the Creator of the Biblical faith in the goodness of creation.

The second important characteristic of the Christian view of man is that he is understood primarily from the standpoint of God, rather than from the uniqueness of his rational faculties or his relation to nature. He is made in the 'image of God'. It has been the mistake of many Christian rationalists to assume that this term is no more than a religious-pictorial expression of what philosophy intends when it defines man as a rational animal. We have previously alluded to the fact that the human spirit has the special capacity of standing continually outside itself in terms of indefinite regression. Consciousness is a capacity for surveying the world and determining action from a governing centre. Self-consciousness represents a further degree of transcendence in which the self makes itself its own object

[1] *ruach*, Hebrew for 'breath, wind, the Spirit'; *nephesh*, Hebrew for 'self'. (Ed.)

[2] Anaxagoras (*c.* 430 B.C.), Greek philosopher. (Ed.)

in such a way that the ego is finally always subject and not object. The rational capacity of surveying the world, of forming general concepts and analysing the order of the world, is thus but one aspect of what Christianity knows as 'spirit'. The self knows the world, in so far as it knows the world, because it stands outside both itself and the world, which means that it cannot understand itself except as it is understood from beyond itself and the world.

This essential homelessness of the human spirit is the ground of all religion; for the self which stands outside itself and the world cannot find the meaning of life in itself or the world. It cannot identify meaning with causality in nature; for its freedom is obviously something different from the necessary causal links of nature. Nor can it identify the principle of meaning with rationality, since it transcends its own rational processes, so that it may, for instance, ask the question whether there is a relevance between its rational forms and the recurrences and forms of nature. It is this capacity of freedom which finally prompts great cultures and philosophies to transcend rationalism, and to seek for the meaning of life in an unconditioned ground of existence. But from the standpoint of human thought this unconditioned ground of existence, this God, can be defined only negatively. This is why mystic religions in general, and particularly the neo-Platonic tradition in Western culture, have one interesting similarity with Christianity and one important difference in their estimate of human nature. In common with Christianity they measure the depth of the human spirit in terms of its capacity for self-transcendence. Thus Plotinus defines *nous* not as Aristotle defines it. For him it is primarily the capacity for self-knowledge and it has no limit short of the eternal. Mysticism and Christianity agree in understanding man from the standpoint of the eternal. But since mysticism leads to an undifferentiated ultimate reality, it is bound to regard particularity, including individuality, as essentially evil. All mystic religions therefore have the characteristic of accentuating individuality, in as far as individuality is inherent in the capacity for self-consciousness emphasized in mysticism and is something more than mere bodily particularity; but all mystic philosophies ultmately lose the very individuality which they first emphasize, because they sink finite particularity in a distinctionless divine ground of existence.

God as will and personality, in concepts of Christian faith, is thus the only possible ground of real individuality, though not the only possible presupposition of self-consciousness. But faith in God as will and personality depends upon faith in His power to reveal Himself. The Christian faith in God's self-disclosure culminating in the revelation of Christ, is thus the basis of the Christian concept of personality and individuality. In terms of this faith man can understand himself as a unity of will which finds its end in the will of God. We thus have in the problem of human nature one of the many indications of the relation of general and special revelation which concerns theology so perennially. The conviction that man stands too completely outside of both nature and reason to understand himself in terms of either without misunderstanding himself, belongs to general revelation in the sense that any astute analysis of the human situation must lead to it. But if man lacks a further revelation of the divine he will also misunderstand himself when he seeks to escape the conditions of nature and reason. He will end by seeking absorption in a divine reality which is at once all and nothing. To understand himself truly means to begin with a faith that he is understood from beyond himself, that he is known and loved of God and must find himself in terms of obedience to the divine will. This relation of the divine to the human will makes it possible for man to relate himself to God without pretending to be God, and to accept his distance from God as a created thing without believing that the evil of his nature is caused by this finiteness. Man's finite existence in the body and in history can be essentially affirmed, as naturalism wants to affirm it. Yet the uniqueness of man's spirit can be appreciated even more than idealism appreciates it, though always preserving a proper distinction between the human and divine. Also the unity of spirit and body can be emphasized in terms of its relation to a Creator and Redeemer who created both mind and body. These are the ultra-rational foundations and presuppositions of Christian wisdom about man.

This conception of man's stature is not, however, the complete Christian picture of man. The high estimate of the human stature implied in the concept of 'image of God' stands in paradoxical juxtaposition to the low estimate of human virtue in Christian thought. Man is a sinner. His sin is defined as rebellion against God. The Christian estimate of human evil is so serious precisely because it places evil at the very centre of human personality—in the will. This evil cannot be regarded complacently as the inevitable consequence of his finiteness or the fruit of his involvement in the contingencies and necessities of nature. Sin is occasioned precisely by the fact that man refuses to admit his 'creatureliness' and to acknowledge himself as merely a member of a total unity of life. He pretends to be more than he is. Nor can he, as in both rationalistic and mystic dualism, dismiss his sins as residing in that part of himself which is not his true self, that is, that part of himself which is involved in physical necessity. In Christianity it is not the eternal man who judges the finite man; but the eternal and holy God who judges sinful man. Nor is redemption in the power of the eternal man who gradually sloughs off finite man. Man is not divided against himself so that the essential man can be extricated from the non-essential. Man contradicts himself within the terms of his true essence. His essence is free self-determination. His sin is the wrong use of his freedom and its consequent destruction.

Man is an individual, but he is not self-sufficing. The law of his nature is love, a harmonious relation of life to life in obedience to the divine centre and source of his life. This law is violated when man seeks to make himself the centre and source of his own life. His sin is therefore spiritual and not carnal, though the infection of rebellion spreads from the spirit to the body and disturbs its harmonies also. Man, in other words, is a sinner not because he is one limited individual within a whole but rather because he is betrayed, by his very ability to survey the whole, to imagine himself the whole.

The fact that human vitality inevitably expresses itself in defiance of the laws of measure can be observed without the presuppositions of the Christian faith. The analysis of this fact in Greek tragedy has already been observed. But it is impossible without the presuppositions of the Christian faith to find the source of sin within man himself. Greek tragedy regards human evil as the consequence of a conflict between vitality and form, between Dionysian and Olympian divinities. Only in a religion of revelation, whose God reveals Himself to man from beyond himself and from beyond the contrast of vitality and form, can man discover the root of sin to be within himself. The essence of man is his freedom. Sin is committed in that freedom. Sin can therefore not be attributed to a defect in his essence. It can only be understood as a self-contradiction, made possible by the fact of his freedom but not following necessarily from it.

Christianity, therefore, issues inevitably in the religious expression of an uneasy conscience. Only within terms of the Christian faith can man not only understand the reality of the evil in himself, but escape the error of attributing that evil to any one but himself. It is possible of course to point out that man is tempted by the situation in which he stands. He stands at the juncture of nature and spirit. The freedom of his spirit causes him to break the harmonies of nature, and the pride of his spirit prevents him from establishing a new harmony. The freedom of his spirit enables him to use the forces and processes of nature creatively; but his failure to observe the limits of his finite existence causes him to defy the forms and restraints of both nature and reason. Human self-consciousness is a high tower looking upon a large and inclusive world. It vainly imagines that it is the large world which it beholds and not a narrow tower insecurely erected amidst the shifting sands of the world.

(FROM: *The Nature and Destiny of Man*, Vol. I, pp. 1–18.)

2 'WHERE A CHRIST IS, AND IS NOT, EXPECTED'

[In this section Niebuhr provides a useful key for classifying and studying the religions of the world. Religions 'where a Christ is expected' are those which take history and time seriously since it is believed that they are vehicles of divine revelation. Judaism and Christianity are examples of such religions. Religions 'where a Christ is not expected' are those where history and time are not taken seriously because they belong to the world of unreality, what the Hindus call *maya* (illusion). Examples of such religions would be Graeco-Roman religion, Hinduism and Buddhism.]

A basic distinction may be made between various interpretations of the meaning of life by noting their attitude towards history. Those which include history in the realm of meaning see it as a process which points and moves towards a fuller disclosure and realization of life's essential meaning. Those which exclude it, do so because they regard history as no more than natural finiteness, from which the human spirit must be freed. They consider man's involvement in nature as the very cause of evil, and define the ultimate redemption of life as emancipation from finiteness. In the one case history is regarded as potentially meaningful, waiting for the ultimate disclosure and realization of its meaning. In the other case it is believed to be essentially meaningless. It may be regarded as a realm of order; but the order is only the subordinate one of natural necessity which affects the meaning of life negatively. It is a mortal coin which must be shuffled off.

The difference in the attitude of various cultures towards history is determined by contradictory estimates of man's transcendence over himself. In the one case it is assumed that since this capacity for self-transcendence represents the highest capacity of the human spirit, the fulfilment of life must naturally consist in man's emancipation from the ambiguities of history. His partial immersion in and partial transcendence over nature must be transmuted into a total transcendence. Some sort of eternity is therefore the goal of human striving in non-historical religions and philosophies; and the eternity which is man's end is the fulfilment of history to the point of being its negation. In this eternity there is 'no separation of thing from thing, no part standing in isolated existence estranged from the rest and therefore nowhere is there any wronging of another'.[1]

In religions which regard history as contributing to the meaning of life the attitude towards man's partial involvement in, and partial transcendence over, the process of nature and

[1] Plotinus, *Enneads,* III, ii:1.

the flux of time is totally different. This ambiguous situation is not regarded as the evil from which man must be redeemed. The evil in the human situation arises, rather, from the fact that men seek to deny or to escape prematurely from the uncertainties of history and to claim a freedom, a transcendence and an eternal and universal perspective which is not possible for finite creatures. The problem of sin rather than finiteness is, in other words, either implicitly or explicitly the basic problem of life. Yet the problem of finiteness is not eliminated. It is recognized that a man who stands in an historical process is too limited in vision to discern the full meaning of that process, and too limited in power to fulfil the meaning, however much the freedom of his knowledge and his power is one element in the stuff of history. Hence the temporal problem of human history and destiny in historical religion is: how the transcendent meaning of history is to be disclosed and fulfilled, since man can discern only partial meanings and can only partially realize the meaning he discerns. In modern corruptions of historical religion this problem is solved very simply by the belief that the cumulative effects of history will endow weak man with both the wisdom and the power to discern and to fulfil life's meaning.

In the more profound versions of historical religion it is recognized, however, that there is no point in history, whatever the cumulations of wisdom and power, in which the finiteness of man is overcome so that he could complete his own life, or in which history as such does not retain the ambiguity of being rooted in nature-necessity on the one hand while pointing towards transcendent, 'eternal' and trans-historical ends on the other hand.

Historical religions are therefore by their very nature prophetic-Messianic. They look forward at first to a point in history and finally towards an eschaton (end) which is also the end of history, where the full meaning of life and history will be disclosed and fulfilled. Significantly, as in the optimistic expectations of a 'day of the Lord' which the first great literary prophet, Amos, found at hand and criticized, these Messianic expectations begin as expressions of national hope and expectations of national triumph. Only gradually it is realized that man's effort to deny and to escape his finiteness in imperial ambitions and power add an element of corruption to the fabric of history and that this corruption becomes a basic characteristic of history and a perennial problem from the standpoint of the fulfilment of human history and destiny. It is recognized that history must be purged as well as completed; and that the final completion of history must include God's destruction of man's abortive and premature efforts to bring history to its culmination.

The basic distinction between historical and non-historical religions and cultures may thus be succinctly defined as the difference between those which expect and those which do not expect a Christ. A Christ is expected wherever history is regarded as potentially meaningful but as still awaiting the full disclosure and fulfilment of its meaning. A Christ is not expected wherever the meaning of life is explained from the standpoint of either nature or supernature in such a way that a transcendent revelation of history's meaning is not regarded as either possible or necessary. It is not regarded as possible when, as in various forms of naturalism, the visions and ambitions of historical existence which point beyond nature are regarded as illusory, and nature-history is believed to be incapable of receiving disclosures of meaning which point beyond itself. It is not regarded as necessary when man's capacity for freedom and self-transcendence is believed to be infinitely extensible until the ambiguities of history are left behind and pure eternity is achieved. The significance of a Christ is that he is a disclosure of the divine purpose, governing history within history. Wherever it is believed that man's capacity to transcend self and history can be dissociated from his finiteness, the meaning of salvation is conceived as essentially redemption from history, obviating any necessity of, or desire for, the fulfilment of man in history, or for the disclosure of history's ultimate meaning.

A Christ is expected wherever history is thought of as a realm of fragmentary revelations of a purpose and power transcending history, pointing to a fuller disclosure of that purpose and power. He is expected because this disclosure is regarded as both possible and necessary. It is regarded as possible because history is known to be something more than the nature-necessity in which it has its roots. It is regarded as necessary because the potential meaningfulness of history is recognized as fragmentary and corrupted. It must be completed and clarified.

The interpretation of the cultures of the world in this fashion according to their possession, or lack, of Messianic expectations, draws upon insights which are possible only after the logic of Messianic expectations has reached its culmination in the Christian belief that these expectations have been fulfilled in Christ. It is not possible to interpret cultures according to their expectation or want of expectation of *a* Christ without drawing upon the faith that *the* Christ has been revealed; for there can be no interpretation of the meaning of life and history without implicitly or explicitly drawing into the interpretation the faith which claims to have found the end of these expectations. This is to say, merely, that there can be no interpretation of history without specific presuppositions and that the interpretation which is being attempted in these pages is based upon Christian presuppositions. The Christian answer to the problem of life is assumed in the discussion of the problem. In that sense our interpretation is, as every interpretation must be in the final analysis, 'dogmatic' or confessional. Yet it is not purely dogmatic or confessional; for it seeks to analyse the question and expectations for which a particular epic of history is regarded as the answer, and also to determine why these questions and expectations are not universal in history. Such an analysis must begin with a further inquiry into the character of non-historical forms of culture which regard Christ as 'foolishness' because they have no questions for which Christ is the answer and no expectations and hopes for which his Cross is the fulfilment.

(FROM: *The Nature and Destiny of Man*, Vol. II, pp. 2–6.)

3 ON MYTH AND ITS PLACE IN THE CHRISTIAN RELIGION

[In this extract from one of what Niebuhr called his 'sermonic essays' he provides a powerful argument for the necessity of myth and metaphor in religious, and especially Christian language. In the course of the argument he discusses in an illuminating way the permanent truth and value of the 'myths' of Creation, 'The Fall of Man', Incarnation and Atonement, Judgement to come. Readers will find it instructive to compare this extract with those by Bultmann and Tillich on 'myth' (see Book 2, pp. 132ff and Book 3, pp. 177ff.).]

Among the paradoxes with which St Paul describes the character, the vicissitudes and the faith of the Christian ministry, the phrase 'as deceivers yet true' is particularly intriguing. Following immediately after the phrase 'by evil report and good report' it probably defines the evil reports which were circulated about him as charges of deception and dishonesty. This charge is refuted with his 'yet true'. But the question arises why the charge is admitted before it is refuted. Perhaps this is done merely for the sake of preserving an unbroken line of paradoxical statements. If this be the case, a mere canon of rhetorical style has prompted a very profound statement. For what is true in the Christian religion can be expressed only in symbols which contain a certain degree of provisional and superficial deception. Every apologist of the Christian faith might well, therefore, make the Pauline phrase his own. We do teach the truth by deception. We are deceivers, yet true.

The necessity for the deception is given in the primary characteristic of the Christian world view. Christianity does not believe that the natural, temporal and historic world is self-derived or self-explanatory. It believes that the ground and the fulfilment of existence lie outside of existence, in an eternal and divine will. But it does not hold, as do many forms of dualism, that there is an eternal world separate and distinct from the temporal world. The relation between the temporal and the eternal is dialectical. The eternal is revealed and expressed in the temporal but not exhausted in it. God is not the sum total of finite occasions and relationships. He is their ground and they are the creation of His will. But, on the other hand, the finite world is not merely a corrupt emanation from the ideal and eternal. Consequently the relation of time and eternity cannot be expressed in simple rational terms. It can be expressed only in symbolic terms. A rational or logical expression of the relationship invariably leads either to a pantheism in which God and the world are identified, and the temporal in its totality is equated with the eternal; or in which they are separated so that a false super-naturalism emerges, a dualism between an eternal and spiritual world without content and a temporal world without meaning or significance.

I

Before analysing the deceptive symbols which the Christian faith uses to express this dimension of eternity in time, it might be clarifying to recall that artists are forced to use deceptive symbols when they seek to portray two dimensions of space upon the single dimension of a flat canvas. Every picture which suggests depth and perspective draws angles not as they are but as they appear to the eye when it looks into depth. Parallel lines are not drawn as parallel lines but are made to appear as if they converged on the horizon; for so they appear to the eye when it envisages a total perspective. Only the most primitive art and the drawings made by very small children reveal the mistake of portraying things in their true proportions rather than as they are seen. The necessity of picturing things as they seem rather than as they are, in order to record on one dimension what they are in two dimensions, is a striking analogy, in the field of space, of the problem of religion in the sphere of time.

Time is a succession of events. Yet mere succession is not time. Time has reality only through a meaningful relationship of its successions. Therefore time is real only as it gives successive expressions of principles and powers which lies outside of it. Yet every suggestion of the principle of a process must be expressed in terms of the temporal process, and every idea of the God who is the ground of the world must be expressed in some term taken from the world. The temporal process is like the painter's flat canvas. It is one dimension upon which two dimensions must be recorded. This can be done only by symbols which deceive for the sake of truth.

Great art faces the problem of the two dimensions of time as well as the two dimensions of space. The portrait artist, for instance, is confronted with the necessity of picturing a character. Human personality is more than succession of moods. The moods of a moment are held together in a unity of thought and feeling, which gives them, however seemingly capricious, a considerable degree of consistency. The problem of the artist is to portray the inner consistency of a character which is never fully expressed in any one particular mood or facial expression. This can be done only by falsifying physiognomic details. Portraiture is an art which can never be sharply distinguished from caricature. A moment of time in a personality can be made to express what transcends the moment of time only if the moment is not recorded accurately. It must be made into a symbol of something beyond itself.

This technique of art explains why art is more closely related to religion than science. Art describes the world not in terms of its exact relationships. It constantly falsifies these relationships, as analysed by science, in order to express their total meaning.

II

The Christian religion may be characterized as one which has transmuted primitive religious and artistic myths and symbols without fully rationalizing them. Buddhism is much more rational than Christianity. In consequence Buddhism finds the finite and temporal world evil. Spinozism is a more rational version of God and the world than the biblical account; but it finds the world unqualifiedly good and identical with God. In the biblical account the world is good because God created it; but the world is not God. Every Christian myth, in one way or another, expresses both the meaningfulness and the incompleteness of the temporal world, both the majesty of God and his relation to the world.

We are deceivers yet true, when we say that God created the world. Creation is a mythical idea which cannot be fully rationalized. It has therefore been an offence to the philosophers who, with the scientists, have substituted the idea of causality for it. They have sought to explain each subsequent event by a previous cause. Such an explanation of the world leads the more naïve thinkers to a naturalism which regards the world as self-explanatory because every event can be derived from a previous one. The more sophisticated philosophers will at least, with Aristotle, seek for a first cause which gives an original impetus to the whole chain of causation. But such a first cause does not have a living relationship with the events of nature and history. It does not therefore account for the emergence of novelty in each new event. No new fact or event in history is an arbitrary novelty. It is always related to a previous event. But it is a great error to imagine that this relationship completely accounts for the new emergence. In both nature and history each new thing is only one of an infinite number of possibilities which might have emerged at that particular juncture. It is for this reason that, though we can trace a series of causes in retrospect, we can never predict the future with accuracy. There is a profound arbitrariness in every given fact, which rational theories of causation seek to obscure. Thus they regard a given form of animal life as rational because they can trace it historically to another form or relate it in terms of genus and species to other types of life. Yet none of these relationships, whether historical or schematic, can eliminate the profound arbitrariness of the givenness of things.

It is therefore true, to account for the meaningfulness of life in terms of the relation of every thing to a creative centre and source of meaning. But the truth of creation can be expressed only in terms which outrage reason. Involved in the idea of creation is the concept of making something out of nothing. The *Shepherd* of Hermas[1] declares 'First of all believe that God is one, who created and set in order all things and caused the universe to exist out of nothing.' This was the constant reiteration of Christian belief, until in very modern times it was thought possible to substitute the idea of evolutionary

[1] A second-century Christian writing. (Ed.)

causation for the idea of creation. The idea of creation out of nothing is profoundly ultrarational; for human reason can deal only with the stuff of experience, and in experience the previous event and cause are seen, while the creative source of novelty is beyond experience.

The idea of creation relates the ground of existence to existence and is therefore mythical rather than rational. The fact that it is not a rational idea does not make it untrue or deceptive. But since it is not rational it is a temptation to deceptions. Every mythical idea contains a primitive deception and a more ultimate one. The primitive error is to regard the early form in which the myth is stated as authoritative. Thus the Christian religion is always tempted to insist that belief in creation also involves belief in an actual forming of man out of a lump of clay, or in an actual creative activity of six days. It is to this temptation that biblical literalism succumbs. But there is also a more ultimate source of error in the mythical statement of religious belief. That is to regard the relation of each fact and event in history to a Divine Creator as obviating the possibility of an organic relation to other facts and events according to a natural order. By this error, which Etienne Gilson[1] calls 'theologism,' Christian theology is constantly tempted to deny the significance of the natural order, and to confuse the scientific analysis of its relationships. At the rise of modern thought Malebranche developed a doctrine of 'occasionalism' which expressed this error of Christian theology in its most consistent form. But it has been a persistent error in Christian thought and one which arises naturally out of the mythical statement of the idea of creation. The error is analogous to that of certain types of art which completely falsify the natural relations of objects in order to express their ultimate significance.

We are deceivers, yet true, when we say that men fell into evil. The story of the fall of man in the Garden of Eden is a primitive myth which modern theology has been glad to disavow, for fear that modern culture might regard belief in it as a proof of the obscurantism of religion. In place of it we have substituted various accounts of the origin and the nature of evil in human life. Most of these accounts, reduced to their

[1] In his *Unity of Philosophical Experience.*

essentials, attribute sin to the inertia of nature, or the hypertrophy of impulses, or to the defect of reason (ignorance), and thereby either explicitly or implicitly place their trust in developed reason as the guarantor of goodness. In all of these accounts the essential point in the nature of human evil is missed, namely that it arises from the very freedom of reason with which man is endowed. Sin is not so much a consequence of natural impulses, which in animal life do not lead to sin, as of the freedom by which man is able to throw the harmonies of nature out of joint. He disturbs the harmony of nature when he centres his life about one particular impulse (sex or the possessive impulse, for instance) or when he tries to make himself, rather than God, the centre of existence. This egoism is sin in its quintessential form. It is not a defect of creation but a defect which becomes possible because man has been endowed with a freedom not known in the rest of creation.

The idea of the fall is subject to the error of regarding the primitive myth of the garden, the apple and the serpent, as historically true. But even if this error is not committed, Christian thought is still tempted to regard the fall as an historical occurrence. The fall is not historical. It does not take place in any concrete human act. It is the presupposition of such acts. It deals with an area of human freedom which, when once expressed in terms of an act, is always historically related to a previous act or predisposition. External descriptions of human behaviour are therefore always deterministic. That is the deception into which those are betrayed who seek to avoid the errors of introspection by purely external descriptions of human behaviour. What Christianity means by the idea of the fall can only be known in introspection. The consciousness of sin and the consciousness of God are inextricably involved with each other. Only as the full dimension of human existence is measured, which includes not only the dimension of historical breadth but the dimension of trans-historical freedom, does the idea of the fall of man achieve significance.

It is interesting to note that Christian theology has usually regarded the fall as an historical occurrence, even when it did not accept the primitive myth of the Garden of Eden. It therefore spoke of a perfection before the fall as if that too were an historical era. Even the sophisticated dialectical theology of Barth and his school speaks of the perfection before the fall as historical, and consequently elaborates a doctrine of human sinfulness which approaches, and sometimes surpasses, the extremism of the historic doctrine of total depravity. The perfection before the fall is an ideal possibility which men can comprehend but not realize. The perfection before the fall is, in a sense, the perfection before the act. Thus we are able to conceive of a perfectly disinterested justice; but when we act our own achievements will fall short of this standard. The rationalists always assume that, since men are able to conceive of perfect standards of justice, such standards will be realized as soon as all men become intelligent enough to conceive them. They do not realize that intelligence offers no guarantee of the realization of a standard, and that the greatest idealists, as well as the most cynical realists or the most ignorant victims of an immediate situation, fall short in their action; nor that such falling short arises not simply from the defect of the mind but from an egoistic corruption of the heart. Self intrudes itself into every ideal, when thought gives place to action. The deceptions to which the idea of the fall give rise are many; and all of them have been the basis of error at some time or other in the history of Christian theology. We are deceivers, yet true in clinging to the idea of the fall as a symbol of the origin and the nature of evil in human life.

III

We are deceivers, yet true, when we affirm that God became man to redeem the world from sin. The idea of eternity entering time is intellectually absurd. This absurdity is proved to the hilt by all the theological dogmas which seek to make it rational. The dogmas which seek to describe the relation of God the Father (the God who does not enter history) and God the son (the God of history) all insist that the Son is equal to the Father and yet is not equal to Him. In the same way all the doctrines of the two natures of Christ assert that he is not less divine for being human and temporal and not less human and temporal for being fully divine. Quite obviously it is impossible to assert that the eternal ground of existence has entered existence and not sacrificed its eternal and unconditioned quality, without outraging every canon of reason. Reason may deal with the conditioned realities of existence in their relationships and it may even point to the fathomless depth of creativity out of which existential forms are born. But it cannot assert that the Divine Creator has come into creation without losing His unconditioned character. The truth that the Word was made flesh outrages all the canons by which truth is usually judged. Yet it is the truth. The whole character of the Christian religion is involved in that affirmation. It asserts that God's word is relevant to human life. It declares that an event in history can be of such a character as to reveal the character of history itself; that without such a revelation the character of history cannot be known. It is not possible to arrive at an understanding of the meaning of life and history without such a revelation. No induction from empirical facts can yield a conclusion about ultimate meaning because every process of induction presupposes some canon and criterion of meaning. That is why metaphysical systems which pretend to arrive at ultimate conclusions about the meaning of life are either covert theologies which unconsciously rationalize some revelation, accepted by faith; or they merely identify rationality with meaning, a procedure which forces them into either pantheism or acosmism. They must either identify the world with God on the supposition that temporal events, fully understood in all their relationships, are transmuted from finiteness and contingency into an unconditioned totality; or they must find the existential world evil in its finiteness because it does not conform in its contingent, existential relationships to a rational idea of unity.

For Christian faith the world is neither perfect nor meaningless. The God who created it also reveals Himself in it. He reveals Himself not only in a general revelation, that is, in the sense that His creation is His revelation; but in a special revelation. A general revelation can only point to the reality of God but not to His particular attributes. A theology which believes only in a general revelation must inevitably culminate in pantheism; because a God who is merely the object of human knowledge and not a subject who communicates with man by His own initiative is something less than God. A knowledge of God which depends only upon a study of the behaviour of the world must inevitably be as flat as the knowledge of any person would be, which depended merely upon the observation of the person's behaviour. The study of human behaviour cannot give a full clue to the meaning of a personality, because there is a depth of freedom in every personality which can only communicate itself in its own 'word.' That word may be related to an analysis. But it is not the consequence of the analysis. Without such a word the picture of any personality would be flat, as the interpretations of the divine which eliminate revelation are flat.

In Christian thought Christ is both the perfect man, 'the second Adam' who had restored the perfection of what man was and ought to be; and the Son of God, who transcends all possibilties of human life. It is this idea which theology sought to rationalize and yet it is a true idea. Human life stands in infinity. Everything it touches turns into infinity. Every moral standard, rigorously analysed, proves to be no permanently valid standard at all short of perfect and infinite love. The only adequate norm of human conduct is love of God and of man, through which all men are perfectly related to each other, because they are all related in terms of perfect obedience and love to the centre and source of their existence. In the same way all evil in human life is derived from an effort to transmute finite values into infinities, to seek infinite power, and infinite wealth and infinite gratification of desire. There is no sharp line between infinity in man and the infinity beyond man and yet there is a very sharp line. Man always remains a creature and his sin arises from the fact that he is not satisfied to remain so. He seeks to turn creatureliness into infinity; whereas his salvation depends upon subjecting his creaturely weakness to the infinite good of God. Christ, who expresses both the infinite possibilities beyond human life, is thus a true revelation of the total situation in which human life stands. There is every possibility of illusion and deception in this statement of the Christian faith. Men may be deceived by the primitive myth of the Virgin Birth and seek to comprehend as a pure historical fact, what is significant precisely because it points beyond history. Or they may seek to explain the dogma of the Incarnation in terms which will make it an article in a philosophical creed. Such efforts will lead to varied deceptions; but the deceptions cannot destroy the truth of the Incarnation.

Yet the revelation of God in the Incarnation is not of itself the redemption. Christianity believes that Christ died to save men from sin. It has a gospel which contains a crucifixion as well as an incarnation, a cross as well as a manger. This doctrine of the atoning death of the Son of God upon the cross has led to many theological errors, among them to theories of substitutionary atonement which outrage the moral sense. There is in fact no theory of the atonement which is quite as satisfying as the simple statements of the vicarious death of Christ in the Gospels. This may mean that faith is able to sense and appropriate an ultimate truth too deep for human reason. This is the foolishness of God which is wiser than the wisdom of men. The modern world has found not only the theories of atonement but the idea of atonement itself absurd. It rebelled not only against theories of a sacrifice which ransomed man from the devil's clutches or of a sacrifice which appeased the anger of a vindictive divine Father; it regarded the very idea of reconciliation between God and man as absurd.

The reason for this simple rejection of the Christian drama of salvation lies in the modern conception of human nature, rather than in any rejection of the theological absurdities attached to the idea of Christ's atoning death. Modern man does not regard life as tragic. He thinks that history is the record of the progressive triumph of good over evil. He does not recognize the simple but profound truth that man's life remains self-contradictory in its sin, no matter how high human culture rises; that the highest expression of human spirituality, therefore, contains also the subtlest form of human sin. The failure to recognize this fact gives modern culture a non-tragic conception of human history. To recognize this fact, and nothing more, is to reduce human history to simple tragedy. But the basic message of Christian faith is a message of hope in tragedy. It declares that when the Christ, by whom the world was made, enters the world, the world will not receive him. 'He came unto his own and his own received him not.' Human existence denies its own deepest and most essential nature. That is tragic. But when that fact is understood, when men cease to make the standards of a sinful existence the norms of life but accept its true norm, even though they fail to obey it, their very contrition opens the eyes of faith. This is the Godly sorrow that worketh repentence. Out of this despair hope is born. The hope is simply this: that the contradictions of human existence, which man cannot surmount, are swallowed up in the life of God Himself. The God of Christian faith is not only creator but redeemer. He does not allow human existence to end tragically. He snatches victory from defeat. He is Himself defeated in history but He is also victorious in that defeat.

There are theologies which interpret this article in the Christian creed as if life were really pure tragedy, but for the atoning love of Christ. But the fact is that the atoning death of Christ is the revelation of ultimate reality which may become the principle of interpretation for all human experience. It is not a principle yielded by experience, but it is applicable to experience and validated by it. It is an actual fact that human life, which is always threatened and periodically engulfed by the evil which human sin creates, is also marvellously redeemed by the transmutation of evil into good. This transmutation is not a human but a divine possibility. No man can, by taking thought, turn evil into good. Yet in the total operations of providence in history this transmutation occurs. The Christian faith consequently does not defy the tragic facts of human existence by a single victory over tragedy; nor does it flee the tragedy of temporal existence into a heavenly escape. These forms of the Christian faith are deceptions.

Most profoundly the atonement of Christ is a revelation of what life actually is. It is tragic from the standpoint of human striving. Human striving can do no better than the Roman law and the Hebraic religion, both the highest of their kind, through which the Lord was crucified. Yet this crucifixion becomes the revelation of that in human history which transcends human striving. And without this revelation, that which is beyond tragedy in life could not have been apprehended.

Without the cross men are beguiled by what is good in human existence into a false optimism and by what is tragic into despair. The message of the Son of God who dies upon the cross, of a God who transcends history and is yet in history, who condemns and judges sin and yet suffers with and for the sinner, this message is the truth about life. It cannot be stated without deceptions; but the truths which seek to avoid the deceptions are immeasurably less profound. Compared to this Christ who died for men's sins upon the cross, Jesus, the good man who tells all men to be good, is more solidly historical. But he is the bearer of no more than a pale truism.

We are deceivers, yet true, when we declare that Christ will come again at the last judgement, that he who was defeated in history will ultimately triumph over it, will become its judge and the author of its new life. No doctrine of Christianity has led to more deceptions and illusions than the hope of the second coming of Christ. This doctrine has been so frequently appropriated and exploited by sectarian fanatics that the Church has been a little ashamed of it. We have made even less of the apocalyptic literature into which Hebraic prophecy culminated and in which Christ was nurtured. The imagery of this literature is so extravagant, and at times so fantastic, that Christian thinkers have been content, on the whole, to leave it alone. Yet the doctrine of Christ's second coming involves all the profoundest characteristics of the Christian religion. It is this doctrine which distinguishes Christianity both from naturalistic utopianism and from Hellenistic otherworldliness. In it the Christian hope of the fulfilment of life is expressed paradoxically and dialectically, holding fast to its essential conception of the relation of time to eternity. History is not regarded as meaningless, as in Greek thought, particularly in later neo-Platonism. For this reason the realm of fulfilment is not above history, in some heaven in which pure form is abstracted from the concrete content of historical existence. The realm of fulfilment is at the end of history. This symbolizes that fulfilment both transcends and is relevant to historical forms. The end of history is not a point in history.

The chronological illusion, that it is a point in history, so characteristic of all myths which point to the trans-historical by a symbol of time, is particularly fruitful of error in the doctrine of the second coming. It has led to fantastic sectarian illusions of every type. Yet it is significant that the dispossessed and disinherited have been particularly prone to these illusions, because they were anxious to express the Christian hope of fulfilment in social as well as in individual terms. Sectarian apocalypticism is closely related to modern proletarian radicalism, which is a secularized form of the latter. In both, the individualism of Christian orthodoxy is opposed with conceptions which place the corporate enterprises of mankind, as well as individuals, under an ultimate judgement and under ultimate possibilities of fulfilment. In these secular and apocalyptic illusions the end of time is a point in time beyond which there will be an unconditioned society. But there is truth in the illusions.

The more bourgeois version of this illusory apocalypticism is the idea of progress in which the unconditioned ground of history is explicitly denied, but an unconditioned fulfilment in terms of infinite duration is implicitly affirmed. The Kingdom of God, as the absolute reign of God, is transmuted into a principle of development, immanent in history itself. Against such a conception Christian thought is forced to maintain as rigorous opposition as against dualistic otherworldliness. The ultimate fulfilment of life transcends the possibilities of human history. There is no hope of overcoming the contradictions, in which life stands, in history. But since these contradictions are not the consequence of mere finiteness and temporality, but the fruits of human freedom, they are not overcome merely by translating the temporal into the eternal. Since they persist in all human striving, fulfilment is not a human but a divine possibility. God must overcome this inescapable contradiction.

Therefore it is Christ who is both the judge of the world and the author of its fulfilment; for Christ is the symbol both of what man ought to be and of what God is beyond man. In Christ we have a revelation of both the human possibilities which are to be fulfilled and the divine power which will fulfil them. In Christ, too, we have the revelation of the significance of human history and of the ground of its meaning which transcends history.

We are therefore deceivers, yet true, when we insist that the

Christ who died on the cross will come again in power and glory, that he will judge the quick and the dead and will establish his Kingdom. We do not believe that the human enterprise will have a tragic conclusion; but the ground of our hope lies not in human capacity but in divine power and mercy, in the character of the ultimate reality, which carries the human enterprise. This hope does not imply that fulfilment means the negation of what is established and developed in human history. Each moment of histody stands under the possibility of an ultimate fulfilment. The fulfilment is neither a negation of its essential character nor yet a further development of its own inherent capacities. It is rather a completion of its essence by an annihilation of the contradictions which sin has introduced into human life.

(FROM: *Beyond Tragedy*, pp. 3–24.)

4 'WE ARE MEN AND NOT GOD'
(On the theology of Karl Barth)

[This extract illustrates the reaction of a leading exponent of 'Anglo-Saxon' theology to the 'Continental' theology of Karl Barth. While welcoming the emphasis on the finality of Christ and his work, especially for a time of crisis, Niebuhr fears that Barth's theology 'tempts the Christian to share the victory and the glory of the risen Lord without participating in the crucifixion of the self'. It could be a temptation, implies Niebuhr, to what Bonhoeffer called 'cheap grace'. See Book 5, pp. 297ff.]

Beyond the traditional differences between confessions at Amsterdam[1] the most marked theological contrast, apparent at the first Assembly of the World Council, was between what was frequently described as the 'Continental theology' and what was with equal inaccuracy known as the 'Anglo-Saxon

[1] The first Assembly of the World Council of Churches was held at Amsterdam in 1948. Barth, Niebuhr and Tillich were present. (Ed.)

approach to theology' Both designations were inaccurate because many Continentals did not share the first approach, and the second was 'Anglo-Saxon' only in the sense that beyond all denominational distinctions in the Anglo-Saxon world, delegates from that world seemed united in their rejection of the Continental position.

Issues Raised by Barth

This position might best be defined as strongly eschatological. This does not mean that it placed its emphasis primarily upon the hope of the culmination of world history in the second coming of Christ, the final judgement, and the general resurrection. If the position is termed eschatological it must be regarded as a form of 'realized eschatology'. Let Karl Bath's words explain the emphasis, since he was the most persuasive spokesman of the position. The assurance, declared Barth, that 'Jesus Christ has already robbed sin, death, the devil and hell of their power and has already vindicated divine and human justice in his person' ought to persuade us 'even on this first day of our deliberations that the care of the church and the care of the world is not our care. Burdened with this thought we could straighten nothing out.' For the final root of human disorder is precisely 'this dreadful, godless, ridiculous opinion that man is the Atlas who is destined to bear the dome of heaven upon his shoulders'.

No christian would quarrel with the affirmation that the Church finds the true and the new beginning of life and history in the revelatory and redemptive power of our Lord's life, death, and resurrection. The questions which arose at Amsterdam were about the conclusions which were drawn from this article of faith. Did not these conclusions tend to rob the Christian life of its sense of responsibility? Did they not promise a victory for the Christian without a proper emphasis upon repentence? And did they not deal in an irresponsible manner with all the trials and perplexities, the judgements and discriminations, the tasks and duties which Christians face in the daily round of their individual and collective life?

The Testimony of St Paul

The first conclusion which Barth drew from the Christian

certainty that Christ has already gained the victory over sin and death was that 'the care of the Church is not our care'. We must rather commit the Church unto the Lord 'who will bring it to pass'. He has called us to be his witnesses but not to be 'his lawyers, engineers, statisticians, and administrative directors'.

One is a little puzzled about this complete rejection of differentiated functions, since the precise point of St Paul's classical chapter on the church as the body of Christ in 1 Corinthians 12 is that there are not only 'diversities of gifts' but also 'differences of administration' and 'diversities of operation' within the church. And St Paul does have a 'care' about the church, which is very relevant to our present ecumenical task. His care is lest diversities of gifts and differences of administration tempt 'the eye to say to the ear, I have no need of thee'. In other words, he is afraid that special gifts and functions within the church may become the occasion of the isolation of one member from another, rather than the basis for their mutual growth in grace. It is in this way that sin enters the church and divides it. If these divisions are to be overcome, must there not be a contrite recognition of the sinful pride in our special gift or function by which we have become divided?

What is that but 'care' about the church? It is the basis of the 'dying with Christ' without which, according to the Scripture, there can be no new and triumphant life with him. The real weakness of this unvarying emphasis upon what we cannot do and upon what Christ has already done is that it tempts the Christian to share the victory and the glory of the risen Lord without participating in the crucifixion of the self, which is the Scriptural presupposition of a new life, for the individual, the church and the nation.

Decrying the Prophetic Function

We are warned with equal emphasis that the 'care of the world is not our care'. We are to beware lest we seem to present a kind of 'Christian Marshall plan'[1] to the nations. This is a wholesome warning against the pet schemes of

[1] The Marshall plan was a scheme initiated by the United States for assisting European countries devastated by the Second World War. (Ed.)

Christian moralists. But does it not annul the church's prophetic function to the nations? Must not the church be busy in 'the pulling down of strongholds, casting down imaginations and every thing that exalteth itself against the knowledge of God and bringing into captivity every thought to the obedience of Christ'?

In such a day as this we are particularly confronted with the fact that nations and empires, proud oligarchies and vainglorious races have been 'wounded' by the divine wrath in the vicissitudes of history and 'have not received correction'. It is a sobering fact that judgement so frequently leads to despair rather than to repentance. It is not within the competence of the Christian church to change despair into repentance. That possibility is a mystery of divine grace. But it *does* belong to the 'care' of the church for the world that it so interpret the judgements under which nations stand, and so disclose their divine origin, that there is a possibility of repentance.

If the gospel is made to mean merely the assurance of God's final triumph over all human rebellion, it may indeed save men from anxious worries. But does it not also save them prematurely from their own perplexities? It prevents them from indulging in the vainglorious belief that they can create the Kingdom of God by their own virtue. But does it remind them that they are 'workers together with Him'? Is this not, in short, a very 'undialectical' gospel in which the 'Yes' of the divine mercy has completely cancelled out the 'No' of the divine judgement against all human pride and pretension?

What Help for Christians?

The second question one is forced to raise about this emphasis is whether it has any guidance or inspiration for Christians in the day-to-day decisions which are the very woof and warp of our existence. Barth insists that we have no 'systems of economic and political principles to offer the world'. We can present it only 'with a revolutionary hope'. This emphasis has its limited validity. Christianity is too simply equated by many with some simple system of 'Christian economics' or 'Christian sociology'. But Barth's teachings seem to mean that we can, as Christians, dispense with the principles of justice which, however faulty, represent the cumulative experience of the race in dealing with the vexing problems of man's relations to his fellows.

We ought indeed to have a greater degree of freedom from all traditions, even the most hallowed, as we seek to establish and re-establish community in our torn world. But freedom over law cannot mean emancipation from the tortuous and difficult task of achieving a tolerable justice. It is certainly not right for Christians to leave it to the 'pagans' of our day to walk the tightrope of our age, which is strung over the abyss of war and tyranny, seeking by patience and courage to prevent war on the one hand and the spread of tyranny on the other, while the Christians rejoice in a 'revolutionary hope' in which all these anxieties of human existence, and the particular anxieties of our age, are overcome proleptically. It is particularly wrong if we suggest to these pagans that we have no immediate counsel in the present perplexity but that we will furnish a 'sign' of the 'coming Kingdom' by some heroic defiance of malignant power, if the situation becomes desperate enough. We will not counsel any community that this or that course might lead to tyranny. We will merely prepare ourselves to defy tyranny when it is full blown.

'Crisis' Theology Gone to Seed

Here there are suggestions of a 'crisis' theology, but not in the connotation originally intended. It is only fair to Barth and to those for whom he speaks to acknowledge gratefully the great contributions which this theology made to the struggle against tyranny in recent decades. Its interpretation of the Christian faith helped to create a heroic heedlessness, a disposition to follow the Scriptural injunction, 'Be careful in nothing'. This resulted in a very powerful witness to Christ in the hour of crisis. But perhaps this theology is constructed too much for the great crises of history. It seems to have no guidance for a Christian statesman for our day. It can fight the devil if he shows both horns and cloven feet. But it refuses to make discriminating judgements about good and evil if the evil shows only one horn or the half of a cloven foot.

There is a special pathos in the fact that so many of the Christian leaders of Germany are inclined to follow this form of flight from daily responsibilities and decisions, because they are trying to extend the virtue of yesterday to cover the problems of today. Yesterday they discovered that the church may be an ark in which to survive a flood. Today they seem so enamored of this special function of the church that they have decided to turn the ark into a home on Mount Ararat and live in it perpetually.

Barth is as anxious to disavow any special responsibilities in our debate with a secular culture on the edge of despair as in our engagement with a civilization on the edge of disaster. We are not to worry about this 'godless' age. It is no more godless than any other age, just as the evil in our day is neither more nor less than that of any previous period. We seem always to be God rather than men in this theology, viewing the world not from the standpoint of the special perplexities and problems of given periods but *sub specie aeternitatis.*

Have We Nothing to Say?

In any event, says Barth, we are not to enter into debate with the secularism of our age. With a special dig at his old opponent Brunner, who had analysed the 'axioms' of secularism to prove that they were filled with idolatry, Barth warned that we had nothing special to say to the godless people of our age which we would not have said in any age. What we have to say to them is that 'Jesus Christ died and rose again for them and has become their divine brother and redeemer'.

Does this mean that St Paul had no right to analyse the meaning of the yearning of his day for the 'unknown God' and prove its relevance for the gospel? When Julian Huxley, for instance, writes a book, *Man in the Modern World*, in which he manages to distil every error of modern man about himself and his destiny, his virtue and his wisdom, is the Christian apologist to refrain from every apologetic assault upon some of the absurdities of these modern beliefs? Is he merely to assure Mr Huxley that Christ died for him, even though Mr Huxley could not, in his present state of belief possibly understand why anyone should need to die for us?

One sees that the church is as rigorously prohibited from turning a furrow in the field of culture as in the field of social relations. Let the church remain an ark, ready to receive those who are fleeing the next flood. If, meanwhile, weeds should grow in the garden of either culture or civilization that is not surprising, since the church knows *a priori* that weeds grow in every human garden.

With the fullest appreciation of what this theology did to puncture the illusions of churchmen, theologians, and moralists, one must insist that this is not the whole gospel. It warned the church rightly that it must bear witness, not to its own power but to the power of God, not to its capacity to build the Kingdom but to the Kingdom which has been established by divine grace.

But the Christian faith, which can easily degenerate into a too simple moralism, may also degenerate into a too simple determinism and irresponsibility when the divine grace is regarded as a way of escape from, rather than a source of engagement with, the anxieties, perplexities, sins, and pretensions of human existence. The certainty of the final inadequacy of the 'wisdom of the world' must not be allowed to become the source of cultural obscurantism. The Christian must explore every promise and every limit of the cultural enterprise. The certainty of the final inadequacy of every form of human justice must not lead to defeatism in our approach to the perplexing problems of social justice in our day. The possibilities as well as the limits of every scheme of justice must be explored. The certainty that every form of human virtue is inadequate in the sight of God must not tempt us to hide our talent in the ground.

One of the tasks of an ecumenical movement is to prevent a one-sided statement of the many-sided truth of the gospel. 'Narrow is the way which leadeth unto life.' There is an abyss on each side of that narrow way. Anyone who is too fearful of the abyss on the one side will fall into the abyss on the other side. We 'Anglo-Saxons' who object to this one-sided emphasis may be corrupted by many Pelagian and semi-Pelagian heresies. We stand in need of correction. But we also have the duty to correct.

We are embarrassed about our correction because we cannot deny that this 'Continental' theology outlines the final pinnacle of the Christian faith and hope with fidelity to the Scriptures. Yet it requires correction, because it has obscured the foothills where human life must be lived. It started its theological assault decades ago with the reminder that we are men and not God, and that God is in the heavens and that we are on earth. The wheel is come full circle. It is now in danger of offering a crown without a cross, a triumph without a battle, a scheme of justice without the necessity of discrimination, a faith which has annulled rather than transmuted perplexity—in short, a too simple and premature escape from the trials and perplexities, the duties and tragic choices, which are the condition of our common humanity. The Christian faith knows of a way through these sorrows, but not of a way around them.

(FROM: D. B. Robertson (Ed.), *Essays in Applied Christianity*, by Reinhold Niebuhr, pp. 168–75.)

5 The Christian Church in a secular age

[Like Bultmann and Bonhoeffer, Niebuhr gave a good deal of thought to the problems of communicating the Christian gospel in an intelligible way to a society whose assumptions are basically 'secular'. Strictly speaking, Niebuhr argues, the Western world is still not yet thoroughgoingly 'secular'. There is too much diffused religiosity (often of a pantheistic kind) and 'religious' humanism (a belief that man has some transcendental significance) for that to be the case. In this kind of 'secularism' there is still a sort of religion since an ultimate trust (cf. Tillich's 'Ultimate Concern') is placed in the possibilities of human intelligence and/or virtue. There is also, significantly a moral fervour and passion for justice in much so-called 'humanism' which reminds one of religion. The basic issue at stake, for Niebuhr, is whether we are to conceive human life and destiny in terms of tragedy (noble, impressive, but doomed to meaninglessness) or in terms of redemption (that there is a 'beyond tragedy'). Tillich expresses the same idea as the choice between 'the courage of resignation' (Stoicism) and 'the courage to be'. (See his *The Courage to be*.)

This extract is a good example of Niebuhr's theological appraisal of the modern political, social and cultural scene. In particular it illustrates his suspicion of a theology which so emphasises human sin and impotence (this is what Niebuhr found in Barth) as to engender a neglect of problems of social justice.]

For the past two hundred years the Christian Church has been proclaiming its gospel in a world which no longer accepted the essentials of the Christian Faith. The Western world, particularly the more advanced industrial nations, has come increasingly under the sway of what has been called a secular culture. Secularism is most succinctly defined as the explicit disavowal of the sacred. The holy in every religion is that reality upon which all things depend, in terms of which they are explained and by which they are judged. It is the ultimate mystery, but also the ultimate source of all meaning. For the Christian Faith holiness is ascribed only to the God who is the Creator, Judge and Redeemer of the world. The world is made and sustained by Him. Its historical realities are thus the fruits of His creative will. The world is judged by Him. Its sins stand under His divine judgement. The world is redeemed by Him. Without His grace mediated through Christ, human existence remains a problem to itself, being unable to escape by any effort of its own from the contradictions of a sinful existence.

The Religion of Secularism

In contrast to this faith, modern secularism has been interpreted by the Christian Church too much in terms of secularism's own disavowal of religious faith. Strictly speaking, there is no such thing as secularism. An explicit denial of the sacred always contains some implied affirmation of a holy sphere. Every explanation of the meaning of human existence must avail itself of some principle of explanation which cannot be explained. Every estimate of values involves some criterion of value which cannot be arrived at empirically. Consequently the avowedly secular culture of today turns out upon close examination to be either a pantheistic religion which identifies existence in its totality with holiness, or a rationalistic humanism for which human reason is essentially god or a vitalistic humanism which worships some unique or particular vital force in the individual or the community as its god, that is, as the object of its unconditioned loyalty.

This latter faith, the product of the romantic movement in Western civilization, is the most obvious form of idolatry. It is also the most explicitly religious. Its emergence, particularly on the European Continent, in these latter days of a dying bourgeois culture, proves the irrelevance of critical categories which imply a simple and unqualified contrast between the religious and the secular. There are no irreligious cultures; and if there were, it could not be assumed that a religious culture is intrinsically superior to an irreligious one. The question is not whether we worship a god. That is not the question, on the one hand, because all men do, whether implicitly or explicitly; and on the other hand, the worship of false gods is in no sense preferable to complete agnosticism, if the latter were possible.

The civilization and culture in which we are called upon to preach the Christian gospel is, in other words, not irreligious, but a devotee of a very old religion, dressed in a new form. It is the old religion of self-glorification. This is a very old religion because it involves the quintessence of human sin, as defined by St Paul in the first chapter of Romans. Speaking of the Gentiles and their culpability in the sight of God he declares: 'So that they are without excuse: because that, when they knew God, they glorified Him not as God, neither were thankful; but became vain in their imaginations, and their foolish heart was darkened. Professing themselves to be wise, they became fools [and what an accurate description that is of the vainglory of our modern era], and changed the glory of the uncorruptible God into an image made like to corruptible man, and to birds and four-footed beasts, and creeping things.'

Every form of modern secularism contains an implicit or explicit self-glorification and deification in the sense described in the Letter to the Romans. Humanistic rationalism, forgetting that human reason as well as human physical existence is a derived, dependent, created and finite reality, makes it into a principle of interpretation of the meaning of life; and believes that its gradual extension is the guarantee of the ultimate destruction of evil in history. It mistakes the image of God in man for God Himself. It does not realize that the freedom by which man is endowed in his rational nature is the occasion for his sin as well as the ground of morality. It does not understand that by this reason nature's harmless will-to-live is transmuted into a sinful will-to-power. It is by this reason that men make pretentious claims for their partial and relative insights, falsely identifying them with absolute truth. Thus rationalism always involves itself in two descending scales of self-deification of humanity in abstract terms ends as the deification of a particular type of man, who supposedly possesses ultimate insights. In Aristotelian rationalism this latter development is expressed in the deification of the aristocrat, whom to glorify the slave exists. In modern rationalism the final result is a glorification of bourgeois perspectives.

The recent emergence of a more explicit type of self-glorification in race, State and nation, in religions of Blut und Boden[1] represents the victory of romanticism over rationalism, to speak in purely cultural terms. More profoundly considered, this romantic development is a cynical reaction to the hypocritical pretensions of the rationalists. Let those of us who live in such parts of Western civilization in which the old rational humanism and universalism is not yet completely disintegrated guard ourselves against premature self-righteous judgements. It may be that our type of humanism represents a more sincere attempt to establish universal values and expresses an honest devotion to European civilization rather than to the defiant strength of a particular nation. But on the other hand, this bourgeois humanism tends to be oblivious to its own partial, national and bourgeois perspectives. Having erroneously identified its truth with the eternal truth, it naturally elicits the reaction of a curious kind of cynical romanticism. It is not without significance that rational humanism is still most robust in the nations which hold a dominant position, politically and economically, in the Western world, more particularly the Anglo-Saxon nations; while what we abhor as primitivistic romanticism flourishes in the less satisfied nations. Hypocrisy and implicit or covert self-glorification are always the particular temptation of the victors; and cynicism and a more explicit self-glorification the sin of the vanquished. The necessity of compensating for outraged self-esteem is the cause

[1] 'Blood and soil'—a reference to Nazism (Ed.).

of this greater degree of explicitness in the deification of self.

The whole story of modern culture might be truly chronicled in terms of the Parable of the Prodigal Son. The more rationalistic humanism is the son in the first stages of his emancipation from his father. The temper of modern culture is expressed quite precisely in the words of the son: 'Father, give me the portion of goods that falleth to me.' Our civilization did not want to recognize its dependence upon a divine father, who is the source of all life and the judge of all human actions. It wanted an autonomous culture. It separated the 'goods that falleth to me' from the divine patrimony and forgot the dangers of anarchy in this independence. The more romantic type of modern humanism, as revealed in the religio-political movements of the Continent, represent a more advanced state of disintegration. Here the son is 'wasting his substance in riotous living', a civilization allowing the vital energies of peoples and nations to express themselves in anarchic conflict with one another, and insisting that any vital or unique energy is morally self-justifying. The 'mighty famine' when the son begins to be in want is still in the future, but our civilization is destined for such a catastrophe as so certain a consequence of the anarchy of its conflicting national passions and ambitions, that one may well speak of it as part of the contemporary picture.

To leave for a moment the Parable of the Prodigal Son, a further reaction to bourgeois rationalism and humanism must be recorded which seeks to eliminate the errors of this dominant form of secularism. I refer to Marxism and the revolt of the proletarians in the Western world against the privileged sections of the community. In this newer form of humanism there is an explicit recognition of the finiteness of the human mind and the relation of human ideals to human interests; to the sinfulness, in short, of all human culture. Yet this very philosophy which sees the pretensions of all 'the wise, the mighty and the noble' so clearly insists that it will be able to arrive at an absolute and universal position. In this creed the life of the proletariat has some mystic union with the absolute.

Here then we have a nice combination of the romantic and the rationalistic strains in modern culture, a glorification of the vitality of the burden bearers of the world as the instrument of an ultimate universalistic humanism; but no recognition that this fateful class is also composed of sinful men and that their sin will become more apparent as soon as they cease to be the oppressed and become the victors. Inasfar as Marxism seeks to establish genuinely universal values it must not be equated with the fascism which defies every common interest in the name of its own self-justifying vitality. Nor can its superiority over the pretentious rationalism of bourgeois life be denied. But unfortunately, as every culture which is not confronted with the one holy God, the Creator, Lord and Judge of the world, it also ends in the sin of self-glorification.

The Message of Repentance

The question is, what shall the Christian Church say to this modern culture, which began its adventure in autonomy with such gay self-assurance, which is already so deeply involved in 'riotous living' and which faces so certain a doom of a mighty famine?

We must, of course, preach the gospel to this, as to every generation. Our gospel is one which assures salvation in the Cross of Christ to those who heartily repent of their sins. It is a gospel of the Cross; and the Cross is a revelation of the love of God only to those who have first stood under it as a judgement. It is in the Cross that the exceeding sinfulness of human sin is revealed. It is in the Cross that we become conscious how, not only what is worst, but what is best in human culture and civilization is involved in man's rebellion against God. It was Roman law, the pride of all pagan civilization, and Hebraic religion, the acme of religious devotion, which crucified the Lord. Thus does the Cross reveal the problem of all human culture and the dilemma of every human civilization.

Repentance is the first key into the door of the Kingdom of God. God resisteth the proud and giveth grace to the humble. Whenever men trust their own righteousness, their own achievements, whenever they interpret the meaning of life in terms of the truth in their own culture or find in their own capacities a sufficient steppingstone to the Holy and the

Divine, they rest their life upon a frail reed which inevitably breaks and leaves their life meaningless.

Perhaps that is why the truest interpretations of the Christian faith have come in moments of history when civilizations were crumbling and the processes of history and the judgements of God had humbled human arrogance. The faith of the Hebrew prophets was thus formulated when the culture religion of Israel was threatened and finally overcome by the mighty civilizations of Assyria and Babylon. Augustine wrote the *City of God* when Roman civilization, once mighty enough to seem identical with civilization itself, had become the helpless victim of barbarians; and the renewal of the Christian gospel in the Protestant Reformation was, historically speaking, the consequence as well as the cause of the crumbling of a once proud medieval civilization. Proud men and successful civilizations find it difficult to know God, because they are particularly tempted to make themselves God. That is why 'not many mighty, not many noble, not many wise after the flesh are called'. Without the godly sorrow that worketh repentance there can be no salvation.

The Message of Hope

Just as the Christian gospel calls the proud to repent, it assures those who despair of a new hope. It is interesting how every religion which imparts a superficial meaning to life, and grounds that meaning in a dubious sanctity, finally issues in despair. Those who make the family their god must despair when the family is proved to be only a little less mortal than the individual. Those who make a god of their nation must despair when the might of their nation crumbles, as every creaturely and sinful might must: 'For we are consumed by thine anger and by thy wrath are we troubled.' That is the despair which awaits many a young nationalistic pagan of Europe today. They might even, if they could see truly, despair in the triumph of their nation, for the nation in triumph is less worthy of reverence than the nation in defeat. Pride accentuates its sins, and there are no sufferings to prompt pity as a handmaiden of love in the heart of the patriot.

Every humanistic creed is a cosmos of meaning sustained by a thin ice on the abysmal deeps of meaninglessness and chaos. Only the faith in God, who has been 'our dwelling place in all generations', and who was God 'before the mountains were brought forth or ever the earth and the world were made', can survive the vicissitudes of history, can rescue human existence from the despair in which it is periodically involved by its sinful pretensions, and the tragic disappointment of its facile hopes.

The fulfilment of life, according to our Christian faith, is possible only through the mercy of God. All superficial questions about the meaning of life, all simple religions which imagine that faith in any god is better than no faith at all, fail to recognize that the ultimate question is not whether life has a meaning (which it must have or no one could live), but whether or not the meaning is tragic. The only serious competitor to Christianity as a spiritual religion is Buddhism, and in Buddhism life is conceived in terms of pure tragedy. Christianity is a faith which takes us through tragedy to beyond tragedy, by way of the Cross to a victory in the Cross. The God whom we worship takes the contradictions of human existence into Himself. This knowledge is a stumbling block to the Jews, and to the Gentiles foolishness, but to them that are called it is the power and the wisdom of God. This is a wisdom beyond human knowledge, but not contrary to human experience. Once known, the truth of the gospel explains our experiences which remain inexplicable on any other level. Through it we are unable to understand life in all of its beauty and its terror, without being beguiled by its beauty or driven to despair by its terror.

Not of the World, but in the World

While the gospel which we preach reveals a world which in its ground and its fulfilment transcends human history, it does not abstract us from this present history with all of its conflicts and tragic disappointments of arrogant hopes. We are in the world, and God's Will, His Judgement and His Mercy impinge upon our daily actions and historic problems. We must bring forth fruits meet for repentance. What can those fruits be but the fruits of 'love, joy, peace?' when the Church proclaims the love commandment to the world as the law of God it must guard against the superficial moralism of telling the world that it can save itself if men will only stop being selfish and learn to be loving. We dare not forget that in us, as well as in those who do not acknowledge the Christian gospel, there is a law in our members that wars against the law that is in our mind. The law of love is not kept simply by being preached. Yet it is the law of life and must be both preached and practised. It is a terrible heresy to suggest that, because the world is sinful, we have a right to construct a Machiavellian politics or a Darwinian sociology as normative for Christians.

What is significant about the Christian ethic is precisely this: that it does not regard the historic as normative. Man may be, as Thomas Hobbes[1] observed, a wolf to his fellowman. But this is not his essential nature. Let Christianity beware, particularly radical Protestanism, that it does not accept the habits of a sinful world as the norms of a Christian collective life. For the Christian only the law of love is normative. He would do well to remember that he is a sinner who has never perfectly kept the law of God. But neither must he forget that he is a child of God who stands under that law. Much of what passes for theological profundity today is no more than a subtle re-enactment of the part of the son in the Lord's Parable who promised to do the father's will and did not, leaving his will to be done by the son who had refused to promise it. How accurately that little parable of Christ pictures the superior passion for human justice of many outside the Church as against those who are in it. Frequently, believing Christians are tempted by their recognition of the sinfulness of human existence to disavow their own responsibility for a tolerable justice in the world's affairs. Justice is not love. Justice presupposes the conflict of life with life and seeks to mitigate it. Every relative justice therefore stands under the judgement of the law of love, but it is also an approximation of it.

A Christian pessimism which becomes a temptation to irresponsibility toward all those social tasks which constantly

[1] **Thomas Hobbes (1588–1679), English philosopher. (Ed.)**

confront the life of men and nations, tasks of ordering the productive labour of men, of adjudicating their conflicts, of arbitrating their divergent desires, of raising the level of their social imagination and increasing the range of their social sympathies, such a pessimism cannot speak redemptively to a world constantly threatened by anarchy and suffering from injustice. The Christian gospel which transcends all particular and contemporary social situations can be preached with power only by a Church which bears its share of the burdens of immediate situations in which men are involved, burdens of establishing peace, of achieving justice, and of perfecting justice in the spirit of love. Thus is the Kingdom of God which is not of this world made relevant to every problem of the world.

The Danger of Profanization

If the problem of presenting the Christian ethic to a non-Christian world without the spirit of self-righteousness is difficult, an even more far-reaching problem is the presentation of the gospel to a secular age. The truths of the Christian gospel are simple and clear. But it is not easy for any human institution to mediate them without pride or hypocrisy; and the Church is a human institution, though it is that institution where it is known that all human life stands under a divine judgement and within a divine mercy. The real difficulty of preaching the gospel of God's mercy to the prodigal son, our modern culture, lies in the temptation to play the part of the elder brother in the Lord's Parable. One might indeed elaborate this Parable without disloyalty to its meaning, with the suggestion that the younger son might well have been prompted to leave his father's house because of the insufferable self-righteousness of the elder brother. At any rate, it is quite obvious that no Christian Church has a right to preach to a so-called secular age without a contrite recognition of the shortcomings of historic Christianity which tempted the modern age to disavow its Christian faith.

Secularism is, on the one hand, the expression of man's sinful self-sufficiency. It may be, on the other hand, a reaction to profanity. Some men are atheists because of a higher implicit theism than that professed by believers. They reject God because His name has been taken in vain, and they are unable to distinguish between His Holiness and its profanization. It is popular today in Christian circles to speak somewhat contemptuously of the errors and illusions of the secular culture which challenged Christianity so optimistically in the last two centuries and finds itself in such confusion today. It would be well to remember, however, that the primary conscious motive of this secularism (whatever may have been its unconscious and more sinful motives) was to break the chains which a profane Christianity had placed upon man.

A profane Christianity, like the elder brother, ostensibly maintains its sense of dependence upon the Father, but it uses this relationship to satisfy a sinful egotism. It falsely identifies its relative and partial human insights with God's wisdom, and its partial and relative human achievements with God's justice. A profane Christianity falsely identifies the Church with the Kingdom of God. Since the historic Church is always touched with human finiteness, is subject to sociological forces and pressures, and victim of the prejudices and illusions of particular ages, any tendency to obscure or deny this fact becomes the final and most terrible expression of human sinfulness. Of that sin no Church has been free.

Protestants may believe, and not without a measure of truth, that this sin of profaning the Holiness of God, of using His Name in vain, is a particular danger in Catholicism, for Catholicism has a doctrine of the Church in which what is human and what is divine in the Church is constantly subject to a confused identification of the one with the other. Yet no historic Christian institution is free of this sin. Every vehicle of God's grace, the preacher of the word, the prince of the Church, the teacher of theology, the historic institution, the written word, the sacred canon, all these are in danger of being revered as if they were themselves divine. The aura of the divine word, which is transmitted through them, falsely covers their human frailties. The Christian Church has never followed St Paul rigorously enough in his disavowal of divinity: 'And when the people saw what Paul had done they lifted up their voices saying, in the speech of Lyconia: The Gods have come down to us in the likeness of men . . . which when the Apostles

Paul and Barnabas heard of they rent their clothes and ran in among the people crying out and saying, Sirs, why do ye these things? We also are men of like passions with you and preach unto you, that ye should turn from these vanities unto the living God, which made heaven and earth and the sea and all things that are therein' (Acts 14:11–15).

Secularism as a Reaction against a Profane Christianity

Modern secularism was forced to resist a profanization of the holiness of God both in the realm of the truth and in the realm of the good, in both culture and ethics. In the realm of culture the Christian religion was tempted to complete the incompleteness of all human culture by authoritative dicta, supposedly drawn from Scripture. It forgot that theology is a human discipline subject to the same relativities as any other human discipline. If modern culture was wrong in regarding the Anselmic axiom '*Credo ut intelligam*'[1] as absurd because it failed to understand that reason cannot function without the presuppositions of faith, Christian culture was wrong in insinuating the specific insights and prejudices of a particular age into the '*credo*'. While modern science was wrong in assuming that its descriptions of detailed historical sequences in nature and history offered an adequate insight into the meaning of life as adequate explanations of detailed sequences and efficient causation.

Thus we have been subjected for centuries to a conflict between a theology which had become a bad science, and a science which implied an unconscious theology, a theology of unconscious presuppositions about the ultimate meaning of life. These presuppositions were doubly wrong. They were wrong in content and erroneous in being implicit rather than explicit. But surely the responsibility for this confusing conflict rests as much with a theology which had become a bad science as with a science which is a bad theology. In one sense all Orthodox Christian theology has been guilty of the sin of profanity. It has insisted on the literal and historic truth of

[1] 'I believe in order to understand' (Ed.).

its myths, forgetting that it is the function and character of religious myth to speak of the eternal in relation to time, and that it cannot therefore be a statement of temporal sequences.

No Christian theology, worthy of its name, can therefore be without gratitude to the forces of modern secularism inasfar as their passion for truth was a passion for God. They failed indeed to recognize that every search for truth begins with a presupposition of faith. They did not know for this reason how vulnerable they were to the sneer of Pilate: 'What is truth?'; and they could not consequently appreciate the affirmation of Christ: 'I am the truth.' But this secularization of truth is no more culpable than the religious profanization of truth which blandly appropriates the truth in Christ for every human vagary and prejudice, for every relative insight and temporal perspective.

The profanity of historic Christianity in regard to the problem of righteousness has been even more grievous than in regard to the problem of truth. Every human civilization is a compromise between the necessities and contigencies of nature and the Kingdom of God with its absolute love commandment. This is as true of a Christian as of an unchristian civilization. In a Christian, as well as in an unchristian civilization, the strong are tempted to exploit the weak, the community is tempted to regard itself as an end in itself, and the rulers are tempted to use their power for their own advantage. When the welter of relative justice and injustice, which emerges out of this conflict and confluence of forces, is falsely covered with the aura of the divine, and when the preservation of such a civilization is falsely enjoined as a holy duty, and when its rebels and enemies are falsely regarded as enemies of God, it is only natural that those who are most conscious of the injustices of a given social order, because they suffer from them, should adopt an attitude of cynical secularism toward the pretensions of sanctity made in behalf of a civilization. A profanization of the holiness of God leads inevitably to an effort to eliminate the sacred from human life. Invariably this effort is partially informed by a covert and implicit sense of the sacred, morally higher than the historical sanctity against which it protests. One need only study the perverted religious intensity of the nineteenth-century Russian nihilists to understand how a warfare against God may be prompted by a prophetic passion for God and scorn for the dubious political divinities which seek to borrow His holiness.

It is impossible to understand the secularism of either the commercial classes or the radical proletarians of the past hundred and fifty years if it is not appreciated to what degree this secularism represents a reaction to the too intimate and organic relation of Christianity with a feudal society. The priest of religion and the landlord of an agrarian society were too closely related to each other and the former was too frequently the apologist and auxiliary gendarme of the latter.

It may seem that this charge falls more heavily upon Catholicism than upon Protestantism, not only because of the historic relation of the former with a medieval culture and feudal civilization, but also because the latter is less prone to identify itself with the detailed economic and political arrangements of any society. But with its higher degree of detachment Protestantism has sometimes also revealed a higher degree of social irresponsibility. It has allowed its pessimism to betray it into a negative sanctification of a given social order on the assumption that any given order is preferable to anarchy and that the disturbance of the *status quo* might lead to anarchy.

Thus Catholicism and Protestantism, between them, have exhausted the possibilities of error in Christianity's relation to society. In either case peace and order through power were estimated too highly and the inevitable injustice of every stabilization of power was judged too leniently. Frequently Christianity was content to regard deeds of personal generosity and charity as adequate expressions of the Christian love commandment within a civilization in which every basic relationship was a complete denial of that commandment.

The secularism both of our modern bourgeois civilization and of the more proletarian civilizations which threaten to replace it, is therefore something more than the religion of self-glorification. It combines this sin with a passion for justice which frequently puts the historic Church to shame. If the Christian Church is to preach its gospel effectively to men of such a culture, it must understand the baffling mixture of a new profanity and resistance to an old profanity which is comprehended in this culture.

JUDGEMENT MUST BEGIN AT THE HOUSE OF GOD

Such a recognition is the clue to the problem of an effective proclamation of the Christian gospel in our day. If we preach repentance, it must be repentance for those who accept the Lord as well as for those who pretend to deny Him. If we preach the judgement of God upon a sinful world, it must be judgement upon us as well as upon those who do not acknowledge His judgements. If we preach the mercy of God, it must be with a humble recognition that we are in need of it as much as those who do not know God's mercy in Christ. If we preach the obligation of the love commandment, the preacher must know that he violates that commandment as well as those who do not consciously accept its obligation. Nothing is cheaper and more futile than the preaching of a simple moralism which is based upon the assumption that the world need only to be told that selfishness is sin and that love is the law of life to beguile it from the anarchy of sin in which it is at present engulfed. Such a moralism, to which the modern Church is particularly prone, is blind to the real tragedy and persistence of sin in the world.

To preach to others and become ourselves castaways is a peril in which all holy business is done. It is a peril to which the Church must succumb if it does not constantly hear the challenge of God to Jeremiah to 'separate the precious from the vile'; to distinguish between what is genuinely the Lord's will and our will, His holiness and our sin in the work of the Christian Church. The Kingdom of God was ushered in by the preaching of John the Baptist. The most profound element in John's message of repentance was expressed in the words, 'And think not to say within yourselves, We have Abraham to our Father; for I say unto you that God is able of these stones to raise up children unto Abraham.'[1] Not only the racial inheritors of a divine promise are tempted to rest complacently in the assurance 'We have Abraham to our Father.' That is a temptation which assails all inheritors of a divine promise, including the Christian Church, the 'Israel of God.' It is wholesome therefore for the Church to stand under the stinging

[1] Matthew 3:9.

rebuke 'God is able of these stones to raise up children unto Abraham,' a rebuke in the form of a statement of fact which history has validated again and again.

If the conscience of the Church feels the relevance to its own life of that rebuke, it can preach the gospel of a holy God, holy in righteousness and in mercy, without making sinful claims for itself in the name of that holiness, and it will be able to speak to the conscience of this generation, rebuking its sins without assuming a role of self-righteousness and overcoming its despair without finding satisfaction in the sad disillusionment into which the high hopes of modernity have issued.

(FROM: *Christianity and Power Politics*, pp. 203–26.)

FOR FURTHER STUDY AND DISCUSSION

1. How would you define 'humanism'? What are the distinguishing features of what Niebuhr calls 'classical humanism'? How do you account for its continuing appeal. (See Albert Camus, *The Myth of Sisyphus* and *The Rebel*.)
2. Is 'tragedy' incompatible with Christian belief? (See Niebuhr's essay 'Christianity and tragedy' in *Beyond Tragedy*.)
3. What meanings do you attach to 'sin', 'original sin', 'the fall of man'?
4. Construct an imaginary discussion between Bultmann, Tillich, Barth and Niebuhr on the subject of 'Myth'.
5. How do you imagine a conversation between Barth, Bonhoeffer and Niebuhr on 'the Church being in the world but not of it' would have gone?

FOR FURTHER READING

Principal Works of Reinhold Niebuhr

Moral Man and Immoral Society: a study in ethics and politics, London, 1932.

An interpretation of Christian ethics, London, 1935.

Beyond Tragedy: essays on the Christian interpretation of history, London, 1937.

Christianity and Power Politics, NewYork, Scribner's, 1940.

The Nature and Destiny of Man. Vols. I and II, London, 1941.

The Children of Light and the Children of Darkness: a vindication of democracy and a critique of its traditional defence, London, 1944.

Discerning the signs of the times: sermons for today and tomorrow, London, 1946.

Faith and history: a comparison of Christian and modern views of history, London, 1949.

The Irony of American History, London, 1952.

Christian realism and political problems, London, 1953.

The Self and the Dramas of History, London, 1955.

The Godly and the Ungodly: essays on the religious and secular dimensions of modern life, London, 1958.

Some Books on Reinhold Niebuhr

Gordon Harland, *The Thought of Reinhold Niebuhr*, New York, 1960.

June Bingham, *Courage to Change*: an introduction to the life and thought of Reinhold Niebuhr, New York, 1961 (very useful for the way it relates the development of Niebuhr's thought to his biography).

FOR GENERAL BACKGROUND READING

John Macquarrie, *Twentieth-century Religious Thought*, 1963.
——, *God-talk*, 1967.
——, *God and Secularity*, 1968.
Frederick Ferré, *Language, Logic and God*, 1962.
——, *Basic Modern Philosophy of Religion*, 1968.
David E. Jenkins, *Guide to the Debate about God*, 1966.
Colin Williams, *Faith in a Secular Age*, 1966.
E. L. Mascall, *The Secularisation of Christianity*, 1965.
H. Gollwitzer, *The Existence of God as confessed by faith*, 1964.
A. M. Ramsey, *God, Christ and the World*, 1969.
T. W. Ogletree, *The Death of God Controversy*, 1966.

5. Dietrich Bonhoeffer

1906–45

BIOGRAPHICAL INTRODUCTION

Dietrich Bonhoeffer was born in 1906 in Breslau which was then in the German province of Silesia but is now, as a result of the last war, incorporated into Poland with the changed name of Wroclaw. There were eight in the family whose background was professional and academic. One brother was killed in the First World War and another, Klaus, executed by the Nazis a fortnight after Dietrich. The father whom Bonhoeffer spoke of as one of the great influences of his life was the first professor of psychiatry in the University of Berlin.

Bonhoeffer's family was not particularly religious. Eberhard Bethge, the friend and biographer of Bonhoeffer, speaks of 'the careful agnosticism of his father and brothers'. Bonhoeffer's own religious convictions, deep though they were, maintained maximum sensitivity to the difficulties and feelings of the unbeliever.

At the age of sixteen Bonhoeffer decided to study theology and entered the University of Berlin. Here he came under the influence of some of the great figures in German liberal protestant theology, among them Adolf von Harnack who impressed Bonhoeffer by his 'intellectual incorruptibility'. After graduation he became a lecturer in the University of Berlin.

The development of Bonhoeffer's mind and beliefs has been divided into three periods. In the first, covering roughly the years 1927–33, he was a student teacher in Berlin. During these years he might almost be said to have worked with the motto of the dramatist Berthold Brecht: 'the truth is concrete'. He was engaged on what Bethge calls the 'quest for the concrete nature of the message'. In other words he was becoming suspicious of the easy generalizations, idealisms, and romanticism of what an American writer has called 'the men of the infinite', those who theorize in terms of abstract principles, especially in ethics, with a careless disregard for facts, particular data and concrete situations. The theological method of Karl Barth, with its insistence on the concrete particularity of the historical Incarnation, greatly influenced Bonhoeffer at this time. He spent two weeks at a Seminar in Bonn conducted by Barth in the summer of 1931. This influence is to be seen in his doctoral thesis which was later to be published as *Sanctorum Communio*. Later on Bonhoeffer was to be more critical of what he called Barth's 'positivism in theology' (see p. 335).

The second formative period in Bonhoeffer's life extends from 1933–40 when he was working as a pastor in Germany and abroad. It was during this period that he published *The Cost of Discipleship* and *Life Together* which represent his early thinking about the character of a truly personal Christian life lived in community. These years also saw his first travels abroad. He was for a time an assistant chaplain at the German church in Barcelona and while there spent a year's leave of absence at the Union Theological Seminary in New York where Reinhold Niebuhr was Professor of Christian Ethics. In a report on this visit Bonhoeffer spoke of Niebuhr as 'one of the most significant and creative of contemporary American theologians' but missed in his work 'a doctrine of the person and redemptive work of Jesus Christ'. This first experience of America was to have a bracing and liberating effect on Bonhoeffer. It was a shock to be in an atmosphere where Germany was not the be-all and the end-all of things theological: 'they find German theology so utterly local, they simply don't understand it here; they laugh at Luther'. But it meant a broadening of his understanding of the problems of the re-union of Christian Churches, relations between Church and state, and race-relations.

This period of Bonhoeffer's life coincided with the rise of the Nazi movement in Germany and the outbreak of war. Bonhoeffer took his stand against the Nazis immediately. Two days after Hitler became chancellor of Germany Bonhoeffer was broadcasting an attack on the Nazi theory of leadership. The broadcast was interrupted. Disheartened by what he saw going on Bonhoeffer came to London as German pastor in charge of two churches. Here he developed further his interests in the ecumenical movement and began his friendship with Dr G. K. A. Bell, Bishop of Chichester. In 1934 came the Barmen Declaration (see Book 1, p. 42) and the formation of the German Confessional Church in opposition to the Nazi-sponsored 'German Christian' Church. Bonhoeffer unhesitatingly came down on the side of the Confessional Church. In 1935 he returned to Germany to take charge of an illegal body, the Confessing Church Seminary at Zingst on the Baltic. This seminary later moved to Finkelwaldt also on the Baltic coast, near Stettin. He started an experimental community, which he called the 'Bruderhaus', and his experience of this lay behind his book *Life Together*. The Bruderhaus Community was dissolved by the Nazis in 1937.

By this time Bonhoeffer was increasingly under the scrutiny of the Gestapo. Reinhold Niebuhr was very anxious to get him out of Germany and succeeded for a short time. Bonhoeffer paid his second visit to America in 1939 but when it appeared that war was inevitable he returned to Germany. He explained why in a letter to Niebuhr:

> 'Sitting here in Dr. Coffin's garden [1] I have had the time to think and to pray about my situation and that of my nation and to have God's will for me clarified. I have come to the conclusion that I have made a mistake in coming to America. I must live through this difficult period of our national history with the Christian people of Germany. I shall have no right to participate in the reconstruction of Christian life in Germany after the war if I do not share the trials of this time with my people. My brothers in the Confessing Synod wanted me to go. They may have been right in urging me to do so; but I was wrong in going. Such a decision each man must make for himself. Christians in Germany will face the terrible alternative of either willing the defeat of their nation in order that Christian civilisation may survive, or willing the victory of their nation and thereby destroying our civilisation. I know which of these alternatives I must choose; *but I cannot make that choice in security.*'

The final period of Bonhoeffer's life covers the years 1940–5, in which he became more and more involved in underground resistance activities. He continued with his writing, as opportunity offered, and it is in this last period that he began his most strenuous thinking about 'Christianity without religion in an adult world'.

[1] Principal of Union Theological Seminary.

In 1942 Bonhoeffer met Dr Bell, the Bishop of Chichester, this time in Stockholm, and he disclosed the plans to overthrow the Nazi regime. The following year he was arrested and imprisoned at Tegel, near Berlin, and it is to this period of captivity that the *Letters and Papers from Prison* belong. They were written to his friend Eberhard Bethge. Following the attempt on Hitler's life in July 1944 he was placed in close confinement in Berlin. Then he was sent to a number of concentration camps, including Buchenwald, and finally was hanged by the SS at Flossenbürg in Bavaria on 9 April 1945 shortly before it was liberated by the Americans.

SELECTIONS

1 'THE EMPIRICAL FORM OF THE CHURCH'

[Bonhoeffer was much concerned with the ambiguous character of the Christian Church. From one point of view it is a religious institution, and sociology can help to analyse and classify the characteristics of such an institution. On the other hand the Church is the 'Body of Christ', the organ of his presence in the world. The Christian religion for Bonhoeffer could never be thought of as a vague mysticism. A real visible historical Incarnation meant taking seriously and realistically the 'real presence' of Christ in his Church.]

(a) *The objective spirit of the Church and the Holy Spirit*

The Church of Jesus Christ actualized by the Holy Spirit is at the present moment really the Church. The communion of saints represented by it is 'in the midst of us'. This proposition gives rise to a twofold question about the empirical Church. There is the question of 'history and the communion of saints', and the question of the *communio peccatorum* within the *sanctorum communio.*[1]

The empirical Church is the organized 'institution' of salvation, having as its focus the cultus with preaching and sacrament, or, in sociological terms, the 'assembly' of the members. It is legally constituted, and links the bestowal of its benefits with the orders of divine service it lays down. It accepts all who submit to these orders, and hence has no guarantee for the inner disposition of its members, but, from the moment it is sanctioned by public opinion and perhaps has even become a political power in the state, it must necessarily reckon with the fact that it will have 'dead members' within it. It is the 'historical result of the work of Jesus Christ' (Seeberg), and as such represents the objective spirit of the Church in its development and being, in transmitted forms and embodiments and in present vitality and effectiveness. The objective spirit, as we saw, is the new spiritual principle springing from

[1] 'Community of sinners'; 'community of saints'. (Ed.)

socialization. The autonomous effectiveness of its will regulates and guides the wills of those partaking of and forming it. It is embodied in certain forms and thereby visibly authenticates its own life. Again, it acts in two directions, that is, it has an intention both in time and in space; it seeks to be effective both in the historical and in the social sphere. It is the bearer of historical tradition, and its action and effects are to include more and more individuals in its scope. It seems as if this sociological structure in the empirical Church should now be studied and analysed as presenting the religious type of community among many types of community. And yet if we did this we should entirely distort the matter. The empirical Church is not identical with a religious community. Rather, as a concrete historical community, in spite of the relativity of its forms, its imperfect and unpretentious appearance, the empirical Church is the Body of Christ, the presence of Christ on earth, for it has his Word. It is possible to understand the empirical Church only by looking down from above, or by looking out from the inside, and not otherwise. Once this fact has been grasped it is of course in principle possible once more to define the Church as a religious community, always bearing in mind that it is really based on God. Thus if we now apply to the Church what we said about the objective spirit, we have the claim of the objective spirit of the Church to be the bearer of the historical work of Jesus Christ and of the social action of the Holy Spirit.

The historical Church claims that it possesses the Holy Spirit and is the effective custodian of the Word of God and of the sacrament. This brings us to the first question, the great body of thought on the problem of the relation of the Spirit of Christ and the Holy Spirit of the *sanctorum communio* to the objective spirit of the empirical Church.

The *sanctorum communio* moved by the Holy Spirit has continually to be actualized in a struggle against two sources of resistance: human imperfection and sin. To equate the two, giving imperfection the weight of sin, or evaluating sin merely as imperfection, is to avoid the seriousness of the Christian concept of sin, and leads either to regarding the Church's sociologically empirical form as sin, or, in the manner of Kant, to viewing the empirical Church only as a manifestation of the non-real, ideal Church of the future or as unattainable in this world. Neither attitude does justice to the empirical Church's historical importance. The first is wrong because Christ entered into history so that the Church is his presence in history. The history of the Church is the hidden centre of world history, and not the history of one educational institution among many. For the Church is Christ existing as the Church. No matter how dubious its empirical form may be, it remains the Church so long as Christ is present in his Word. Thereby we acknowledge that God has willed the Church's historical life, in the sense that it is intended to perfect itself. The Body of Christ is just as much a real presence in history as it is the standard for its own history. This brings us once again to what was said at the beginning of our inquiry, about the normative character of basic ontic[1] relationships. In the sphere of Christian ethics it is not what ought to be that effects what is, but what is effects what ought to be.

(FROM: *Sanctorum Communio*, pp. 144–6.)

2 'CHEAP AND COSTLY GRACE'

[By 'cheap grace' Bonhoeffer meant a merely theoretical acceptance of Christianity, fluent no doubt in its verbal expression, but having no real awareness of the personal commitment, obedience and discipline involved. It is possible, for example, to pay all the correct lip-service to the Christian doctrine of redemption in such a way as to remain insensitive to the problems raised by human suffering and injustice. Bonhoeffer pays tribute to monasticism as an attempt to 'follow' Christ but criticizes it for becoming a way of salvation *from* the world, rather than *in* and *for* it. Luther he praises for restoring the belief that the imitation of Christ is not a man-made endeavour to copy Christ but a letting oneself be lived through by the Spirit of God who 'conforms' human beings to the likeness of Christ.]

[1] Basic relationships of being. (Ed.)

Cheap grace is the deadly enemy of our Church. We are fighting today for costly grace.

Cheap grace means grace sold on the market like cheap-jack's wares. The sacraments, the forgiveness of sin, and the consolations of religion are thrown away at cut prices. Grace is represented as the Church's inexhaustable treasury, from which she showers blessings with generous hands, without asking questions or fixing limits. Grace without price; grace without cost! The essence of grace, we suppose, is that the account has been paid in advance; and, because it has been paid, everything can be had for nothing. Since the cost was infinite, the possibilities of using and spending it are infinite. What would grace be if it were not cheap?

Cheap grace means grace as a doctrine, a principle, a system. It means forgiveness of sins proclaimed as a general truth, the love of God taught as the Christian 'conception' of God. An intellectual assent to that idea is held to be of itself sufficient to secure remission of sins. The Church which holds the correct doctrine of grace has, it is supposed, *ipso facto* a part in that grace. In such a Church the world finds a cheap covering for its sins; no contrition is required, still less any real desire to be delivered from sin. Cheap grace therefore amounts to a denial of the living Word of God, in fact, a denial of the Incarnation of the Word of God.

Cheap grace means the justification of sin without the justification of the sinner. Grace alone does everything, they say, and so everything can remain as it was before. 'All for sin could not atone.' The world goes on in the same old way, and we are still sinners 'even in the best life' as Luther said. Well, then, let the Christian live like the rest of the world, let him model himself on the world's standards in every sphere of life, and not presumptuously aspire to live a different life under grace from his old life under sin. That was the heresy of the enthusiasts, the Anabaptists[1] and their kind. Let the Christian beware of rebelling against the free and boundless grace of God and desecrating it. Let him not attempt to erect a new religion of the letter by endeavouring to live a life of

[1] The name given to a number of Protestant groups in the sixteenth century who emphasized 'believers baptism' rather than the baptism of infants. (Ed.)

obedience to the commandments of Jesus Christ! The world has been justified by grace. The Christian knows that and takes it seriously. He knows he must strive against this indispensable grace. Therefore—let him live like the rest of the world! Of course he would like to go and do something extraordinary, and it does demand a good deal of self-restraint to refrain from the attempt and content himself with living as the world lives. Yet it is imperative for the Christian to achieve renunciation, to practise self-effacement, to distinguish his life from the life of the world. He must let grace be grace indeed, otherwise he will destroy the world's faith in the free gift of grace. Let the Christian rest content with his worldliness and with this renunciation of any higher standard than the world. He is doing it for the sake of the world rather than for the sake of grace. Let him be comforted and rest assured in his possession of this grace—for grace alone does everything. Instead of following Christ, let the Christian enjoy the consolations of his grace! That is what we mean by cheap grace, the grace which amounts to the justification of sin without the justification of the repentant sinner who departs from sin and from whom sin departs. Cheap grace is not the kind of forgiveness of sin which frees us from the toils of sin. Cheap grace is the grace we bestow on ourselves.

Cheap grace is the preaching of forgiveness without requiring repentance, baptism without Church discipline, Communion without confession, absolution without personal confession. Cheap grace is grace without discipleship, grace without the cross, grace without Jesus Christ, living and incarnate.

Costly grace is the treasure hidden in the field; for the sake of it a man will gladly go and sell all that he has. It is the pearl of great price to buy which the merchant will sell all his goods. It is the kingly rule of Christ, for whose sake a man will pluck out the eye which causes him to stumble, it is the call of Jesus Christ at which the disciple leaves his nets and follows him.

Costly grace is the gospel which must be *sought* again and again, the gift which must be *asked* for, the door at which a man must *knock*.

Such grace is *costly* because it calls us to follow, and it *is grace* because it calls us to follow *Jesus Christ*. It is costly because it costs a man his life, and it is grace because it gives a man the only true life. It is costly because it condemns sin, and grace because it justifies the sinner. Above all, it is *costly* because it cost God the life of his Son: 'ye were bought at a price', and what has cost God much cannot be cheap for us. Above all, it is *grace* because God did not reckon his Son too dear a price to pay for our life, but delivered him up for us. Costly grace is the Incarnation of God.

Costly grace is the sanctuary of God; it has to be protected from the world, and not thrown to the dogs. It is therefore the living word, the Word of God, which he speaks as it pleases him. Costly grace confronts us as a gracious call to follow Jesus, it comes as a word of forgiveness to the broken spirit and the contrite heart. Grace is costly because it compels a man to submit to the yoke of Christ and follow him; it is grace because Jesus says: 'My yoke is easy and my burden is light.'

On two separate occasions Peter received the call, 'Follow me'. It was the first and last word Jesus spoke to his disciple (Mark 1:17; John 21:22). A whole life lies between these two calls. The first occasion was by the lake of Gennesareth, when Peter left his nets and his craft and followed Jesus at his word. The second occasion is when the Risen Lord finds him back again at his old trade. Once again it is by the lake of Gennesareth, and once again the call is: 'Follow me.' Between the two calls lay a whole life of discipleship in the following of Christ. Half-way between them comes Peter's confession, when he acknowledged Jesus as the Christ of God. Three times Peter hears the same proclamation that Christ is his Lord and God—at the beginning, at the end, and at Caesarea Philippi. Each time it is the same grace of Christ which calls to him 'Follow me' and which reveals itself to him in his confession of the Son of God. Three times on Peter's way did grace arrest him, the one grace proclaimed in three different ways.

This grace was certainly not self-bestowed. It was the grace of Christ himself, now prevailing upon the disciple to leave all and follow him, now working in him that confession which to the world must sound like the ultimate blasphemy, now inviting Peter to the supreme fellowship of martyrdom for the

Lord he had denied, and thereby forgiving him all his sins. In the life of Peter grace and discipleship are inseparable. He had received the grace which costs.

As Christianity spread, and the Church became more secularized, this realization of the costliness of grace gradually faded. The world was christianized, and grace became its common property. It was to be had at low cost. Yet the Church of Rome did not altogether lose the earlier vision. It is highly significant that the Church was astute enough to find room for the monastic movement, and to prevent it from lapsing into schism. Here on the outer fringe of the Church was a place where the older vision was kept alive. Here men still remembered that grace costs, that grace means following Christ. Here they left all they had for Christ's sake, and endeavoured daily to practise his rigorous commands. Thus monasticism became a living protest against the secularization of Christianity and the cheapening of grace. But the Church was wise enough to tolerate this protest, and to prevent it from developing to its logical conclusion. It thus succeeded in relativizing it, even using it in order to justify the secularization of its own life. Monasticism was represented as an individual achievement which the mass of the laity could not be expected to emulate. By thus limiting the application of the commandments of Jesus to a restricted group of specialists, the Church evolved the fatal conception of the double standard—a maximum and a minimum standard of Christian obedience. Whenever the Church was accused of being too secularized, it could always point to monasticism as an opportunity of living a higher life within the fold, and thus justify the other possibility of a lower standard of life for others. And so we get the paradoxical result that monasticism, whose mission was to preserve in the Church of Rome the primitive Christian realization of the costliness of grace, afforded conclusive justification for the secularization of the Church. By and large, the fatal error of monasticism lay not so much in its rigorism (though even here there was a good deal of misunderstanding of the precise content of the will of Jesus) as in the extent to which it departed from genuine Christianity by setting up itself as the individual achievement of a select few, and so claiming a special merit of its own.

When the Reformation came, the providence of God raised Martin Luther to restore the gospel of pure, costly grace. Luther passed through the cloister; he was a monk, and all this was part of the divine plan. Luther had left all to follow Christ on the path of absolute obedience. He had renounced the world in order to live the Christian life. He had learnt obedience to Christ and to his Church because only he who is obedient can believe. The call to the cloister demanded of Luther the complete surrender of his life. But God shattered all his hopes. He showed him through the Scriptures that the following of Christ is not the achievement or merit of a select few, but the divine command to all Christians without distinction. Monasticism had transformed the humble work of discipleship into the meritorious activity of the saints, and the self-renunciation of discipleship into the flagrant spiritual self-assertion of the 'religious'. The world had crept into the very heart of the monastic life, and was once more making havoc. The monk's attempt to flee from the world turned out to be a subtle form of love for the world. The bottom having thus been knocked out of the religious life, Luther laid hold upon grace. Just as the whole world of monasticism was crashing about him in ruins, he saw God in Christ stretching forth his hand to save. He grasped that hand in faith, believing that 'after all, nothing we can do is of any avail, however good a life we live'. The grace which gave itself to him was a costly grace, and it shattered his whole existence. Once more he must leave his nets and follow. The first time was when he entered the monastery, when he had left everything behind except his pious self. This time even that was taken from him. He obeyed the call, not through any merit of his own, but simply through the grace of God. Luther did not hear the word: 'Of course you have sinned, but now everything is forgiven, so you can stay as you are and enjoy the consolations of forgiveness.' No, Luther had to leave the cloister and go back to the world, not because the world in itself was good and holy, but because even the cloister was only a part of the world.

Luther's return from the cloister to the world was the worst blow the world had suffered since the days of early Christianity. The renunciation he made when he became a monk was child's play compared with that which he had to make when he returned to the world. Now came the frontal assault. The only way to follow Jesus was by living in the world. Hitherto the Christian life had been the achievement of a few choice spirits under the exceptionally favourable conditions of monasticism; now it is a duty laid on every Christian living in the world. The commandment of Jesus must be accorded perfect obedience in one's daily vocation of life. The conflict between the life of the Christian and the life of the world was thus thrown into the sharpest possible relief. It was a hand-to-hand conflict between the Christian and the world.

It is a fatal misunderstanding of Luther's action to suppose that his rediscovery of the gospel of pure grace offered a general dispensation from obedience to the command of Jesus, or that it was the great discovery of the Reformation that God's forgiving grace automatically conferred upon the world both righteousness and holiness. On the contrary, for Luther the Christian's worldly calling is sanctified only in so far as that calling registers the final radical protest against the world. Only in so far as the Christian's secular calling is exercised in the following of Jesus does it receive from the gospel new sanction and justification. It was not the justification of sin, but the justification of the sinner that drove Luther from the cloister back into the world. The grace he had received was costly grace. It was grace, for it was like water on parched ground, comfort in tribulation, freedom from the bondage of a self-chosen way, and forgiveness of all his sins. And it was costly, for, so far from dispensing him from good works, it meant that he must take the call to discipleship more seriously than ever before. It was grace because it cost so much, and it cost so much because it was grace. That was the secret of the gospel of the Reformation—the justification of the sinner.

Yet the outcome of the Reformation was the victory, not of Luther's perception of grace in all its purity and costliness, but of the vigilant religious instinct of man for the place where grace is to be obtained at the cheapest price. All that was needed was a subtle and almost imperceptible change of emphasis, and the damage was done. Luther had taught that man cannot stand before God, however religious his works and ways may be, because at bottom he is always seeking his own interests. In the depth of his misery, Luther had grasped by faith the free and unconditional forgiveness of all his sins. That experience taught him that this grace had cost him his very life, and must continue to cost him the same price day by day. So far from dispensing him from discipleship, this grace only made him a more earnest disciple. When he spoke of grace, Luther always implied as a corollary that it cost him his own life, the life which was now for the first time subjected to the absolute obedience of Christ. Only so could he speak of grace. Luther had said that grace alone can save; his followers took up his doctrine and repeated it word for word. But they left out its invariable corollary, the obligation of discipleship. There was no need for Luther always to mention that corollary explicitly for he always spoke as one who had been led by grace to the strictest following of Christ. Judged by the standard of Luther's doctrine, that of his followers was unassailable, and yet their orthodoxy spelt the end and destruction of the Reformation as the revelation on earth of the costly grace of God. The justification of the sinner in the world degenerated into the justification of sin and the world. Costly grace was turned into the cheap grace without discipleship.

Luther had said that all we can do is of no avail, however good a life we live. He had said that nothing can avail us in the sight of God but 'the grace and favour which confers the forgiveness of sin'. But he spoke as one who knew that at the very moment of his crisis he was called to leave all that he had a second time and follow Jesus. The recognition of grace was his final, radical breach with his besetting sin, but it was never the justification of that sin. By laying hold of God's forgiveness, he made the final, radical renunciation of a self-willed life, and this breach was such that it led inevitably to a serious following of Christ. He always looked upon it as the answer to a sum, but an answer which had been arrived at by God, not by man. But then his followers changed the 'answer' into the data for a calculation of their own. That was the root of the trouble. If grace is God's answer, the gift of Christian life, then we cannot for a moment dispense with following Christ. But if grace is the data for my Christian life, it means that I set out to live the Christian life in the world with all my sins justified beforehand. I can go and sin as much as I like, and rely on this grace to forgive me, for after all the world is justified in principle by grace. I can therefore cling to my bourgeois secular existence, and remain as I was before, but with the added assurance that the grace of God will cover me. It is under the influence of this kind of 'grace' that the world has been made 'Christian', but at the cost of secularizing the Christian religion as never before. The antithesis between the Christian life and the life of bourgeois respectability is at an end. The Christian life comes to mean nothing more than living in the world and as the world, in being no different from the world, in fact, in being prohibited from being different from the world for the sake of grace. The upshot of it all is that my only duty as a Christian is to leave the world for an hour or so on a Sunday morning and go to church to be assured that my sins are all forgiven. I need no longer try to follow Christ, for cheap grace, the bitterest foe of discipleship, which true discipleship must loathe and detest, has freed me from that. Grace as the data for our calculations means grace at the cheapest price, but grace as the answer to the sum means costly grace. It is terrifying to realize what use can be made of a genuine evangelical doctrine. In both cases we have the identical formula—'justification by faith alone'. Yet the misuse of the formula leads to the complete destruction of its very essence.

At the end of a life spent in the pursuit of knowledge Faust has to confess:

'I now do see that we can nothing know'.

That is the answer to a sum, it is the outcome of a long experience. But as Kierkegaard observed, it is quite a different thing when a freshman comes up to the university and uses the same sentiment to justify his indolence. As the answer to a sum it is perfectly true, but as the initial data it is a piece of self-deception. For acquired knowledge cannot be divorced from the existence in which it is acquired. The only man who has the right to say that he is justified by grace alone is the man who has left all to follow Christ. Such a man knows that the call to discipleship is a gift of grace, and that the call is inseparable from the grace. But those who try to use this grace as a dispensation from following Christ are simply deceiving themselves.

But, we may ask, did not Luther himself come perilously

near to this perversion in the understanding of grace? What about his *Pecca fortiter, sed fortius fide et gaude in Christo* ('Sin boldly, but believe and rejoice in Christ more boldly still')? You are a sinner, anyway, and there is nothing you can do about it. Whether you are a monk or a man of the world, a religious man or a bad one, you can never escape the toils of the world or from sin. So put a bold face on it, and all the more because you can rely on the *opus operatum* of grace. Is this the proclamation of cheap grace, naked and unashamed, the *carte blanche* for sin, the end of all discipleship? Is this a blasphemous encouragement to sin boldly and rely on grace? Is there a more diabolical abuse of grace than to sin and rely on the grace which God has given? Is not the Roman Catechism quite right in denouncing this as the sin against the Holy Ghost?

If we are to understand this saying of Luther's, everything depends on applying the distinction between the data and the answer to the sum. If we make Luther's formula a premiss for our doctrine of grace, we are conjuring up the spectre of cheap grace. But Luther's formula is meant to be taken, not as the premiss, but as the conclusion, the answer to the sum, the copingstone, his very last word on the subject. Taken as the premiss, *pecca fortiter* acquires the character of an ethical principle, a principle of grace to which the principle of *pecca fortiter* must correspond. That means the justification of sin, and it turns Luther's formula into its very opposite. For Luther 'sin boldly' could only be his very last refuge, the consolation for one whose attempts to follow Christ had taught him that he can never become sinless, who in his fear of sin despairs of the grace of God. As Luther saw it, 'sin boldly' did not happen to be a fundamental acknowledgement of his disobedient life; it was the gospel of the grace of God before which we are always and in every circumstance sinners. Yet that grace seeks us and justifies us, sinners though we are. Take courage and confess your sin, says Luther, do not try to run away from it, but believe more boldly still. You are a sinner, so be a sinner, and don't try to become what you are not. Yes, and become a sinner again and again every day, and be bold about it. But to whom can such words be addressed, except to those who from the bottom of their hearts make a daily renunciation of sin and of every barrier which hinders them from following Christ, but who nevertheless are troubled by their daily faithlessness and sin? Who can hear these words without endangering his faith but he who hears their consolation as a renewed summons to follow Christ? Interpreted in this way, these words of Luther become a testimony to the costliness of grace, the only genuine kind of grace there is.

Grace interpreted as a principle, *pecca fortiter* as a principle, grace at a low cost, is in the last resort simply a new law, which brings neither help nor freedom. Grace as a living word, *pecca fortiter* as our comfort in tribulation and as a summons to discipleship, costly grace is the only pure grace, which really forgives sins and gives freedom to the sinner.

We Lutherans have gathered like eagles round the carcase of cheap grace, and there we have drunk of the poison which has killed the life of following Christ. It is true, of course, that we have paid the doctrine of pure grace divine honours unparalleled in Christendom, in fact we have exalted that doctrine to the position of God himself. Everywhere Luther's formula has been repeated, but its truth perverted into self-deception. So long as our Church holds the correct doctrine of justification, there is no doubt whatever that she is a justified Church! So they said, thinking that we must vindicate our Lutheran heritage by making this grace available on the cheapest and easiest terms. To be 'Lutheran' must mean that we leave the following of Christ to legalists, Calvinists and enthusiasts—and all this for the sake of grace. We justified the world, and condemned as heretics those who tried to follow Christ. The result was that a nation became Christian and Lutheran, but at the cost of true discipleship. The price it was called upon to pay was all too cheap. Cheap grace had won the day.

But do we also realize that this cheap grace has turned back upon us like a boomerang? The price we are having to pay today in the shape of the collapse of the organized Church is only the inevitable consequence of our policy of making grace available to all at too low a cost. We gave away the word and sacraments wholesale, we baptized, confirmed, and absolved a whole nation unasked and without condition. Our humanitarian sentiment made us give that which was holy to the scornful and unbelieving. We poured forth unending streams of grace. But the call to follow Jesus in the narrow way was hardly ever heard. Where were those truths which impelled the early Church to institute the catechumenate which enabled a strict watch to be kept over the frontier between the Church and the world, and afforded adequate protection for costly grace? What had happened to those warnings of Luther's against preaching the gospel in such a manner as to make men rest secure in their ungodly living? Was there ever a more terrible or disastrous instance of the Christianizing of the world than this? What are those three thousand Saxons put to death by Charlemagne compared with the millions of spiritual corpses in our country today? With us it has been abundantly proved that the sins of the fathers are visited upon the children unto the third and fourth generations. Cheap grace has turned out to be utterly merciless to our Evangelical Church.

This cheap grace has been no less disastrous to our own spiritual lives. Instead of opening up the way to Christ it has closed it. Instead of calling us to follow Christ, it has hardened us in our disobedience. Perhaps we had once heard the gracious call to follow him, and had at this command even taken the first few steps along the path of discipleship in the discipline of obedience, only to find ourselves confronted by the word of cheap grace. Was that not merciless and hard? The only effect that such a word could have on us was to bar our way to progress, and seduce us to the mediocre level of the world, quenching the joy of discipleship by telling us that we were following a way of our own choosing, that we were spending our strength and disciplining ourselves in vain—all of which was not merely useless, but extremely dangerous. After all, we were told, our salvation had already been accomplished by the grace of God. The smoking flax was mercilessly extinguished. It was unkind to speak to men like this, for such a cheap offer could only leave them bewildered and tempt them from the way to which they had been called by Christ. Having laid hold on cheap grace, they were barred for ever from the knowledge of costly grace. Deceived and weakened, men felt that they were strong now that they were in possession of this cheap grace—whereas they had in fact lost the power to live the life of discipleship and obedience. The word of cheap grace has been the ruin of more Christians than any commandment of works.

In our subsequent chapters we shall try to find a message for those who are troubled by this problem, and for whom the word of grace has been emptied of all its meaning. This message must be spoken for the sake of truth, for those among us who confess that through cheap grace they have lost the following of Christ and further, with the following of Christ, have lost the understanding of costly grace. To put it quite simply, we must undertake this task because we are now ready to admit that we no longer stand in the path of true discipleship. We confess that, although our Church is orthodox as far as her doctrine of grace is concerned, we are no longer sure that we are members of a Church which follows its Lord. We must therefore attempt to recover a true understanding of the mutual relation between grace and discipleship. The issue can no longer be evaded. It is becoming clearer every day that the most urgent problem besetting our Church is this: How can we live the Christian life in the modern world?

Happy are they who have reached the end of the road we seek to tread, who are astonished to discover the by no means self-evident truth that grace is costly just because it is the grace of God in Jesus Christ. Happy are the simple followers of Jesus Christ who have been overcome by his grace, and are able to sing the praises of the all-sufficient grace of Christ with humbleness of heart. Happy are they who, knowing that grace, can live in the world without being of it, who, by following Jesus Christ, are so assured of their heavenly citizenship that they are truly free to live their lives in this world. Happy are they who know that discipleship simply means the life which springs from grace, and that grace simply means discipleship. Happy are they who have become Christians in this sense of the word. For them the word of grace has proved a fount of mercy.

(FROM: *The Cost of Discipleship*, pp. 35–47.)

3 Positive Christology

[A Christian doctrine of the Incarnation, Bonhoeffer insisted, must be realistic. This needs saying, he believed, because Christians have in their history hesitated to say, for instance, that Christ was born in the way that we are, or that he had exactly the same human nature as ours. On the latter point some Christians have said that the human nature assumed by Christ in the Incarnation was perfect ('unfallen'). Against this Bonhoeffer insists that Christians must make it quite clear that the Incarnation for them means that Christ shared in an unqualified way human nature as we know it. This meant among other things that there was an element of the incognito about the Incarnation. It was possible, that is, to mistake him for an ordinary man.]

1. *The Incarnate*

The question may not run 'How is it possible to conceive of the Incarnate?', but 'Who is he?' He is not adopted by God, and he is not clothed in human characteristics. He is the God who has become man as we have become man. He lacks nothing that is man's. There is nothing offered by this world or by men which Jesus Christ did not take. The protest against *enhypostasia*[1] must be maintained. Jesus Christ had his own human individual hypostasis[2] and human mode of existence. The man that I am, Jesus also was. Of him alone it is really true that nothing human remained alien to him. Of this man we say, 'This is God for us'.

This does not mean that we know, say, at an earlier stage quite apart from Jesus Christ, what and who God is, and then apply it to Christ. We have a direct statement of identity; whatever we can say here is prompted by a look at him, or, better, is compelled by this man. Neither does it mean that the statement 'This man is God' adds anything to his manhood. That is the essential point. *Per contra,* it could be argued that something was added to the man Jesus that we do not have, namely Godhead. And this is right. But we must be care-

[1] The idea that in the Incarnation Christ assumed human nature in general rather than the human nature of an individual. (Ed.)

[2] A difficult word to translate adequately: here almost 'personality'. (Ed.)

ful here. The union of God and man in Christ is not to be conceived of in terms of essence or *ousia*. The Godhead of Jesus is not an extension of his manhood. Nor it is something contiguous to his manhood, which Jesus goes on to achieve. The statement 'This man is God' touches on Jesus vertically from above. It takes nothing from him and adds nothing to him. It simply qualifies the whole man Jesus as God. It is God's judgement and Word on this man. But this qualification, this judgement and Word of God which 'comes from above' is in turn not to be thought of as something which is added. Rather than being understood as an addition, this Word of God coming from above is in fact the man Jesus Christ himself. And because Jesus Christ is also God's judgement on himself, he points at the same time both to himself and to God.

An attempt is thus made to avoid the union of two demonstrable isolated entities. Jesus, the man, is believed in as God. And he is believed in as the man, and not despite his manhood, or in addition to it. Faith in the Word ignites in the man Jesus. Jesus Christ is not God in a divine *ousia;* he is not God in a demonstable and describable way; he is God in faith. There is no such thing as this divine essence. If Jesus Christ is to be described as God, then we may not speak of this divine essence, of his omnipotence and his omniscience, but we must speak of this weak man among sinners, of his cradle and his cross. When we consider the Godhead of Jesus, then above all we must speak of his weakness. In christology one looks at the whole historical man Jesus and says of him, 'He is God'. One does not first look at a human nature and then beyond it to a divine nature; one meets the one man Jesus Christ, who is fully God.

The accounts of the birth and the baptism of Jesus stand side by side. The birth points wholly to Jesus himself. The baptism points to the Holy Spirit coming from above. The difficulty of taking the birth narrative and the baptism narrative together is a consequence of the doctrine of the two natures. But the two accounts are not a doctrine of two natures. If we disregard this doctrine, the one story deals with the presence of the Word of God in Christ and the other with the descent of the Word of God on Jesus. The child in the cradle is the whole God; see Luther's christology in the Christmas hymns. The call at the baptism is a confirmation of the first event; there is no adoptionism[1] in it. The cradle shows the man who is God, the baptism shows in respect of Jesus the God who calls.

So if we speak of Jesus Christ as God, we may not speak of him as the representative of an idea of God who possesses the properties of omniscience and omnipotence (there is no such thing as this abstract divine nature!); we must speak of his weakness, of the cradle and the cross; and this man is no abstract God.

Strictly speaking, we should really talk, not about the Incarnation, but only about the Incarnate One. An interest in the Incarnation raises the question 'How?' The question 'How?' thus underlies the hypothesis of the Virgin Birth. It is both historically and dogmatically questionable. The biblical evidence for it is uncertain. If the biblical evidence gave decisive evidence for the real fact, there might be no particular significance in the dogmatic obscurity. The doctrine of the Virgin Birth is meant to express the incarnation of God and not just the fact of the Incarnate One. But does it not miss the decisive point of the incarnation by implying that Jesus has *not* become man wholly as we are? The question remains open, just as and just because it is already open in the Bible.

The Incarnate One is the glorified God. 'The Word was made flesh and we beheld his glory.' God glorifies himself in man. That is the ultimate mystery of the Trinity. The humanity is taken up into the Trinity; not since eternity, but 'from now to all eternity'. The glorification of God in the flesh is now at the same time the glorification of man, who is to have life with the trinitarian God for eternity. So it is incorrect to see the incarnation of God as a judgement of God on man. God remains the Incarnate One even at the last judgement. The incarnation is the message of the glorification of God who sees his honour in being man. It must be observed that the incarnation is primarily a real revelation of the creator in the

[1] The idea that Jesus was an ordinary man who was 'adopted' into Godhead, rather like the divinization of heroes in Greek and Roman mythology. (Ed.)

creature, and not a veiled revelation. Jesus Christ is the unveiled image of God.

The incarnation of God may not be thought of as being derived from an idea of God where, say, the manhood already belongs to the idea of God as in the case of Hegel.[1] The biblical testimony, 'We saw his glory', is meant here. If the incarnation is thus regarded as the glorification of God we may go on again to slip in a speculative idea of God, which derives the incarnation as necessary from the idea of God. A speculative basis for the doctrine of the incarnation in an idea of God would pervert the free relationship between the creator and the creature into a logically necessary one. The incarnation is contingent. God freely binds himself to the creature, and freely glorifies himself in the Incarnate. Why does that sound strange and improbable? Because the revelation of the incarnation in Jesus Christ is not a visible glorification of God. Because this Incarnate one is also the Crucified.

2. *The Humiliated One and the Exalted One*

In considering humiliation and exaltation, we are not investigating the divine and human natures, but the way God exists as man. We do not know a Godhead and a manhood each in its own nature. We are concerned with the way in which the one who has been made man exists. Thus 'humiliation' does not mean a state where the Incarnate One is more man and less God, in other words a stage in the limitation of God. Neither does exaltation mean a state where he is more God and less man. In humiliation and exaltation, Jesus remains fully man and fully God. The statement 'This is God' must be made of the Humiliated One in just the same way as it is made of the Exalted One.

We say of the Humiliated One, 'This is God'. He makes none of his divine properties manifest in his death. On the contrary, all we see is a man doubting in God as he dies. But of this man we say, 'This is God'. Anyone who cannot do this does not know the meaning of 'God became man'. In the incarnation, God reveals himself without concealment. Not the Logos, the Godhead or the manhood of Christ, but the whole person of the God-man is in the humiliation. He veils himself

[1] G. W. F. Hegel (1770–1831), German philosopher. (Ed.)

in the concealment of this scandal. The principle of the humiliation is not Christ's humanity but the 'likeness of flesh' (Rom. 8:3). With the exaltation, this is done away with, but Christ's manhood remains eternal.

The question is no longer, *How* can God be humiliated man? but rather, *Who* is the humiliated God-man? The doctrine of the incarnation and the doctrine of the humiliation must be strictly distinguished from each other. The mode of existence of humiliation is an act of the Incarnate. That does not, of course, mean that he can be separated in time from the act of the incarnation; the God-man in history is always already the humiliated God-man, from the cradle to the cross.

In what way is this special mode of existence of the humiliation expressed? In the fact that Christ takes sinful flesh. The humiliation is made necessary by the world under the curse. The incarnation is relative to the first creation, the humiliation to fallen creation. In the humiliation, Christ enters the world of sin and death of his own free will. He enters it in such a way as to hide in it in weakness and not to be known as God-man. He does not enter in the royal clothes of a 'Form of God'. The claim which he raises as God-man in this form must provoke antagonism and hostility. He goes incognito as a beggar among beggars, as an outcast among the outcast, despairing among the despairing, dying among the dying. He also goes as sinner among the sinners, yet in that he is *peccator pessimus*[1] (Luther), as sinless among the sinners, And here the central problem of christology lies.

The doctrine of the sinlessness of Jesus is not one *locus* among others. It is a central point on which all that has been said is decided. The question runs: Did Jesus, as the humiliated God-man, fully enter into human sin? Was he a man with sins like ours? If not, was he then man at all? If not, can he then help at all? And if he was, how can he help us in our predicament, as he is in the same predicament?

It is vital here to understand what the 'likeness of flesh' can mean. It means the real image of human flesh. His flesh is our flesh. Liability to sin and self-will are an essential part of our flesh. Christ became involved in the predicament of the whole flesh. But to what extent does he differ from us? In the

[1] The worst sinner. (Ed.)

first place, not at all. He is man as we are, he is tempted on all sides as we are, indeed far more dangerously than we are. In his flesh, too, was the law that is contrary to God's will. He was not the perfectly good man. He was continually engaged in struggle. He did things which outwardly sometimes looked like like sin. He was angry, he was harsh to his mother, he evaded his enemies, he broke the law of his people, he stirred up revolt against the rulers and the religious men of his country. He entered man's sinful existence past recognition.

But everything depends on the fact that it is *he* who took the flesh with its liability to temptation and self-will. *He* did this and that, which seem to the onlooker to be sin and failure, and must be evaluated as such. Because it is *he*, these statements, of course, appear in a different light. It is really human flesh that he bore—but because *he* bears it, this flesh is robbed of its rights. He pronounces the verdict on his action. He has anguish as we do; it is his anguish. He is tempted as we are, but because *he* is condemned, we are saved through him. In the light of this 'He' the harshest and most scandalous expressions about this humiliated God-man must be ventured and tolerated. He was really made sin for us, and crucified as the *peccator pessimus*. Luther says that he is himself robber, murderer and adulterer as we are, for he bears our sin, and in so doing describes the ultimates foundation of all christological statements. As the one who bears our sin, and no one else, he is sinless, holy, eternal, the Lord, the Son of the Father.

There can be no balancing of the two expressions 'sinner' and 'sinless', as though one could still separate the Humiliated One from the likeness of flesh. He is fully man; he gives the law its due and is judged, *and* robs sin of its force. He is completely in the likeness of flesh and under condemnation as we are, and yet he is without sin. The likeness of flesh with its realm of sin is related to him, but it is related to him, who is yet without sin. Without reaching an equilibrium we must say: *He*, not the likeness of flesh, is without sin; but he does not will to be distinguished from this likeness of flesh. Christology cannot get round this paradox.

The assertion of the sinlessness of Jesus fails if it has in mind observable acts of Jesus. His deeds are done in the likeness of flesh. They are not sinless, but ambiguous. One can and should see good and bad in them. If a man wishes to be incognito, one insults him if one says to him: I have both seen you and seen through you (Kierkegaard). So we should not justify Jesus' sinlessness by his actions. The assertion of the sinlessness of Jesus in his actions is no demonstrable moral judgement but a statement of belief that it is *he* who does these ambiguous actions, *he* who is eternally without sin. Faith acknowledges that the One who is tempted, is the victor, the One who struggles is the Perfect One, the Unrighteous One is the Righteous One, the Rejected, the Holy One. Even the sinlessness of Jesus is incognito, 'Blessed is he who is not offended in me' (Matt. 11:6).

The humiliated God-man is a stumbling block for the Jews, i.e., or the pious man. His historical ambiguity is a stumbling block. The pious man, the righteous man does not act as *he* did. The claim which this man raises, that he is not only a pious man but the Son of God, is incomprehensible to the pious man because it breaks every law: 'The men of old have said . . . but I . . .' The authority he assumes is incomprehensible: 'But I say to you' (Matt. 5:21), and 'Your sins are forgiven you' (Matt. 9:2). That is the essence of the scandal. Were Jesus not wholly man, but of a divinized nature, the claim might well have been allowed. Had he done the signs which were demanded of him for proof, men would probably have believed in him. But just when it came to the point of signs and wonders, he retreated into his incognito and refused to give any visible attestation. In this way he makes a stumbling block. But everything depends on this. Had he answered the question put to him about his authority with a miracle, then it would not be true that he was wholly man as we are. At the decisive moment, in the question about Christ, the exception would have been made. So the nearer the revelation, the thicker the concealment must be; the more urgent the question about Christ, the more impenetrable the incognito.

That means that the form of scandal is the very one which makes belief in Christ possible. In other words, the form of humiliation is the form of the *Christus pro nobis*. In this Christ proved himself by miracles, we would 'believe' the visible theopathy of the Godhead, but it would not be belief in the *Christus pro me*. It would not be inner conversion, but acknowledgement. Belief in miracles is belief in a visible epiphany. Nothing happens in me if I assert my belief in miracles. There is only faith where a man so surrenders himself to the humiliated God-man as to stake his life on him, even when this seems against all sense. Faith is where the attempt to have security from something visible is rejected. In that case, it is faith in God and not in the world. The only assurance that faith tolerates is the Word itself which comes to me through Christ.

Anyone who looks for signs of verification remains by himself. He is not changed. Anyone who recognizes the Son through the scandal is a believer in the New Testament sense. He sees the *Christus pro nobis*, he is reconciled and made new. The stumbling block in the incognito and the ambivalent form of the *Christus pro nobis* is at the same time the unceasing temptation of faith. The temptation, however, teaches us to pay heed to the Word (Isa. 28 : 19). And from the Word comes faith.

How are we to understand the fact that Jesus nevertheless does miracles? Are they not a breaching of the incognito? If the incognito has once slipped, is it not all a mockery? Are we, with liberal theology, to regard miracle as a phenomenon of the age? Or must we not at least return to the doctrine of the two natures? Must we not recognize a *genus maiestaticum*?[1] The miracles are no breaching of the incognito. The ancient religious world is full of miracle workers and healers. Jesus is not alone in this. The realm of miracle is not identical with the realm of God. True, the miracles may exceed normal everyday happenings, but they are only on another level within the created world. The concept which goes with miracle is not that of God, but that of magic. Magic remains within the world. If Jesus does miracles, he preserves his incognito within the magical picture of the world. It is not miracle which accredits him as the Son of God in the New Testament. On the contrary, his authority is taken to be demonic.

Only the believing community recognizes the approach of the kingdom in the miracles of Jesus. It does not see only magic and false claims here. But the incognito is not done away

[1] *Genus maiestaticum*: a reference to the Lutheran teaching that in the Incarnate Christ the human nature took on divine attributes. (Ed.)

with for the unbeliever. The unbeliever sees magic and an ambiguous world. The believer says, 'Here is the kingdom of God.' Our age no longer lives in a magical world, but it is still inclined to take miracles as an unequivocal manifestation of the divine. But miracle remains ambiguous if it happens, and it needs to be explained. It *is* explained by both believer and unbeliever. The believer sees in it the prelude to the divine action at the end of the world. He sees, bound up with the incognito, something of the glory of God. 'We saw his glory' (John 1 : 14). But the non-believer sees nothing.

The Humiliated One is present to us only as the Risen and Exalted One. We know that he is the God-man in incognito only through the resurrection and the exaltation. As believers, we always have the incognito as an already penetrated incognito, we have the child in the cradle as the one who is eternally present, the one laden with guilt as the Sinless One. But the converse must also be valid. We cannot get round the scandal by means of the resurrection. We have the Exalted One only as the Crucified, the Sinless One only as the one laden with guilt, the Risen One only as the Humiliated One. Were this not so, the *pro nobis* would be done away with, there would be no faith. Even the resurrection is not a penetration of the incognito. Even the resurrection is ambiguous. It is only believed in where the stumbling block of Jesus has not been removed. Only the disciples who followed Jesus saw the resurrection. Only blind faith sees here. They believe as those who do not see, and in this faith they see. 'Blessed are they who do not see and yet believe' (John 20 : 29).

Between humiliation and exaltation the historical fact of the empty tomb lies oppressively starkly. What is the significance of the account of the empty tomb before the account of the resurrection? Is it the decisive fact of christology? If it was really empty, then is Christ not risen and our faith vain? It seems as though our faith in the resurrection were bound up with the account of the empty tomb. Is our faith then in the last resort only faith in the empty tomb?

This is and remains a last stumbling block which the person who believes in Christ must accept in one way or the other. Empty or not empty, it remains a stumbling block. We are not sure of its historicity. The Bible itself reveals the stumbling block in showing how hard it was to prove that the disciples had not perhaps stolen the body. Even here we cannot evade the realm of ambiguity. We cannot get round it anywhere. Jesus has entered even the testimony of Scripture in the form of a stumbling block. Even as the Risen One, he does not break through his incognito. He only breaks through it when he returns in glory. Then the Incarnate is no longer the Lowly One. Then the decision over faith and unbelief has already been made. Then the manhood of God is really and only the glorification of God.

We know all this now only from our encounter with the Lowly One. The Church goes its own way of lowliness with this Lowly One. It cannot strive for a visible confirmation of its way while it renounces itself at every step. But as the lowly Church, it may not look at itself in vain conceit, as though its its lowliness were visible proof that Christ was present there. Lowliness is no proof, at least it is not a proof that one can refer to. There is no law or principle here which the Church has to follow; this is a fact, in short, God's way with the Church. As Paul says of himself that he can be either exalted or lowly so long as it happens for the sake of Christ, so too the church can be exalted and lowly, so long as it follows Christ's way. This way is the enemy of the proud, whether they wrap themselves in purple robes or set the martyrs crown upon their heads. The Church always looks only to the humiliated Christ, whether it be exalted or lowly.

It is not good if the Church boasts of its lowliness too hastily. It is equally bad if it boasts of its power and influence too hastily.

It is only good if the Church humbly acknowledges its sins, allows itself to be forgiven and acknowledges its Lord. Every day it must receive the will of God afresh from Christ. It receives it because of the presence of the Incarnate, Lowly and Exalted One. Every day this Christ once again becomes a stumbling block for its own hopes and wishes. Every day it comes anew to the sentence, 'You will all be offended because of me' (Matt. 26:31), and every day it holds anew to the promise, 'Blessed is he who is not offended in me' (Matt. 11:6).

(FROM: *Christology*, pp. 106–18.)

4 'Ethics as Formation'

[Bonhoeffer's *Ethics* is a significant attempt to reconstruct for the twentieth century the Christian ideal of the imitation of Christ. Every since Luther's criticism of it the *imitatio Christi* as an ethical pattern had been suspect in German protestantism. Luther criticized it because it had been taken in an antiquarian way as a literal attempt to mimic the Christ of the gospels. Luther also feared that it would be regarded as some kind of heroic moral endeavour to be like Christ which a man could attain by his own efforts apart from grace. For these reasons he preferred the term 'conformation to Christ' rather than 'imitation of Christ', as a way of bringing out that it is Christ, through the Spirit who brings Christians into some likeness to himself. Bonhoeffer takes up this phrase and seeks to show that far from being a vague abstract ideal it is embodied in the concrete realities of community and personal life and that conformation to Christ is compatible with the freedom and separate individuality of the human person.]

Conformation

The word 'formation' arouses our suspicion. We are sick and tired of Christian programmes and of the thoughtless and superficial slogan of what is called 'practical' Christianity as distinct from 'dogmatic' Christianity. We have seen that the formative forces in the world do not arise from Christianity at all and that the so-called practical Christianity is at least as unavailing in the world as is the dogmatic kind. The word 'formation', therefore, must be taken in quite a different sense from that to which we are accustomed. And in fact the Holy Scriptures speak of formation in a sense which is at first entirely unfamiliar to us. Their primary concern is not with the forming of a world by means of plans and programmes. Whenever they speak of forming they are concerned only with the one form which has overcome the world, the form of Jesus Christ. Formation can come only from this form. But here again it is not a question of applying directly to the world the teaching of Christ or what are referred to as Christian principles, so that the world might be formed in accordance with these. On the contrary, formation come only by being drawn in into the form of Jesus Christ. It comes only as formation in His likeness, as *conformation* with the unique form of His who was made man, was crucified, and rose again.

This is not achieved by dint of efforts 'to become like Jesus', which is the way in which we usually interpret it. It is achieved only when the form of Jesus Christ itself works upon us in such a manner that it moulds our form in its own likeness (Gal. 4:19). Christ remains the only giver of forms. It is not Christian men who shape the world with their ideas, but it is Christ who shapes men in conformity with Himself. But just as we misunderstood the form of Christ if we take Him to be essentially the teacher of a pious and good life, so, too, we should misunderstand the formation of man if we were to regard it as instruction in the way in which a pious and good life is to be attained. Christ is the Incarnate, Crucified and Risen One whom the Christian faith confesses. To be transformed in His image (2 Cor. 3:18, Phil. 3:10, Rom. 8:29 and 12:2)—this is what is meant by the formation of which the Bible speaks.

To be conformed with the Incarnate—that is to be a real man. It is man's right and duty that he should be man. The quest for the superman, the endeavour to outgrow the man within the man, the pursuit of the herioc, the cult of the demigod, all this is not the proper concern of man, for it is untrue. The real man is not an object either for contempt or for deification, but an object of the love of God. The rich and manifold variety of God's creation suffers no violence here from false uniformity or from the forcing of men into the pattern of an ideal or a type or a definite picture of the human character. The real man is at liberty to be his Creator's creature. To be conformed with the Incarnate is to have the right to be the man one really is. Now there is no more pretence, no more hypcrisy or self-violence, no more compulsion to be something other, better and more ideal than what one is. God loves the real man. God became a real man.

To be formed in the likeness of the Crucified—this means being a man sentenced by God. In his daily existence man carries with him God's sentence of death, the necessity of dying before God for the sake of sin. With his life he testifies that nothing can stand before God save only under God's sentence and grace. Every day man dies the death of a sinner. Humbly he bears the scars on his body and soul, the marks of the wounds which sin inflicts on him. He cannot raise himself up above any other man or set himself to be the greatest of all sinners. He can excuse the sin of another, but never his own. He bears all the suffering imposed on him, in the knowledge that it serves to enable him to die with his own will and to accept God's judgement upon him. But in surrendering himself to God's judgement upon him and against him he is himself just in the eyes of God. In the words of K. F. Hartmann's poem, 'it is in suffering that the Master imprints upon our minds and hearts his own all-valid image'.

To be conformed with the Risen One—that is to be a new man before God. In the midst of death he is in life. In the midst of sin he is righteous. In the midst of the old he is new. His secret remains hidden from the world. He lives because Christ lives, and lives in Christ alone. 'Christ is my life' (Phil. 1:21). So long as the glory of Christ is hidden, so long, too, does the glory of his new life remain 'hidden with Christ in God' (Col. 3:3). But he who knows espies already here and there a gleam of what is to come. The new man lives in the world like any other man. Often there is little to distinguish him from the rest. Nor does he attach importance to distinguishing himself, but only to distinguishing Christ for the sake of his brethren. Transfigured though he is in the form of the Risen One, here he bears only the sign of the cross and the judgement. By bearing it willingly he shows himself to be the one who has received the Holy Spirit and who is united with Jesus Christ in incomparable love and fellowship.

The form of Jesus Christ takes form in man. Man does not take on an independent form of his own, but what gives him form and what maintains him in the new form is always solely the form of Jesus Christ Himself. It is therefore not a vain imitation or repetition of Christ's form but Christ's form itself which takes form in man, And again, man is not transformed into a form which is alien to him, the form of God, but into his own form, the form which is essentially proper to him. Man becomes man because God became man. But man does not become God. It is not he, therefore, who was or is able to accomplish his own transformation, but it is God who changes his form into the form of man, so that man may become, not indeed God, but, in the eyes of God, man.

In Christ there was re-created the form of man before God. It was an outcome of the place or the time, of the climate or the race, of the individual or the society, or of religion or of taste, but quite simply of the life of mankind as such, that mankind at this point recognized its image and its hope. What befell Christ had befallen mankind. It is a mystery, for which there is no explanation, that only a part of mankind recognize the form of their Redeemer. The longing of the Incarnate to take form in all men is as yet still unsatisfied. He bore the form of man as a whole, and yet He can take form only in a small band. These are His Church.

'Formation' consequently means in the first place Jesus's taking form in His Church. What takes form here is the form of Jesus Christ Himself. The New Testament states the case profoundly and clearly when it calls the Church the Body of Christ. The body is the form. So the Church is not a religious community of worshippers of Christ but is Christ Himself who has taken form among men. The Church can be called the Body of Christ because in Christ's Body man is really taken up by Him, and so too, therefore, are all mankind. The Church, then, bears the form which is in truth the proper form of all humanity. The image in which she is formed is the image of man. What takes place in her takes place as an example and substitute for all men. But it is impossible to state clearly enough that the Church, too, is not an independent form by herself, side by side with the form of Christ, and that she, too, can therefore never lay claim to an independent character, title, authority or dignity on her own account and apart from Him. The Church is nothing but a section of humanity in which Christ has really taken form. What we have here is utterly and completely the form of Jesus Christ and not some other form side by side with Him. The Church is the man in Christ, incarnate, sentenced and awakened to new life. In the first instance, therefore, she has essentially nothing whatever to do with the so-called religious functions of man, but with the whole man in his existence in the world with all its implications. What matters in the Church is not religion but the form of Christ, and its taking form amidst a band of men. If we allow ourselves to lose sight of this, even for an instant, we inevitably relapse into that programme-planning for the ethical or religious shaping of the world, which was where we set out from.

We have now seen that it is only with reference to the form that we can speak of formation in a Christian and ethical sense. Formation is not an independent process or condition which can in some way or other be detached from this form. The only formation is formation by and into the form of Jesus Christ. The point of departure for Christian ethics is the body of Christ, the form of Christ in the form of the Church, and formation of the Church in conformity with the form of Christ. The concept of formation acquires its significance, indirectly, for all mankind only if what takes place in the Church does in truth take place for all men. But this again does not mean that the Church is set up, so to speak, as a model for the world. One can speak of formation and of world only if mankind is called by name in its true form, which is its own by right, which it has already received, but which it merely fails to understand and accept, namely, the form of Jesus Christ, which is proper to man, and if in this way, in anticipation as one might say, mankind is drawn in into the Church. This means, then, that even when we speak in terms of the formation of the world we are referring solely to the form of Jesus Christ.

The form of Christ is one and the same at all times and in all places. And the Church of Christ also is one and the same throughout all generations. And yet Christ is not a principle in accordance with which the whole world must be shaped. Christ is not the proclaimer of a system of what would be good today, here and at all times. Christ teaches no abstract ethics such as must at all costs be put into practice. Christ was not essentially a teacher and legislator, but a man, a real man like ourselves. And it is not therefore His will that we should in our time be the adherents, exponents and advocates of a definite doctrine, but that we should be men, real men before God. Christ did not, like a moralist, love a theory of good, but He loved the real man. He was not, like a philosopher, interested in the 'universally valid', but rather in that which is of help to the real and concrete human being.

What worried Him was not, like Kant, whether 'the maxim of an action can become a principle of general legislation', but whether my action is at this moment helping my neighbour to become a man before God. For indeed it is not written that God became an idea, a principle, a programme, a universally valid proposition or a law, but that God became man. This means that though the form of Christ certainly is and remains one and the same, yet it is willing to take the form in the real man, that is to say, in quite different guises. Christ does not dispense with human reality for the sake of an idea which demands realization at the expense of the real. What Christ does is precisely to give effect to reality. He affirms reality. And indeed He is Himself the real man and consequently the foundation of all human reality. And so formation in conformity with Christ has this double implication. The form of Christ remains one and the same, not as a general idea but in its own unique character as the incarnate, crucified and risen God. And precisely for the sake of Christ's form the form of the real man is preserved, and in this way the real man receives the form of Christ.

The Concrete Place

This leads us away from any kind of abstract ethic and towards an ethic which is entirely concrete. What can and must be said is not what is good once and for all, but the way in which Christ takes form among us here and now. The attempt to define that which is good once and for all has, in the nature of the case, always ended in failure. Either the proposition was asserted in such general and formal terms that it retained no significance as regards its contents, or else one tried to include in it and elaborate the whole immense range of conceivable contents, and thus to say in advance what would be good in every single conceivable case; this led to a casuistic system so unmanageable that it could satisfy the demands neither of general validity nor of concreteness. The concretely Christian ethic is beyond formalism and casuistry. Formalism and casuistry set out from the conflict between the good and the real, but the Christian ethic can take for its point of departure the reconciliation, already accomplished, of the world with God and the man Jesus Christ and the acceptance of the real man by God.

But the question of how Christ takes form among us here and now, or how we are conformed with His form, contains within itself still further difficult questions. What do we mean by 'among us', 'now' and 'here'? If it is impossible to establish for all times and places what is good, then the question still arises for what times and places can any answer at all be given to our enquiry. It must not remain in doubt for a single moment that any one section to which we may now turn our attention is to be regarded precisely as a section, as a part of the whole of humanity. In every section of his history man is simply and entirely the man taken upon Himself by Christ. And for this reason whatever may have to be said about this section will always refer not only to this part but also to the whole. However, we must now answer the question regarding the times and places of which we are thinking when we set out to speak of formation through the form of Christ. These are in the first place quite generally the times and places which in some way concern us, those of which we have experience and which are reality for us. They are the times and places which confront us with concrete problems, set us tasks and charge us with responsibility. The 'among us', the 'now' and 'here' is therefore the region of our decisions and encounters. This region undoubtedly varies very greatly in extent according to the individual, and it might consequently be supposed that these definitions could in the end be interpreted so widely and vaguely as to make room for unrestrained individualism. What prevents this is the fact that by our history we are set objectively in a definite nexus of experiences, responsibilities and decisions from which we cannot free ourselves again except by an abstraction. We live, in fact, within this nexus, whether or not we are in every respect aware of it. Furthermore, this nexus is characterized in a quite peculiar manner by the fact that until our own days its consciously affirmed and recognized underlying basis has been the form of Christ. In our historical identity, therefore, we stand already in the midst of Christ's taking form, in a section of human history which He himself has chosen. It is consequently in this sense that we regard the west as the region for which we wish to speak and must speak, the world of the peoples of Europe and America in so far as it is already united through the form of Jesus Christ. To take a narrower view or to limit our consideration to Germany, for example, would be to lose sight of the fact that the form of Christ is the unity of the Western nations and that for this reason no single one of these nations can exist by itself or even be conceived as existing by itself. And to take a wider view would be to overlook the mysterious fact of the self-containedness of tbe Western world.

The purpose of what follows is not indeed to develop a programme for shaping or formation of the Western world. What is intended is rather a discussion of the way in which in this Western world the form of Christ takes form. This means that the discussion must be neither abstract nor casuistic, but entirely concrete. It must be insisted that no other form may be placed side by side with the form of Jesus Christ, for He alone is the subduer and reconciler of the world. Only this one form can help. And so whatever concrete assertion may have to be made here today about the way in which this form takes form amongst us, it must be referred quite strictly to this form of Jesus Christ. Moreover, in the incarnation of Christ the assurance is given us that Christ is willing to take form amongst us here and today.

Ethics as formation, then, means the bold endeavour to speak about the way in which the form of Jesus Christ takes form in our world, in a manner which is neither abstract nor casuistic, neither programmatic nor purely speculative. Concrete judgements and decisions will have to be ventured here. Decision and action can here no longer be delegated to the personal conscience of the individual. Here there are concrete commandments and instructions for which obedience is demanded.

Ethics as formation is possible only upon the foundation of the form of Jesus Christ which is present in His Church. The Church is the place where Jesus Christ's taking form is proclaimed and accomplished. It is this proclamation and this event that Christian ethics is designed to serve.

(FROM: *Ethics*, pp. 80–8.)

5 'This-worldliness and Other-worldliness'

[Bonhoeffer believed that one of the urgent needs of the twentieth century was a reconstructed doctrine of the spiritual life. The word 'spiritual', however, he would have been suspicious of, because in Christian history it has often been assumed that that is most 'spiritual' which is most removed from the earthly, the material, the bodily, the sexual. This for Bonhoeffer constituted a radical denial of the Incarnation and, moreover, a blasphemous attempt to try and be more 'spiritual' than God who did not by-pass the material world but accepted it and used it.]

. . . And on the Christian aspect of the matter, there are some lines that say

> . . . that we remember what we would forget,
> that this poor earth is not our home.

That is indeed something essential, but it must come last of all. I believe that we ought so to love and trust God in our *lives*, and in all the good things that he sends us, that when the time comes (but not before!) we may go to him with love, trust, and joy. But, to put it plainly, for a man in his wife's arms to be hankering after the other world is, in mild terms, a piece of bad taste, and not God's will. We ought to find and love God in what he actually gives us; if it pleases him to allow us to enjoy some overwhelming earthly happiness, we mustn't try to be more pious than God himself and allow our happiness to be corrupted by presumption and arrogance, and by unbridled religious fantasy which is never satisfied with what God gives. God will see to it that the man who finds him in his earthly happiness and thanks him for it does not lack reminder that earthly things are transient, that it is good for him to attune his heart to what is eternal, and that sooner or later there will be times when he can say in all sincerity, 'I wish I were home'. But everything has its time, and the main thing is that we keep step with God, and do not keep pressing on a few steps ahead—nor keep dawdling a step behind. It's presumptuous to want to have everything at once—matrimonial bliss, the cross, and the heavenly Jerusalem, where they neither marry nor are given in marriage. 'For everything there is a season' (Eccles. 3:1); everything has its time: 'a time to weep, and a time to laugh; . . . a time to embrace, and a time to refrain from embracing; . . . a time to rend, and a time to sew; . . . and God seeks again what is past.' I suspect that these last words mean that nothing that is past is lost, that God gathers up again with us our past, which belongs to us. So when we are seized by a longing for the past—and this may happen when we least expect it—we may be sure that it is only one of the man 'hours' that God is always holding ready for us. So we oughtn't to seek the past again by our own efforts, but only with God . . .

. . . I think we honour God more if we gratefully accept the life that he gives us with all its blessings, loving it and drinking it to the full, and also grieving deeply and sincerely when we have impaired or wasted any of the good things of life (some people denounce such an attitude, and think it is bourgeois, weak, and sensitive), than if we are insensitive to life's blessings and may therefore also be insensitive to pain . . .

. . . What I mean is that God wants us to love him eternally with our whole hearts—not in such a way as to injure or weaken our earthly love, but to provide a kind of *cantus firmus*[1] to which the other melodies of life provide the counterpoint. One of these contrapuntal themes (which have their own complete independence but are yet related to the *cantus firmus*) is earthly affection . . .

Now for some further thoughts about the Old Testament. Unlike the other oriental religions, the faith of the Old Testament isn't a religion of redemption. It's true that Christianity has always been regarded as a religion of redemption. But isn't this a cardinal error, which separates Christ from the Old Testament and interprets him on the lines of the myths about redemption? To the objection that a crucial importance is given in the Old Testament to redemption (from Egypt, and later from Babylon—cf. Deutero-Isaiah) it may be answered that the redemptions referred to here are *historical*, i.e., on *this* side of death, whereas everywhere else the myths about redemption are concerned to overcome the barrier of death.

[1] Basic theme. (Ed.)

Israel is delivered out of Egypt so that it may live before God as God's people on earth. The redemption myths try unhistorically to find an eternity after death. Sheol[1] and Hades are no metaphysical constructions, but images which imply that the 'past', while it still exists, has only a shadowy existence in the present.

The decisive factor is said to be that in Christianity the hope of resurrection is proclaimed, and that that means the emergence of a genuine religion of redemption, the main emphasis now being on the far side of the boundary drawn by death. But it seems to me that this is just where the mistake and the danger lie. Redemption now means redemption from cares, distress, fears, and longings, from sin and death, in a better world beyond the grave. But is this really the essential character of the proclamation of Christ in the gospels and by Paul? I should say it is not. The difference between the Christian hope of resurrection and the mythological hope is that the former sends a man back to his life on earth in a wholly new way which is even more sharply defined than it is in the Old Testament. The Christian, unlike the devotees of the redemption myths, has no last line of escape available from earthly tasks and difficulties into the eternal, but, like Christ himself ('My God, why hast thou forsaken me?'), he must drink the earthly cup to the dregs, and only in his doing so is the crucified and risen Lord with him, and he crucified and risen with Christ. This world must not be prematurely written off; in this the Old and New Testaments are at one. Redemption myths arise from human boundary-experiences, but Christ takes hold of a man at the centre of his life.

(FROM: *Letters and Papers from Prison*, pp. 168–9, 191–2, 303, 336–7.)

[1] Hebrew word for Hades. (Ed.)

6 'Religionless Christianity'

[In his later period Bonhoeffer pondered deeply on the question raised by Barth of the relationship between Christianity and religion (see Book 1, pp. 59ff.). Bonhoeffer suspected that religion is commonly thought of in a very primitive way as the satisfaction of the human need for security and significance and as a lazy way of dealing with the gaps in our knowledge. Hence the 'God of the gaps' type of religion where God is used as a term to fill in a gap in our ignorance which cannot yet be explained by scientific or other investigation. In all this, Bonhoeffer saw religion being used in relation to human weakness or ignorance, involving salvation *from* rather than *for* the world. He could see in Christianity however, the resources for a religion which relates to man in his strength, achievement and enterprise. He was moving towards a new version of man as made in the image of God: man as 'procreator' acting by and on behalf of the Creator to use and enjoy creation.]

. . . What is bothering me incessantly is the question what Christianity really is, or indeed who Christ really is, for us today. The time when people could be told everything by means of words, whether theological or pious, is over, and so is the time of inwardness and conscience—and that means the time of religion in general. We are moving towards a completely religionless time; people as they are now simply cannot be religious any more. Even those who honestly describe themselves as 'religious' do not in the least act up to it, and so they presumably mean something quite different by 'religious'.

Our whole nineteen-hundred-year-old Christian preaching and theology rest on the 'religious *a priori*' of mankind. 'Christianity' has always been a form—perhaps the true form—of 'religion'. But if one day it becomes clear that this *a priori* does not exist at all, but was a historically conditioned and transient form of human self-expression, and if therefore man becomes radically religionless—and I think that that is already more or less the case (else how is it, for example, that this war, in contrast to all previous ones, is not calling forth any 'religious' reaction?)—what does that mean for 'Christianity'?

It means that the foundation is taken away from the whole of what has up to now been our 'Christianity', and that there remain only a few 'last survivors of the age of chivalry', or a few intellectually dishonest people, on whom we can descend as 'religious'. Are they to be the chosen few? Is it on this dubious group of people that we are to pounce in fervour, pique, or indignation, in order to sell them our goods? Are we to fall upon a few unfortunate people in their hour of need and exercise a sort of religious compulsion on them? If we don't want to do all that, if our final judgement must be that the Western form of Christianity, too, was only a preliminary stage to a complete absence of religion, what kind of situation emerges for us, for the Church? How can Christ become the Lord of the religionless as well? Are there religionless Christians? If religion is only a garment of Christianity—and even this garment has looked very different at different times—then what is a religionless Christianity?

Barth, who is the only one to have started along this line of thought, did not carry it to completion, but arrived at a positivism of revelation,[1] which in the last analysis is essentially a restoration. For the religionless working man (or any other man) nothing decisive is gained here. The questions to be answered would surely be: What do a church, a community, a sermon, a liturgy, a Christian life mean in a religionless world? How do we speak of God—without religion, i.e., without the temporally conditioned presupposition of metaphysics, inwardness, and so on? How do we speak (or perhaps we cannot now even 'speak' as we used to) in a 'secular' way about 'God'? In what way are we 'religionless-secular' Christians, in what way are we the ἐκ-κλησία, those who are called forth, not regarding ourselves from a religious point of view as specially favoured, but rather as belonging wholly to the world? In that case Christ is no longer an object of religion, but something quite different, really the Lord of the world. But what does that mean? What is the place of worship and prayer in a religionless situation? Does the secret discipline, or alternatively the difference (which I have suggested to you before) between penultimate and ultimate, take on a new importance here? . . .

[1] See Book 1, pp. 85ff.

. . . The Pauline question whether περιτομή [circumcision] is a condition of justification seems to me in present-day terms to be whether religion is a condition of salvation. Freedom from περιτομή is also freedom from religion. I often ask myself why a 'Christian instinct' often draws me more to the religionless people than to the religious, by which I don't in the least mean with any evangelizing intention, but, I might almost say, 'in brotherhood'. While I'm often reluctant to mention God by name to religious people—because that name somehow seems to me here not to ring true, and I feel myself to be slightly dishonest (it's particularly bad when others start to talk in religious jargon; I then dry up almost completely and feel awkward and uncomfortable)—to people with no religion I can on occasion mention him by name quite calmly and as a matter of course. Religious people speak of God when human knowledge (perhaps simply because they are too lazy to think) has come to an end, or when human resources fail—in fact it is always the *deus ex machina* that they bring on to the scene, either for the apparent solution of insoluble problems, or as strength in human failure—always, that is to say, exploiting human weakness or human boundaries. Of necessity, that can go on only till people can by their own strength push these boundaries somewhat further out, so that God becomes superfluous as a *deus ex machina*. I've come to be doubtful of talking about any human boundaries (is even death, which people now hardly fear, and is sin, which they now hardly understand, still a genuine boundary today?). It always seems to me that we are trying anxiously in this way to reserve some space for God; I should like to speak of God not on the boundaries but at the centre, not in weaknesses but in strength; and therefore not in death and guilt but in man's life and goodness. As to the boundaries, it seems to me better to be silent and leave the insoluble unsolved. Belief in the resurrection is *not* the 'solution' of the problem of death. God's 'beyond' is not the beyond of our cognitive faculties. The transcendence of epistemological theory has nothing to do with the transcendence of God. God is beyond in the midst of our life. The Church stands, not at the boundaries where human powers give out, but in the middle of the village. That is how it is in the Old Testament, and in this sense we still read the

New Testament far too little in the light of the Old. How this religionless Christianity looks, what form it takes, is something that I'm thinking about a great deal.

A few more words about 'religionlessness'. I expect you remember Bultmann's essay on the 'demythologizing' of the New Testament?[1] My view of it today would be, not that he went 'too far', as most people thought, but that he didn't go far enough. It's not only the 'mythological' concepts, such as miracle, ascension, and so on (which are not in principle separable from the concepts of God, faith, etc.), but 'religious' concepts generally, which are problematic. You can't, as Bultmann supposes, separate God and miracle, but you must be able to interpret and proclaim *both* in a 'non-religious' sense. Bultmann's approach is fundamentally still a liberal one (i.e., abridging the gospel), whereas I'm trying to think theologically.

What does it mean to 'interpret in a religious sense'? I think it means to speak on the one hand metaphysically, and on the other hand individualistically. Neither of these is relevant to the biblical message or to the man of today. Hasn't the individualistic question about personal salvation almost completely left us all? Aren't we really under the impression that there are more important things than that question (perhaps not more important than the *matter* itself, but more important than the *question*!)? I know it sounds pretty monstrous to say that. But, fundamentally, isn't this in fact biblical? Does the question about saving one's soul appear in the Old Testament at all? Aren't righteousness and the Kingdom of God on earth the focus of everything, and isn't it true that Rom. 3:24 ff. is not an individualistic doctrine of salvation, but the culmination of the view that God alone is righteous? It is not with the beyond that we are concerned, but with this world as created and preserved, subjected to laws, reconciled, and restored. What is above this world is, in the gospel, intended to exist *for* this world; I mean that, not in the anthropocentric sense of liberal, mystic pietistic, ethical theology,

[1] 'New Testament and Mythology', Whitsun 1941, first printed in the supplements to *Evangelische Theologie* the same year; there is an English translation in *Kerygma and Myth* (ed. H. W. Bartsch), SPCK, p. 1–41. See Book 2, pp. 132ff.

but in the biblical sense of the creation and of the incarnation, crucifixion, and resurrection of Jesus Christ.

Barth was the first theologian to begin the criticism of religion, and that remains his really great merit; but he put in its place a positivist doctrine of revelation which says, in effect, 'Like it or lump it': virgin birth, Trinity, or anything else; each is an equally significant and necessary part of the whole, which must simply be swallowed as a whole or not at all. That isn't biblical. There are degrees of knowledge and degrees of significance; that means that a secret discipline must be restored whereby the *mysteries* of the Christian faith are protected against profanation. The positivism of revelation makes it too easy for itself, by setting up, as it does in the last analysis, a law of faith, and so mutilates what is—by Christ's incarnation!—a gift for us. In the place of religion there now stands the Church—that is in itself biblical—but the world is in some degree made to depend on itself and left to its own devices, and that's the mistake.

. . . We are to find God in what we know, not in what we don't know; God wants us to realize his presence, not in unsolved problems but in those that are solved. That is true of the relationship between God and scientific knowledge, but it is also true of the wider human problems of death, suffering, and guilt. It is now possible to find, even for these questions, human answers that take no account whatever of God. In point of fact, people deal with these questions without God (it has always been so), and it is simply not true to say that only Christianity has the answers to them. As to the idea of 'solving' problems, it may be that the Christian answers are just as unconvincing—or convincing—as any others. Here again, God is no stop-gap; he must be recognized at the centre of life, not when we are at the end of our resources; it is his will to be recognized in life, and not only when death comes; in health and vigour, and not only in suffering; in our activities, and not only in sin. The ground for this lies in the revelation of God in Jesus Christ. He is the centre of life, and he certainly didn't 'come' to answer our unsolved problems.

(FROM: *Letters and Papers from Prison*, pp. 279–81, 281–2, 285–6, 311–12.)

7 'Man Come of Age'

[Bonhoeffer, in this extract, continues his reflections on the consequences for Christian belief of the realization that religion is not necessary for the underpinning of man's self-confidence. Christian apologists have often thought it essential to dwell on man's anxiety and despair before coming to the 'good news' of the gospel. In passing, Bonhoeffer calls in question Tillich's assumption that all men feel the pressure of certain 'ultimate questions' (life after death, judgement, etc.) which point towards religion. Increasingly, man 'come of age' is content to ignore such questions and because he has been brought up to expect God in the spectacular and astounding is ill-equipped to discover him in the ordinary and seemingly ineffectual.]

The movement that began about the thirteenth century (I'm not going to get involved in any argument about the exact date) towards the autonomy of man (in which I should include the discovery of the laws by which the world lives and deals with itself in science, social and political matters, art, ethics, and religion) has in our time reached an undoubted completion. Man has learnt to deal with himself in all questions of importance without recourse to the 'working hypothesis' called 'God'. In questions of science, art, and ethics this has become an understood thing at which one now hardly dares to tilt. But for the last hundred years or so it has also become increasingly true of religious questions; it is becoming evident that everything gets along without 'God'—and, in fact, just as well as before. As in the scientific field, so in human affairs generally, 'God' is being pushed more and more out of life, losing more and more ground.

Roman Catholic and Protestant historians agree that it is in this development that the great defection from God, from Christ, is to be seen; and the more they claim and play off God and Christ against it, the more the development considers itself to be anti-Christian. The world that has become conscious of itself and the laws that govern its own existence has grown self-confident in what seems to us to be an uncanny way. False developments and failures do not make the world doubt the necessity of the course that it is taking, or of its development; they are accepted with fortitude and detachment as part of the bargain, and even an event like the present war is no exception. Christian apologetic has taken the most varied forms of opposition to this self-assurance. Efforts are made to prove to a world thus come of age that it cannot live without the tutelage of 'God'. Even though there has been surrender on all secular problems, there still remain the so-called 'ultimate questions'—death, guilt—to which only 'God' can give an answer, and because of which we need God and the Church and the pastor. So we live, in some degree, on these so-called ultimate questions of humanity. But what if one day they no longer exist as such, if they too can be answered 'without God'? Of course, we now have the secularized offshoots of Christian theology, namely existentialist philosophy and the psychotherapists, who demonstrate to secure, contented, and happy mankind that it is really unhappy and desperate and simply unwilling to admit that it is in a predicament about which it knows nothing, and from which only they can rescue it. Wherever there is health, strength, security, simplicity, they scent luscious fruit to gnaw at or to lay their pernicious eggs in. They set themselves to drive people to inward despair, and then the game is in their hands. That is secularized methodism. And whom does it touch? A small number of intellectuals, of degenerates, of people who regard themselves as the most important thing in the world, and who therefore like to busy themselves with themselves. The ordinary man, who spends his everyday life at work and with his family, and of course with all kinds of diversions, is not affected. He has neither the time nor the inclination to concern himself with his existential despair, or to regard his perhaps modest share of happiness as a trial, a trouble, or a calamity.

The attack by Christian apologetic on the adulthood of the world I consider to be in the first place pointless, in the second place ignoble, and in the third place unchristian. Pointless, because it seems to me like an attempt to put a grown-up man back into adolescence, i.e., to make him dependent on things on which he is, in fact, no longer dependent, and thrusting him into problems that are, in fact, no longer problems to him. Ignoble, because it amounts to an attempt to exploit man's weakness for purposes that are alien to him and to which he has not freely assented. Unchristian, because it confuses Christ with one particular stage in man's religiousness, i.e., with a human law. More about this later.

But first, a little more about the historical position. The question is: Christ and the world that has come of age. The weakness of liberal theology was that it conceded to the world the right to determine Christ's place in the world; in the conflict between the Church and the world it accepted the comparatively easy terms of peace that the world dictated. Its strength was that it did not try to put the clock back, and that it genuinely accepted the battle (Troeltsch), even though this ended with its defeat.

Defeat was followed by surrender, and by an attempt to make a completely fresh start based on the fundamentals of the Bible and the Reformation. Heim[1] sought, along pietist and methodist lines, to convince the individual man that he was faced with the alternative 'despair or Jesus'. He gained 'hearts'. Althaus[2] (carrying forward the modern and positive line with a strong confessional emphasis) tried to wring from the world a place for Lutheran teaching (ministry) and Lutheran worship, and otherwise left the world to its own devices. Tillich set out to interpret the evolution of the world (against its will) in a religious sense—to give it its shape through religion. That was very brave of him, but the world unseated him and went on by itself; he, too, sought to understand the world better than it understood itself; but it felt that it was completely misunderstood, and rejected the imputation. (Of course, the world *must* be understood better than it understands itself, but not 'religiously' as the religious socialists wanted.)

Barth was the first to realize the mistake that all these attempts (which were all, in fact, still sailing, though unintentionally, in the channel of liberal theology) were making in leaving a clear space for religion in the world or against the world. He brought in against religion the God of Jesus Christ,

[1] Karl Heim, one of Bonhoeffer's theological teachers at Tübingen. (Ed.).

[2] Paul Althaus, German theologian who supported the Nazi-sponsored German Christians. (Ed.)

'*pneuma* against *sarx*'. That remains his greatest service (his *Epistle to the Romans*, second edition, in spite of all the neo-Kantian egg-shells). Through his later dogmatics, he enabled the Church to effect this distinction, in principle, all along the line. It was not in ethics, as is often said, that he subsequently failed—his ethical observations, as far as they exist, are just as important as his dogmatic ones—; it was that in the non-religious interpretation of theological concepts he gave no concrete guidance, either in dogmatics or in ethics. There lies his limitation, and because of it his theology of revelation has become positivist, a 'positivism of revelation', as I put it.

Now for a few more thoughts on our theme. I'm only gradually working my way to the non-religious interpretation of biblical concepts; the job is too big for me to finish just yet.

On the historical side: There is one great development that leads to the world's autonomy. In theology one sees it first in Lord Herbert of Cherbury,[1] who maintains that reason is sufficient for religious knowledge. In ethics it appears in Montaigne[2] and Bodin[3] with their substitution of rules of life for the commandments. In politics Machiavelli[4] detaches politics from morality in general and founds the doctrine of 'reasons of state'. Later, and very differently from Machiavelli, but tending like him towards the autonomy of human society, comes Grotius,[5] setting up his natural law as international law, which is valid *etsi deus non daretur*,[6] 'even if there were no God'. The philosophers provide the finishing touches: on the one hand we have the deism of Descartes,[7] who holds that the world is a mechanism, running by itself with no interference from God; and on the other hand the pantheism of Spinoza,[8] who says that God is nature. In the last resort, Kant[9] is a

[1] Lord Herbert of Cherbury (1583–1648), a forerunner of the English deists who held that reason and revelation were synonymous. (Ed.)

[2] Michel de Montaigne (1533–1592), French essayist. (Ed.)

[3] Jean Bodin (1530–1596), French political philosopher. (Ed.)

[4] Niccolo Machiavelli (1469–1527), Italian political philosopher. (Ed.)

[5] Hugo Grotius (1583–1645 , Dutch jurist and theologian. (Ed.)

[6] 'without assuming there to be a God.' (Ed.)

[7] Réne Descartes (1596–1650), French philosopher and scientist. (Ed.)

[8] Baruch Spinoza (1632–77), Dutch Jewish philosopher. (Ed.)

[9] Immanuel Kant (1724–1804), German philosopher. (Ed.)

deist, and Fichte[1] and Hegel[2] are pantheists. Everywhere the thinking is directed towards the autonomy of man and the world.

(It seems that in the natural sciences the process begins with Nicolas of Cusa[3] and Giordano Bruno[4] and the 'heretical' doctrine of the infinity of the universe. The classical *cosmos* was finite, like the created world of the Middle Ages. An infinite universe, however it may be conceived, is self-subsisting, *etsi deus non daretur*. It is true that modern physics is not as sure as it was about the infinity of the universe, but it has not gone back to the earlier conceptions of its finitude.)

God as a working hypothesis in morals, politics, or science, has been surmounted and abolished; and the same thing has happened in philosophy and religion (Feuerbach!).[5] For the sake of intellectual honesty, that working hypothesis should be dropped, or as far as possible eliminated. A scientist or physician who sets out to edify is a hybrid.

Anxious souls will ask what room there is left for God now; and as they know of no answer to the question, they condemn the whole development that has brought them to such straits. I wrote to you before about the various emergency exits that have been contrived; and we ought to add to them the *salto mortale* [death-leap] back into the Middle Ages. But the principle of the Middle Ages is heteronomy in the form of clericalism; a return to that can be a counsel of despair, and it would be at the cost of intellectual honesty. It's a dream that reminds one of the song *O wüsst' ich doch den Weg zurück, den weiten Weg ins Kinderland*.[6] There is no such way—at any rate not if it means deliberately abandoning our mental integrity; the only way is that of Matt. 18:3,[7] i.e., through repentance, through *ultimate* honesty.

[1] Johann Gotlieb Fichte (1762–1814), German philosopher. (Ed.)

[2] G. W. F. Hegel (1770–1831), German philosopher. (Ed.)

[3] Nicolas of Cusa (*c.* 1400–64), German philosopher and mystic. (Ed.)

[4] Giordano Bruno (1548–1600), Italian philosopher. (Ed.)

[5] Ludwig Feuerbach (1804–72), German philosopher. (Ed.)

[6] 'If only I knew the way back, the long way into the land of childhood.'

[7] 'Unless you turn and become like children, you will never enter the kingdom of heaven.'

And we cannot be honest unless we recognize that we have to live in the world *etsi deus non daretur*. And this is just what we do recognize—before God! God himself compels us to recognize it. So our coming of age leads us to a true recognition of our situation before God. God would have us know that we must live as men who manage our lives without him. The God who is with us is the God who forsakes us (Mark 15:34).[1] The God who lets us live in the world without the working hypothesis of God is the God before whom we stand continually. Before God and with God we live without God. God lets himself be pushed out of the world on to the cross. He is weak and powerless in the world, and that is precisely the way, the only way, in which he is with us and helps us. Matt. 8:17[2] makes it quite clear that Christ helps us, not by virtue of his omnipotence, but by virtue of his weakness and suffering.

Here is the decisive difference between Christianity and all religions. Man's religiosity makes him look in his distress to the power of God in the world: God is the *deus ex machina*. The Bible directs man to God's powerlessness and suffering; only the suffering God can help. To that extent we may say that the development towards the world's coming of age outlined above, which has done away with a false conception of God, opens up a way of seeing the God of the Bible, who wins power and space in the world by his weakness. This will probably be the starting-point for our 'secular interpretation'.

(FROM: *Letters and Papers from Prison*, pp. 325–8, 359–61.)

[1] 'My God, my God, why hast thou forsaken me?'

[2] 'This was to fulfil what was spoken by the prophet Isaiah, "He took our infirmities and bore our diseases".'

8 'Participation in the Suffering of God'

[Christian theology in its classical phase would have shrunk from all talk about 'the sufferings of God'. Suffering meant being acted upon by exterior forces outside one's control and it was difficult to see how one could reconcile belief in God's omnipotence and self-sufficiency with talk about his 'suffering'. But there was the problem of the crucifixion which necessitated Christians saying that in some sense God suffered. Eastern orthodox theology has always held that suffering in the sense of sacrificial self-giving love is of the essence of God. God empties himself in creation, in Incarnation and in re-creation (redemption). It seems that Bonhoeffer was moving towards a fresh expression of this belief in his presentation of the Christian life as one of self-giving love in the real (not idealized or romanticized) world. This is to share in the self-giving love of God who, at cost ('suffering') makes the world genuinely real to himself by, for example, giving himself to real history in Christ.]

. . . Man is summoned to share in God's sufferings at the hands of a godless world.

He must therefore really live in the godless world, without attempting to gloss over or explain its ungodliness in some religious way or other. He must live a 'secular' life, and thereby share in God's sufferings. He *may* live a 'secular' life (as one who has been freed from false religious obligations and inhibitions). To be a Christian does not mean to be religious in a particular way, to make something of oneself (a sinner, a penitent, or a saint) on the basis of some method or other, but to be a man—not a type of man, but the man that Christ creates in us. It is not the religious act that makes the Christian, but participation in the sufferings of God in the secular life. That is *metanoia*[1]: not in the first place thinking about one's own needs, problems, sins, and fears, but allowing oneself to be caught up into the way of Jesus Christ, into the messianic event, thus fulfilling Isa. 53. Therefore 'believe in the gospel', or, in the words of John the Baptist, 'Behold, the Lamb of God, who takes away the sin of the world' (John

[1] 'Repentance'. (Ed.)

1:29). (By the way, Jeremias[1] has recently asserted that the Aramaic word for 'lamb' may also be translated 'servant'; very appropriate in view of Isa. 53!)

This being caught up into the messianic sufferings of God in Jesus Christ takes a variety of forms in the New Testament. It appears in the call to discipleship, in Jesus' table-fellowship with sinners, in 'conversions' in the narrower sense of the word (e.g., Zacchaeus), in the act of the woman who was a sinner (Luke 7)—an act that she performed without any confession of sin, in the healing of the sick (Matt. 8:17; see above), in Jesus' acceptance of children. The shepherds, like the wise men from the East, stand at the crib, not as 'converted sinners', but simply because they are drawn to the crib by the star just as they are. The centurion of Capernaum (who makes no confession of sin) is held up as a model of faith (cf. Jairus). Jesus 'loved' the rich young man. The eunuch (Acts 8) and Cornelius (Acts 10) are not standing at the edge of an abyss. Nathaniel is 'an Israelite indeed, in whom there is no guile' (John 1:47). Finally, Joseph of Arimathea and the women at the tomb. The only thing that is common to all these is their sharing in the suffering of God in Christ. That is their 'faith'. There is nothing of religious method here. The 'religious act' is always something partial; 'faith' is something whole, involving the whole of one's life. Jesus calls men, not to a new religion, but to life.

But what does this life look like, this participation in the powerlessness of God in the world? I will write about that next time, I hope. Just one more point for today. When we speak of God in a 'non-religious' way, we must speak of him in such a way that the godlessness of the world is not in some way concealed, but rather revealed, and thus exposed to an unexpected light. The world that has come of age is more godless, and perhaps for that very reason nearer to God, than the world before its coming of age.

I discovered later, and I'm still discovering right up to this moment, that it is only by living completely in this world that one learns to have faith. One must completely abandon any attempt to make something of oneself, whether it be a saint,

[1] Joachim Jeromias, contemporary German New Testament Scholar. (Ed.)

or a converted sinner, or a churchman (a so-called priestly type!), a righteous man or an unrighteous one, a sick man or a healthy one. By this-worldliness I mean living unreservedly in life's duties, problems, successes and failures, experiences and perplexities. In so doing we throw ourselves completely into the arms of God, taking seriously, not our own sufferings, but those of God in the world—watching with Christ in Gethsemane. That, I think, is faith; that is *metanoia*; and that is how one becomes a man and a Christian (cf. Jer. 45!). How can success make us arrogant, or failure lead us astray, when we share in God's sufferings through a life of this kind?

(FROM: *Letters and Papers from Prison*, pp. 361–2, 369–70.)

9 'Outline for a Book'

[This extract gives the famous synopsis of a book which Bonhoeffer was planning to write. This was obviously going to expand his thoughts on 'man's coming of age', 'wordliness', Christ as 'the man for others', and the church as the 'servant' imitator of Christ. Already there have been many attempts to finish Bonhoeffer's book for him but one has the feeling that like Schubert's 'Unfinished Symphony' the 'Outline for a book' will remain one of the great fragments of human endeavour.]

I should like to write a book of not more than 100 pages, divided into three chapters:

1. A Stocktaking of Christianity.
2. The Real Meaning of Christian Faith.
3. Conclusions.

Chapter 1 to deal with:

(*a*) The coming of age of mankind (as already indicated). The safeguarding of life against 'accidents' and 'blows of fate'; even if these cannot be eliminated, the danger can be reduced. Insurance (which, although it lives on 'accidents', seeks to mitigate their effects) as a western phenomenon. The aim: to be independent of nature. Nature was formerly conquered by spiritual means, with us by technical organization of all kinds. Our immediate environment is not nature, as formerly, but organization. But with this protection from nature's menace there arises a new one—through organization itself.

But the spiritual force is lacking. The question is: What protects us against the menace of organization? Man is again thrown back on himself. He has managed to deal with everything, only not with himself. He can insure against everything, only not against man. In the last resort it all turns on man.

(*b*) The religionlessness of man who has come of age. 'God' as a working hypothesis, as a stop-gap for our embarrassments, has become superfluous (as already indicated).

(*c*) The Protestant church: Pietism as a last attempt to maintain evangelical Christianity as a religion; Lutheran orthodoxy, the attempt to rescue the Church as an institution for salvation; the Confessing Church: the theology of revelation; a δὸς μοὶ ποῦ στῶ[1] over against the world, involving a 'factual' interest in Christianity; art and science searching for their origin. Generally in the Confessing Church: standing up for the Church's 'cause', but little personal faith in Christ. 'Jesus' is disappearing from sight. Sociologically: no effect on the masses—interest confined to the upper and lower middle classes. A heavy incubus of difficult traditional ideas. The decisive factor; the Church on the defensive. No taking risks for others.

(*d*) Public morals—as shown by sexual behaviour.

Chapter 2.

(*a*) God and the secular.

(*b*) Who is God? Not in the first place an abstract belief in God in his omnipotence etc. That is not a genuine experience of God but a partial extension of the world. Encounter with Jesus Christ. The experience that a transformation of all human life is given in the fact that 'Jesus is there only for others'. His 'being there for others' is the experience of transcendence. It is only this 'being there for others', maintained till death, that is the ground of his omnipotence, omniscience,

[1] 'Grant me to be able to stand.' (Ed.)

and omnipresence. Faith is participation in this being of Jesus (incarnation, cross, and resurrection). Our relation to God is not a 'religious' relationship to the highest, most powerful, and best Being imaginable—that is not authentic transcendence—but our relation to God is a new life in 'existence for others', through participation in the being of Jesus. The transcendental is not infinite and unattainable tasks, but the neighbour who is within reach in any given situation. God in human form—not, as in oriental-religions, in animal form, monstrous, chaotic, remote, and terrifying, nor in the conceptual forms of the absolute, metaphysical, infinite, etc., nor yet in the Greek divine human form of 'man in himself', but 'the man for others', and therefore the Crucified, the man who lives out of the transcendent.

(*c*) Interpretation of biblical concepts on this basis. (Creation, fall, atonement, repentance, faith, the new life, the last things.)

(*d*) Cultus. (Details to follow later, in particular on cultus and 'religion'.)

(*e*) What do we really believe? I mean, believe in such a way that we stake our lives on it? The problem of the Apostles' Creed? 'What *must* I believe?' is the wrong question; antiquated controversies, especially those between the different sects; the Lutheran versus Reformed,[1] and to some extent the Roman Catholic versus Protestant, are now unreal. They may at any time be revived with passion, but they no longer carry conviction. There is no proof of this, and we must simply take it that it is so. All that we can prove is that the faith of the Bible and Christianity does not stand or fall by these issues. Karl Barth and the Confessing Church have encouraged us to entrench ourselves persisently behind the 'faith of the Church', and evade the honest question as to what we ourselves really believe. That is why the air is not quite fresh, even in the Confessing Church. To say that it is the Church's business, not mine, may be a clerical evasion, and outsiders always regard it as such. It is much the same with the dialectical assertion that I do not control my own faith, and that it is therefore not for me to say what my faith is. There may be a place for all these considerations, but they do

[1] i.e., Calvinist. (Ed.)

not absolve us from the duty of being honest with ourselves. We cannot, like the Roman Catholics, simply identify ourselves with the Church. (This, incidentally, explains the popular opinion about Roman Catholics' insincerity.) Well then, what do we really believe? Answer: see (*b*), (*c*), and (*d*).

Chapter 3.
Conclusions:

The Church is the Church only when it exists for others. To make a start, it should give away all its property to those in need. The clergy must live solely on the free-will offerings of their congregations, or possibly engage in some secular calling. The Church must share in the secular problems of ordinary human life, not dominating, but helping and serving. It must tell men of every calling what it means to live in Christ, to exist for others. In particular, our own Church will have to take the field against the vices of *hubris*, power-worship, envy, and humbug, as the roots of all evil. It will have to speak of moderation, purity, trust, loyalty, constancy, patience, discipline, humility, contentment, and modesty. It must not underestimate the importance of human example (which has its origin in the humanity of Jesus and is so important in Paul's teaching); it is not abstract argument, but example, that gives its word emphasis and power. (I hope to take up later this subject of 'example' and its place in the New Testament; it is something that we have almost entirely forgotten.) Further: the question of revising the creeds (the Apostles' Creed); revision of Christian apologetics; reform of the training for the ministry and the pattern of clerical life.

All this is very crude and condensed, but there are certain things that I'm anxious to say simply and clearly—things that we so often like to shirk. Whether I shall succeed is another matter, especially if I cannot discuss it with you. I hope it may be of some help for the Church's future.

(FROM: *Letters and Papers from Prison*, pp. 380–3).

FOR FURTHER STUDY AND DISCUSSION

1 Throughout his theology, Bonhoeffer was concerned with the nature and rôle of the Church. On the one hand he had a high doctrine of the Church as 'the formation of Christ', and on the other an acute sense of how certain images of the Church (as the 'great lord', for example, or the holder of all certain truth) could get in the way. Is Bonhoeffer's image of the Church as the 'servant' adequate? Can one relate the concept of the 'Body of Christ' to the empirical Church?
2 Bonhoeffer's *Ethics* attempts to relate belief about Christ to Christian ethics and the pattern of the Christian life. Is this the way to bring out the distinctive character of the Christian conception of the good life?
3 Is it sufficient to think of Christ as 'the man for others'? How does this relate to traditional Christian teaching about Christ?
4 Imagine you had invited Barth, Tillich, Bultmann and Bonhoeffer for an evening and the conversation turned to the subject of the meaning of the Bible for modern man. How do you think the conversation would have gone?
5 Did Bonhoeffer in his interpretation of the Christian life as 'a participation in the sufferings of God' run the risk of turning Christianity into a tragedy?
6 Can Christianity do without 'religion'?

FOR FURTHER READING

The Life of Bonhoeffer

1965 *No Rusty Swords* (Collected Works. Volume I).
1966 *The Way to Freedom* (Collected Works. Volume II).
1966 *I Knew Dietrich Bonhoeffer* (edited by W. D. Zimmermann and R. G. Smith).
1968 Mary Bosanquet, *The Life and Death of Dietrich Bonhoeffer*.
1970 E. Bethge, *Dietrich Bonhoeffer* (likely to remain the standard biography).

Principal Works of Bonhoeffer

Sanctorum Communio (Berlin and Frankfurt/Oder 1930 ET 1963).
Act and Being (Munich 1956) ET 1962.
Christology (Munich 1960) ET 1960.
Creation and Temptation (Munich 1937 and 1953) ET 1955 and 1959.
The Cost of Discipleship (Munich 1937) ET 1948.
Life Together (Munich 1939) ET 1954.
Ethics (Munich 1949) ET 1955.
Letters and Papers from Prison (Munich 1951) ET 1955.

Some Books about Bonhoeffer

A. Dumas, *Dietrich Bonhoeffer : theologian of reality*, 1971. (To date the best book on Bonhoeffer's theology.)
Martin E. Marty (ed.), *The Place of Bonhoeffer*, 1963.
R. Gregor Smith (ed.), *World Come of Age*, 1967. (Contains the valuable Chicago lectures of Eberhard Bethge on 'The Challenge of Dietrich Bonhoeffer's Life and Theology' and important comments on Bonhoeffer by Barth and Bultmann.)
John A. Phillips, *The Form of Christ in the World*, 1967. (A study of Bonhoeffer's Christology.)

FOR GENERAL BACKGROUND READING

John Macquarrie, *Twentieth-century Religious Thought*, 1963.
——, *God-talk*, 1967.
——, *God and Secularity*, 1968.
Frederick Ferré, *Language, Logic and God*, 1962.
——, *Basic Modern Philosophy of Religion*, 1968.
David E. Jenkins, *Guide to the Debate about God*, 1966.
Colin Williams, *Faith in a Secular Age*, 1966.
E. L. Mascall, *The Secularisation of Christianity*, 1965.
H. Gollwitzer, *The Existence of God as confessed by faith*,
A. M. Ramsey, *God, Christ and the World*, 1969.
1964.
T. W. Ogletree, *The Death of God Controversy*, 1966.